MW00986702

SLAVE STORIES

LAW, REPRESENTATION, AND GENDER IN THE DANISH WEST INDIES

SLAVE STORIES

Law, Representation, and Gender in the Danish West Indies

Gunvor Simonsen

Aarhus University Press

Slave Stories
Law, Representation, and Gender in the Danish West Indies
© The author and Aarhus University Press

Cover design: Hanne Kolding
Cover illustration: © Mary's Fancy, St. Croix, painting
unknown artist, possibly Fritz Melbye, c. 1840 (courtesy of
Museet for Søfart, the Maritime Museum of Denmark)
Type setting: Narayana Press
Type: Arno Pro
Printed at Narayana Press, Gylling
Printed in Denmark 2017

ISBN 978 87 7124 917 0

Aarhus University Press
Finlandsgade 29
8200 Aarhus N
Denmark
www.unipress.dk

International distributors:
Gazelle Book Services Ltd.
White Cross Mills
Hightown, Lancaster, LA1 4XS
United Kingdom
www.gazellebookservices.co.uk

ISD
70 Enterprise Drive
Bristol, CT 06010
USA
www. isdistribution.com

Published with the financial support of
Den Hielmstierne-Rosencroneske Stiftelse
E. Lerager Larsens Fond
Konsul George Jorck og Hustru Emma Jorck's Fond
Landsdommer V. Gieses Legat
Lillian og Dan Finks Fond
Prof. Ludvig Wimmer og Hustrus Legat

CONTENTS

LIST OF FIGURES

LIST OF ILLUSTRATIONS

Legal Power and Gendered Voices in the Danish West Indies

In 1799, the enslaved woman Sally appeared before Christiansted Lower Court in St. Croix of the Danish West Indies (today the US Virgin Islands). She was charged with attempted murder of her common law husband. The road that led to Sally's trial was long and winding. It began when she walked to Christiansted town to complain to Governor General Wilhelm Anton Lindemann about the treatment the slaves received on Bonne Esperance Estate where she worked as a field hand. Sally's complaint resulted in the fining of the estate administrator, but it also led to the investigation that implicated her in a murder attempt on her husband, Leander. During her trial, Sally stated that she was innocent. She emphasized that she "loved Leander" and "wished that she could live with him" forever. Yet Leander was unfaithful and maintained a second wife. Sally explained that it was Leander's "infidelity" that had led her to burn down his house and mix marl in his drinking water. All her deeds had been done "for him," Sally claimed; indeed her feelings were so strong that she was "unable to leave him."[1]

Judge Brown of Christiansted Lower Court drew heavily on Sally's court testimony when he drafted his verdict, but he disregarded the main thrust of her argument: Sally claimed that she had no intention of causing harm to the man she loved. During the trial, Sally admitted that she felt "jealous" and "revengeful" towards Leander, and she confessed that she harbored feelings of "hatred" against her overseer. These were the elements of Sally's testimony that Brown chose to repeat in his verdict. Disregarding Sally's main claim, he picked her statement apart and chose only those bits and pieces that allowed him to issue a death sentence.[2]

Though unusual, Sally's testimony was not unique in the Danish West Indian courts. Indeed, this book is about Sally and the many other enslaved men and women who appeared in the courts of Christiansted jurisdiction in St. Croix from the 1750s until the abolition of slavery in the Danish West Indies in 1848. Representational processes that included slave depositions were central to litigation in

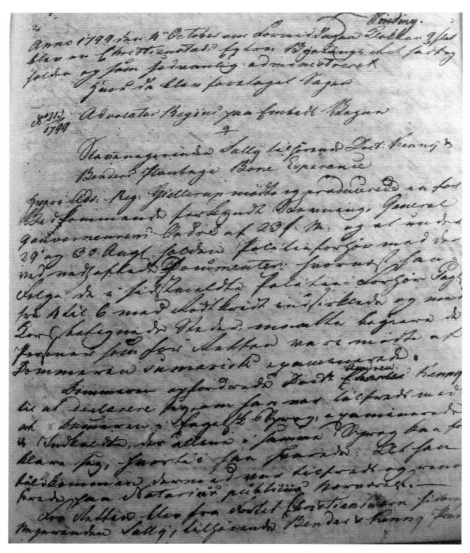

Detail of the court book containing the testimony of the enslaved woman Sally, 1799.

The folio-sized *retsprotokol*, i.e. the court protocol, containing the transcript of the statement Sally gave in Christiansted Lower Court on October 4, 1799. On the following pages, Sally explained that she "loved" her husband and she related how she had attempted to deal with what she understood to be his infidelity.

the Danish West Indies in the eighteenth and nineteenth centuries. Thousands of enslaved men and women appeared in the Danish West Indian courts. What they said was meticulously recorded by the royal judges and scribes. Today, the judicial records pertaining to or including slaves in the jurisdiction of Christiansted, St. Croix, take up more than 190 large volumes in the *Rigsarkiv*, the National Archives in Copenhagen, Denmark. These volumes comprise a substantive, tangible sign of the important role that slaves' words played in the Danish Atlantic legal institutions during the eighteenth and nineteenth centuries.[3] In these courts, the testimonies of enslaved men and women were part of long, tortuous, and inclusive trials that were decided through the ingenious interpretations of schooled jurists.

Sally's court appearance points to the inclusive element of the processes of representation that took place in the Danish West Indian courts. Several identity markers were attributed to slaves who entered the courtroom. Sally was described as a "negress," belonging to "Bonne Esperance Estate," "born on St. Eustatius," who "did not know her age" and did not "confess to any religion." Like other slaves appearing in court, Sally was labeled according to her sex, skin color, faith, age, birthplace, and owner. Such labels were used to distinguish one slave from another. Usually enslaved people did not have the possibility of adding further layers of meaning to the sketchy portraits they engendered. This was not the case with gender. As Sally's story illustrates, gender provided a narrative opening that enslaved Africans and Afro-Caribbeans could sometimes use to establish themselves as subjects before the Danish West Indian courts. Though slaves and judges had very different preconceived ideals of manliness and womanliness, they shared a concern for the ways in which gender ideologies came into play in Atlantic slavery. This common concern paved the way for a broken, distorted, and unequal dialogue in the courts of Christiansted in St. Croix.[4]

Yet dialogue seldom amounted to tangible influence in the Danish Atlantic legal system. Sally's trial and verdict illustrate a central argument of this book. In *Slave Stories* I argue that legal power in the Danish West Indies should be understood as both inclusive and repressive. On the one hand, the court's procedural practices included statements by enslaved Africans and Afro-Caribbeans, particularly when they portrayed themselves as Christian men and women living industrious and respectable lives. On the other hand, the self-portraits and stories developed by slaves seldom affected trial outcomes. Judges developed reading practices that allowed them to reach guilty verdicts in most trials. In the Danish West Indian courts, inclusive procedures and repressive verdicts went hand in hand and enabled slaves to tell their stories while simultaneously allowing judges to sentence them harshly afterwards.

13

Slave Stories aims to broaden our understanding of the place of enslaved Africans and Afro-Caribbeans in the legal institutions of the Atlantic slave societies and does so by analyzing, among other things, how gendered ideas and practices were mobilized by the enslaved and their judges during and after trials. My focus on the Danish West Indian legal system, which relied on the procedural traditions of continental Europe, helps to show that slaves' experiences with the law varied across the Atlantic world. I argue that the legitimacy of justice in the Danish West Indies was based on a peculiar inclusion of slave testimony rather than on its formal exclusion from the legal process. On the whole, *Slave Stories* offers a brutal and painful history. In the Danish West Indian courtrooms there is no grand story to be found of Africans and Afro-Caribbeans who, by having a voice, obtained some sort of agency and achieved justice. Slaves spoke, but to little avail. Instead, imprisonment, flogging, transportation, and death were the usual destinies of these men and women. And yet their stories remain to remind us that slaves strove to represent themselves as dignified, reasonable men and women in their encounters with the Danish West Indian judiciary.

The questions I ask and the interpretations I offer in what follows rely on and debate with the work of other scholars of law and gender in the Atlantic world. Parallel to the focus on slave law that has characterized Atlantic legal history, legal records are now being opened up to the analysis of specific legal practices and the reconstruction of the voices that enslaved men and women raised in their encounters with the judges of slavery.[5] The British Caribbean, and to some degree Anglophone America, saw the development of legal systems and courts in which scribes seldom recorded the statements provided by the enslaved.[6] In the older British Caribbean colonies, like Barbados, Antigua and Jamaica, specific slave courts were established that excluded enslaved men and women from the procedural routines of ordinary courts. Yet in colonial societies dominated by civil law systems, such as the former Dutch colonies Berbice, Essequibo and Demerara and the former French (alternately Spanish) colony Louisiana, legal cultures and institutions emerged in which slaves' depositions were recorded. Likewise, Danish West Indian judicial institutions incorporated slave depositions into the processes of litigation.[7]

As specific legal practices in the Atlantic slave societies are opened up to historical enquiry, historians have confronted the question of how to read legal transcripts. Many studies have concentrated on the exceptionally gruesome trials that took place in the aftermath of slave rebellions, conspiracies, and alleged plots, rather than on the ordinary, everyday legal practices of slavery. With torture and white panic looming in the background, historians have chosen different interpretative paths. Some have argued that the statements made by the enslaved, already sentenced to death, can be trusted precisely because these men and women no longer had any reason to lie. Others have insisted that enslaved men and women said "what they thought would help them escape."[8] Instead of evaluating the veracity of slave testimony, however, Sally's story suggests that it may also be fruitful to read everyday slave testimonies as evidence of the narrative skills, imaginative universe, and intellectual trajectories of enslaved men and women rather than as more or less true representations of enslaved reality.[9] Sally may have provided reliable evidence, she may have attempted to strategically shape her defense, or she may have done a little of each; regardless, she also told a story about love and partnership within slavery. To understand her testimony and the court statements of the many enslaved men and women who appeared in the courts of Christiansted in St. Croix of the Danish West Indies, it is central both to examine the processes of representation that made particular themes and storylines possible while keeping others out of earshot and to detail when representation became so twisted that it turned into misrepresentation, distortion, and repression.

Sally was not alone in her concern with the place of marriage during slavery. Historians of Atlantic gender regimes have established that gendered ideologies informed labor regimes, experiences of domination, and strategies of resistance in the diverse slave societies of the Atlantic world. During Atlantic slavery, strong and multifarious pressures were brought to bear on the gender ideologies and practices that enslaved men and women brought with them, maintained, and adapted in the Americas. Atlantic slavery was hinged on an ideology that invested Africans and their descendants, particularly women, with abnormal bodies and deviant forms of sexuality.[10] In *Slave Stories*, I ask how Sally and other enslaved women and men engaged with and negotiated the gendered pressures they encountered in the Danish West Indies during the, roughly, one hundred years from the 1750s until emancipation in 1848. I do so by reconstructing the voices, or narrative practices, that enslaved people developed in the Danish West Indian legal institutions, and I argue that these narratives were central to the legal encounters that took place in Christiansted in St. Croix.

The concern with enslaved 'voices' that informs this study has long been at the heart of Atlantic gender history precisely because the colonial "archives do not allow women enslaved in early American colonies to speak," as Jennifer Morgan recently noted in relation to the British colonies.[11] Historians focused specifically on the Caribbean slave societies have also noted that enslaved Africans and Afro-Caribbeans seldom partook in the representational processes that constitute colonial archives.[12] This observation reflects the obstacles involved in locating

The eastern Caribbean islands, including the Danish islands, c. 1777, indicated by the yellow circle. Map from Christian Georg Andreas Oldendorp, *Geschichte der Mission der evangelischen Brüder auf den caraibischen Inseln S. Thomas, S. Croix und S. Jan*, vol. I, ed. Bossart, Johann Jakob (Barby, 1777).

historical sites that included enslaved men and women in calligraphic processes. Christiansted's courts, as Sally's testimony illustrates, were among such sites. Here, representation was a daily routine, but — as we shall see — it went hand in hand with distortion and the exclusion of particular experiences, as witnessed by, for instance, the censorship exerted in cases concerning interracial sexuality and rape in the Danish West Indian courts.

The notion of 'voice', while slippery, points to the interpretative practices developed among enslaved Africans and their descendants as they confronted the harsh world of Atlantic slavery. It allows us to think about how "slaves saw themselves and their world."[13] Therefore, it suggests how enslaved men and women confronted the repressive epistemologies developed collectively by a variety of European agents, including slave traders, owners, overseers, doctors, missionaries, travelers, scientists, and colonial judges. Employed in this way, voice as a metaphor signifies an attempt to embrace the myriad ways by which enslaved men and women made sense of their lives in bondage.[14] Or, put another way, historians talk about voices as a means of reconstructing the historical subjectivities of enslaved people.[15]

The reconstruction of slave voices, then, is intimately connected to the study of enslaved men and women as subjects with a specific sense of self as both individuals and as members of communities, or, in the words of Michel-Rolph Trouillot, "as subjects, that is, as voices aware of their vocality."[16] Yet the subject as a concept is twofold. On the one hand, the subject is conditioned by his or her subjection to others; on the other hand, she or he has experiences, knowledge, and the ability to perform a certain degree of self-definition. Although these aspects of subjectivity are intertwined, the idea of the enslaved voice emphasizes the self-constructive element of subjectivity.[17] Sally's experiences on Bonne Esperance Estate in 1799 were shaped by the regime of racial slavery that undergirded plantation production in St. Croix. Sally's husband, Leander, was the estate driver. She — as many other women in St. Croix — worked in the cane fields, and their conflict about Leander's second wife was shaped by their different positions on the estate. However, when Sally appeared in Christiansted Lower Court in 1799, she portrayed herself as a woman who was rightly upset by her husband's illicit behavior; she did not, that is, explain herself through reference to her position as an enslaved Afro-Caribbean.

Although I emphasize the contributions made by enslaved Africans and Afro-Caribbeans to legal proceedings, at times at the expense of focusing on elite legal discourses, it is clear that the voices raised by the enslaved in the Danish West Indian courts were shaped in multiple ways by the legal setting in which they emerged. The complicated representational processes involving enslaved Africans and their descendants in the Atlantic world have also been noted by literary scholars concerned with autobiographical literature, such as the works of Olaudah Equiano, Ottabah Cugoano, and Mary Prince, ex-slaves who wrote in the late eighteenth and early nineteenth centuries.[18] These authors were, in different ways, participating in the development of abolitionist discourses and have been understood as "[i]mpossible witnesses," a phrasing which clearly warns us against assuming that slave testimony mirrors the realities of slave life.[19] Indeed, it is important to note that the notion of voice, and the interpretative results it generates, cannot readily be understood as a shortcut to the perspectives of enslaved men and women. Nevertheless, it may bring us closer to the worlds of enslaved men and women than we would have been if we ignored the concept altogether.[20]

Enslaved men and women told stories in the courts of Christiansted in St. Croix, and, taken together, these stories — a notion I use to disengage slave testimony from its tenuous relationship to the events and episodes it presumes to describe — allow us to reconstruct the narrative practices that emerged among many enslaved men and women in St. Croix during the hundred year period from the mid-eighteenth to the mid-nineteenth century. Understood as such, *Slave Stories* may be considered one chapter in a troubled history of ideas of enslaved men and women in the Danish West Indies. It draws us closer to the hopes, fears, and desires entertained by enslaved men and women in the Danish West Indies, to their views and opinions, and it seeks to establish some of the ideational horizons entertained by slaves as they sought to find their feet in the harsh world of Danish West Indian slavery.

In the Danish West Indian courts, as in a number of other courts in the Caribbean and the wider Atlantic world, enslaved men and women were heard and their statements were recorded. It is from this observation that *Slave Stories* sets out to explore how and why slaves' statements were recorded and in what way slaves' statements in the Danish West Indian courts can be understood to contain their changing, gendered stories.

In *Slave Stories*, I use the terms African and Afro-Caribbean to designate people born in Africa or people of African descent born in the Caribbean. I have often preferred these terms to, for instance, 'blacks' since they underline the processes of dislocation and relocation that conditioned social existence for enslaved people in St. Croix. Nonetheless, it is not always possible to distinguish people born in Africa from those born in the Caribbean for which reason I often use both terms. In contemporary Danish West Indian texts, enslaved people were mostly described as '*negere*' and '*negerinder*', 'negroes' and 'negresses', and in the pages that follow I maintain this usage in translations of contemporary texts. As I have been less interested in the shifting identity of Europeans and Euro-Caribbeans in the

Danish West Indies, I mostly describe them as white West Indians, or Europeans and, if relevant, as Danes.

Translations from manuscript sources and other Danish language texts have been completed by me unless otherwise noted. In the eighteenth and nineteenth centuries, Danish texts were often composed of long and convoluted sentences. In my translations I have not attempted to completely remove this structure. Instead, I have often opted for a textually close, but occasionally inelegant translation.

CHAPTER 1

The Many Gendered World
of Slaves and Judges

In 1828, Thomas, driver on Hermon Hill Estate, west of the town of Christiansted in St. Croix, found his horse dead, hanged in the bush. Judge Frederiksen of
Christiansted Police Court investigated the incident, and, after some time, the
enslaved man Limmerich emerged as the main culprit. According to witnesses,
the dispute began because Thomas had rebuked Limmerich for having two wives.
Following this incident, Thomas' horse was killed. During the trial, a slave witness
established Thomas as an advocate for Christian ideals on Hermon Hill. Thomas
disapproved of polygyny, referred to the Christian God in conversations with his
underlings, and strove to settle the conflict with Limmerich quietly. In contrast,
Limmerich, one witness related, failed to behave "as a man" and hanged the horse
instead of confronting Thomas directly.

   Yet other witnesses related that Thomas and Limmerich had been involved
in a fierce obeah battle regarding masculine authority. The concept of obeah had
probably arrived in St. Croix from the British Caribbean during the late eighteenth
century. Obeah covered a "complex of shamanistic practices derived from various parts of Africa," yet Danish observers, as well as other Europeans, found it
notoriously difficult to define.[21] During the investigation of the conflict between
Thomas and Limmerich, one witness brought a bottle with a yellow fluid to the
court and explained that Limmerich used this "obeah" to strengthen himself.
Another explained that Thomas spoke with "arrogance," threatening to "cool"
Limmerich — a term that in other cases was used by slaves to describe the calm-
ing influence of obeah on aggressive managers and overseers.[22] These witnesses
emphasized that one of Limmerich's wives had encouraged him to behave as a
"man" and refrain from implicating others in the killing of the horse even if he was
to be hanged. While none of the slaves of Hermon Hill explicated the meaning of
the hanged horse (an act that could be understood as an elaborate form of shadow
catching, an obeah ritual known throughout the English-speaking Caribbean in

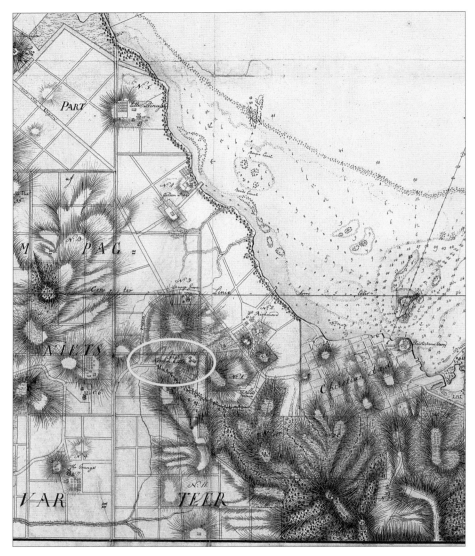

Detail of map of Christiansted and surrounding estates, by Peter Lotharius Oxholm, 1778.
The yellow circle shows Hermon Hill Estate, just west of Christiansted town (courtesy of *Rigsarkivet*,
the Danish National Archives).

which objects symbolizing death were employed to catch souls and cause death), they referred to ideals of manliness and marriage to explain and understand Limmerich's acts.[23] And, as the depositions show, Hermon Hill's slaves did not agree on what proper marital life should look like, and they certainly did not agree on how men should handle their intimate affairs. Some argued that Christian ways were manly; others saw masculine behavior primarily in connection with African-Atlantic spiritual forces.

The depositions made by the slaves of Hermon Hill point to the overlapping and competing gendered ideals and practices that shaped the encounter between enslaved men and women and judges in the Danish West Indies. However, the trial prose in the case against the slaves at Hermon Hill also illustrates that the gendered stories crafted by enslaved men and women cannot be understood as transparent descriptions of the events under scrutiny. Judge Frederiksen found it extremely difficult to obtain any information about the case. Therefore, he ordered that provisions be withheld from the estate's slaves; he also ordered the flogging of some of the witnesses — a decision that, as we shall see, broke with normal procedure in the 1830s. Hungry, perhaps starving, and injured, some of the enslaved deponents may have shaped their testimonies to satisfy Frederiksen's need for knowledge.

Nonetheless, in the trial proceedings against Limmerich, slaves and judges juggled narratively with several gender regimes. Ideals of Christian monogamous marital life, African elite traditions of polygyny, African-Atlantic spiritual regulation of slaves' intimate affairs, *and* Judge Frederiksen's belief in the wild and unregulated nature of African sexuality can all be read in the layered depositions recorded by the court scribe in 1828. In this way, the investigation of a dead horse brought the many gendered ideals that circulated in the harsh world of Danish West Indian slavery in the nineteenth century to Christiansted Police Court.[24]

Slavery and Sugar in the Danish West Indies

In 1828, when the fight between Thomas and Limmerich was examined in Christiansted Police Court, St. Croix, the largest island in the Danish West Indies, which also included the islands of St. Thomas and St. John, had been a place of intensive sugar cultivation and production for many decades. Danish colonization had begun in the late seventeenth century, resulting in the colonization of St. Thomas in 1672 by the Danish West India and Guinea Company. Later, in 1718, St. John was occupied, and, in 1733, St. Croix was bought from the French. In 1754-55, the Danish-Norwegian double monarchy (reduced to a Danish monarchy after 1814) took over the Danish West Indies and established an institutional structure, including a legal system, that resembled similar institutions in Denmark.[25] In 1848, slavery was abolished after a successful uprising in St. Croix. The islands remained Danish colonial possessions until they were sold to the United States of America in 1917.

The Danish West Indies was a cosmopolitan place in the eighteenth and nineteenth centuries. Europeans and Africans from all over the Atlantic world crowded the islands and ensured that a single insular, national tradition would never dominate island life. This was, as historian Neville Hall has argued, an "empire without dominion."[26] The Danish state could not settle its colonial possessions with its own subjects and therefore Danes and Danish culture were never dominant in the islands. White society included people from England, Scotland, Ireland, the Netherlands, France, the German principalities, and Denmark-Norway, yet English-speakers came to dominate island life from the mid-eighteenth century onward, when St. Croix, an island of eighty-five square miles, developed into a full-blown sugar island.[27]

From the mid-eighteenth to the early nineteenth century enslaved Africans were imported in large numbers to support the expanding sugar estates in the Danish West Indies. Africans arrived to the islands from other Caribbean islands and from the long West African coastline stretching from Senegambia to Angola. In 1755, the land in St. Croix had been parceled out and most had been sold.[28] Now estate owners began to consolidate their properties. Many turned from cotton production to sugar, and they bought more land and more slaves.[29] In the 1750s, Danish sugar planter Reimert Haagensen, who lived in St. Croix from 1739 to 1751 and initially held a position as a government bookkeeper, estimated that an ideal sugar estate would need about fifty slaves; around 1800 such estimates had grown to one hundred.[30] These numbers were ideals and most estates had fewer workers. In 1792, 70 percent of the 197 estates in St. Croix had fewer than one hundred slaves, while 25 percent had between one and two hundred, and very few plantations, such as La Grange with 288 and Princesse with 397 enslaved workers, had more.

Danish West Indian estate owners, particularly those in St. Croix who engaged in sugar production, imported enslaved Africans to labor on their plantations and provide a broad range of auxiliary services in Christiansted and Frederiksted, the urban centers of the island. From the mid-eighteenth century to the turn of the century, the purchase of enslaved Africans resulted in an average yearly increase in the slave population of 3 percent, with numbers growing from approximately 15,000 in 1755 to 35,000 around 1800, despite high mortality. Slave trading was particularly intensive in St. Croix with its expanding production. Three years after the purchase of St. Croix, in 1736, 137 enslaved people lived on the island; in 1743 the number had grown to 1,700 and continued to grow until the 1770s when the population had reached 23-24,000 individuals. In the last decade of the eighteenth century, slave auctions were expanding and sales were again increasing. This late eighteenth-century increase was, ironically, caused by the royal edict of 1792 that abolished Danish participation in the transatlantic slave trade by 1803. The edict specified a ten years grace period during which the state would subsidize the purchase of slaves, particularly women, while also removing the head-tax for female field laborers. As a result, the slave population of St. Croix grew to approximately 27,000 men, women, and children in 1804.[31]

Abolition changed, but did not ease, conditions for enslaved Africans and their descendants on St. Croix's plantations. The soil began to show signs of exhaustion and international sugar prices fell rapidly after the Napoleonic wars of the early nineteenth century. Between 1800 and 1848 sugar production fell by approximately 30 percent in St Croix, while the enslaved population declined by about 40 percent. Yet the size of land planted with cane shrank by merely 10 percent in the same period, a sign that enslaved men and women now had to work harder to sustain production levels. Meanwhile, they faced heavily indebted masters who, haunted by the prospect of bankruptcy, had little reason or ability to improve the lot of their workers. Indeed, the number of estates in St. Croix fell from 181 to 132 in the first half of the nineteenth century. Some estates became part of larger plantations, and slaves risked being moved to a different section of the property; other estates were turned into less labor-intensive cattle pens, a decision that presumably caused indebted owners to move or sell estate slaves.[32]

The volatile sugar economy and the horrendous conditions on St. Croix' plantations ensured that demographical decline continued after the abolition of the transatlantic slave trade in the early nineteenth century. Loved ones, husbands, wives, children, kin, and friends died because of crippling work, undernourishment, and the aggressive disease environment of the West Indies. Although death had been an enduring element of slaves' daily lives, a condition that shaped both experiences and dreams, in the eighteenth century, the way in which death shaped life changed in the nineteenth century. Now high death rates, for the first time, resulted in a steady demographic decline because new Africans no longer arrived to replace those who died. The enslaved population in St. Croix fell from about 27,000 in 1804 to about 16,700 in 1848. Presumably, it became even harder to replace lost loved ones and partners. There were simply fewer and fewer people with whom enslaved men and women could create bonds of affection.[33]

African-Atlantic Gender Ideals

Africans and Afro-Caribbeans in the Danish West Indies were confronted with many, often contradictory, practices and ideals of gender and sexuality, but they also brought ideals of how femininity and masculinity ought to shape life from their various home communities in West Africa and West Central Africa to St. Croix.[34] In the West Indies, these homeland bonds were described by an elaborate language of 'nations,' developed in collaboration with Moravian missionaries, among others, during the eighteenth and early nineteenth centuries. At least fifty such nations were represented in St. Croix.[35] Some of these were more significant than others; from the 1760s to the 1820s, large numbers of Africans described themselves as Mandingo and Bambara from Senegambia; Amina from the Gold Coast; Watyi from the Slave Coast; Igbo, Kalabari, and Mokko from the Bight of Biafra; and Kongo and Loango from West Central Africa.[36] The full sweep of African nations, some large, some minuscule, indicates that while many enslaved found people with whom they could share or attempt to share language, meaning, and cosmology, others found themselves utterly dislocated and alone.

The intensive cultivation of most of the land in St. Croix meant that Africans and their descendants did not live in isolation on sugar estates. Many enslaved people created friendships, established families, and got into conflicts, not only with enslaved people from their own estate, but also with people from the surrounding estates who either spoke their own language or a language they knew.[37] At night they walked along narrow paths and crossed estate boundaries to meet fellow slaves from neighboring estates.[38] And, just as they met people with whom they could share and develop ideas, they also met Africans and Afro-Caribbeans who did not share their language, their specific set of memories, and their particular outlook on their West Indian predicament.[39]

The various nations were part of the identity practices that guided Africans when they arrived in St. Croix during the eighteenth and early nineteenth centuries. As historian Louise Sebro has shown, some enslaved Africans passed their national identity on to their children while others were able to adopt the national label they found most fitting for their position in the Caribbean.[40] Enslaved Africans and Afro-Caribbeans used nations both to identify themselves and to recognize others. In 1774, Sam identified himself as a "Coast Mandingo," in 1777, Attje teamed up with a "compatriot" when he ran away, and in 1798, Endevour explained that he was born on "the coast of Guinea by Fort Wilhelmine."[41] Fifteen years later, in 1813, Regina related that she was "born in Congo in Guinea."[42] Likewise, the transatlantic passage shaped identity. When Edinburg and Jenny were interrogated in 1773, Edinburg explained that they had arrived in the West Indies on the same ship, and, in 1815, Juliana made sure to mention that she had been born during the Atlantic passage.[43] Other enslaved people used the nation as a way to characterize and identify others. So, in 1758, Catta from St. John Estate explained that the estate slaves had obtained poison from a sorcerer, named Gomma, a "Congo negro," whose language one of the other parties to the trial understood "rather well," and, in 1815, William identified a runaway as "an Igbo negro."[44]

The language of nation and homeland was a living tool in the hands of enslaved men and women. It was a way of forming bonds, establishing knowledge, and pursuing dreams. In 1758, when twelve slaves were accused of plotting an escape to Puerto Rico, they thought they were going to a "country, where one lives well and in freedom like in Guinea." In 1774, the enslaved man Sam related that he had "learned from his father in Guinea" how to prepare an herbal bath that brought luck. Indeed, African experiences and languages were shared to establish bonds of understanding that crossed the borders between more narrow African identities; it was an alternative, or rather a parallel, to the regime of racial slavery that shaped life in the Danish West Indies.

By necessity, enslaved Africans in the Danish West Indies adjusted to and became familiar with African traditions beyond their own. In 1778, during a trial against the slave woman Mariana, the enslaved woman Felicity related that she spoke the language "*Gibiitoh*" with all her owner's slaves and with fellow inmates in Christiansværn, the fort securing the town of Christiansted, which also served as the colony prison. Witnesses explained that Felicity carried the name "*Seoind* or *Zui*" when addressed in "*Gibiitoh*." Mariana also spoke "*Gibiitoh*," but she explained that it was not her native language. Felicity had taught her to speak it during the many evenings they had spent together.[45] Presumably, Mariana's experience was common. Neither slaves nor judges could hope to reproduce their homeland's traditions in the Danish West Indies. In St. Croix, they primarily communicated in English-Creole, although some enslaved people preferred to speak the Dutch-Creole that had developed in the early years of Danish colonization of St. Thomas. Others, like Felicity and Mariana, communicated in West African languages.

It was in this multinational world, confronted with the racial and gendered ideologies and practices that emerged with Atlantic slavery, that enslaved Africans developed, came to share, and argued over ideas about marriage and adultery. The Moravian mission inspector, Christian Andreas Oldendorp, who was commissioned to write a history of the Church's substantial Caribbean mission in 1766, left one of the most detailed descriptions of African lives in the Caribbean

in the eighteenth century. Having spent eighteen months in the Danish West
Indies in 1767-68, Oldendorp related that Africans and Afro-Caribbeans accepted premarital, flirtatious relationships and described such relationships as
"*skelmtrek*," an term which, according to Oldendorp, denoted "immoral things."
However, he also noted that Africans and Afro-Caribbeans condemned married
people who went astray and characterized their acts as "*overspeel*" (adultery) in
Dutch-Creole.[46] According to Oldendorp, Africans arranged marriages following
the norms and traditions of their homelands. This meant that a man who wished
to marry would first speak to the woman's parents, if she had any. If the parents
and the woman accepted, the couple was married. In Oldendorp's view this occurred without any ceremonies, though those who could afford it celebrated with
a banquet and a dance.[47]

Oldendorp did not make do with mere observations of Africans in the Danish
West Indies. He also conducted group interviews with representatives of around
thirty African nations. These interviews offer a glimpse of how African members
of the Moravian congregation shared recollections of their African life within the
institutional framework provided by the Church. During their conversations with
Oldendorp, the Christian converts painted Africa as an idealized site of harmony
and order. Invited to speak in general terms about their homeland, they established
a consensus about what constituted marriage and adultery rather than express
insecurity or ambivalence about how to understand and evaluate marital conflicts.
They conjured up Africa as a place where relationships between men and women
were regulated by strict behavioral codes. Marriage was part of the reproduction of family, kinship, and lineage affiliations. A marriage was arranged through
negotiations between the groom-to-be and the family of the bride. Each group
of interviewees depicted specific practices. The Mandingo group, for instance,
related that a groom would have to endow his would be in-laws with gifts, and
the Kalabari group reported that a man would have to pay for the upbringing of
his wife-to-be. Yet all of the groups stressed that marriage involved the exchange
of wealth between families and bound families together through kinship ties.[48]

The regulation of adultery appeared as strict and transparent in the interviewees' accounts as African marriage rituals were orderly. As they spoke, and were
later represented by Oldendorp, the interviewees came to share a past in which
adultery was easy to define, unacceptable, and rigidly investigated by priests who
possessed reliable spiritual-legal powers and led ordeals — involving, for example,
potions, movable objects, and fire — to identify the transgressors. Each group
described the specific punishments that they remembered. The Amina group
stated that adulterers were punished with everything from torture and painful

death to a fine, and the Mandingo interviewees explained that a man who had committed adultery would be fined or sold into slavery.[49] Again, particularities were developed against a shared belief in the wrongfulness of adultery.

Conflicts and disagreements regarding marital behavior, obligations, and rights were not included in this tradition of Moravian and African memory making. Indeed, the possibility of divorce, a formal act highly dependent on the interpretation of spousal behavior, was not mentioned by any of Oldendorp's informants nor did the word divorce appear in the Dutch-Creole dictionary compiled by Oldendorp in the 1760s. Nevertheless, divorce was a possibility in many West and West Central African societies. Among the Loango in West Central Africa, for example, spouses could have their conflicts tried before a court headed by a female official called the Makunda. For the Fon, on the Slave Coast, divorce was also a possibility for common women and, similarly, the Anlo-Ewe, also on the Slave Coast, could divorce, although it became more difficult during the eighteenth century.[50]

Tenuous evidence suggests that a legal-spiritual infrastructure, informed by African-Atlantic traditions and allowing enslaved men and women to sanction the break of marital norms, may have been available in St. Croix during the eighteenth and early nineteenth centuries. In the 1760s, Oldendorp described legal tribunals headed by sorcerers who detected crime through divination and ordeals.[51] Similar judicial practices were also present in the Danish West Indies in the nineteenth century; and would be categorized as obeah at this point. In 1815, the free woman of color Jenny Almeyda intended her slaves to undergo an obeah ritual, a *"duddlido* test" in order to discover a thief among them. Although the trial never came to pass — Almeyda was arrested — she explained that the test consisted of placing a robe, tied with the leaves and flowers of the Flamboyant, i.e., *delonix regia*, around the neck of the suspects. The rope, Almeyda explained, had "the force that it would tighten around the neck of the culprit and remove his breath and in this manner the thief will be detected."[52] Likewise, Qvamina was sought out by both enslaved and free people for his ability to pinpoint thieves by divining with cards in 1825.[53] Although there are no examples of adulterers discovered through such procedures, their presence evinces that, at least some, enslaved Cruzians developed their own procedures for crime identification and examination.

Marginalizing Gender

In the Danish West Indies, as in the other Caribbean slave societies, the majority of enslaved men and women worked together in the cane fields, and although women constituted a growing proportion of fieldworkers beginning in the early nineteenth century, fieldwork never became an exclusively female domain.[54] Working days were long, ten to eleven hours, and longer during harvest — in the months from January to August. During these long days of strenuous labor, enslaved men and women worked side-by-side in gangs wherein gendered differences were marginalized.[55] For many West African men and women, labor organization, particularly fieldwork, in the West Indies challenged the gendered labor regime they knew from their home communities.[56] Indeed, men would have understood fieldwork as intimately related to a female sphere, while many African women would have seen the expropriation of their produce by male slave owners as a collapse of the gendered division of the economy they knew at home.[57]

For Danish legal experts in the West Indies, the presence of women in the cane fields also challenged the complementary gender order they would have known in rural Denmark. In Denmark, conditions for small farmers changed dramatically during the eighteenth century with the abolition of adscription for the male peasant population in 1788. Yet the gendered division of work in agricultural households remained relatively fixed during both the eighteenth and nineteenth centuries. Male farmers headed their households, gathered with other village farmers to organize cultivation, and were responsible for fieldwork — both on their own fields and on the fields of the noble estates. Although women also participated in agricultural production, for instance in hay staking and in the beating of grain, they were mainly occupied in rural households with heavy tasks such as food preparation and preservation; carding, spinning, sewing and knitting; mucking among and feeding farm animals; milking; and tending to the kitchen garden. The organization of agricultural labor in the West Indies, where most men and women worked together in the cane fields, contrasted starkly with Danish and, more broadly, European labor traditions.[58]

The organization of plantation labor made aggressive inroads into the ways in which enslaved people performed their lives as men and women and was supported by the institutionalization of chattel slavery. As in other Atlantic slave societies, Danish West Indian chattel slavery made it difficult for enslaved men and women to establish relationships independent of their masters. Slaves' intimate lives, marriages, parenthood, and kinship ties were subject to the decisions of their masters and mistresses and could be broken at will. This was not simply an abstract possibility. For enslaved men and women, the St. Croix domestic slave market spread uncertainty and fear. During the late eighteenth and the early nineteenth centuries, one out of ten slaves risked sale decennially, and most slaves were sold alone, without family, kin, or friends. For people enslaved on sugar estates a sale could mean that they were moved long distances, losing the chance of maintaining regular contact with their loved ones. For instance, this happened to the enslaved at Mount Welcome Estate, owned by John Brenner in 1816-17. Despite their collective attempt at preventing their sale, John Brenner sold forty of his sixty slaves in 1817, presumably to work in the cane fields on other estates.[59]

In the Danish West Indies, the chattel principle was formulated in 1733 when Governor Philip Gardelin proclaimed the first comprehensive Danish West Indian slave code, which was to shape prosecution until the 1830s. Gardelin declared that "negroes" were "made slaves by God himself" and they were to be regarded as nothing more than their masters' "money." With this proclamation, drawing on the highest authority of European society, the Christian God, Gardelin turned men, women, and children into epicene capital, a category that had little, if any, room for a gendered inflection.[60] Like Gardelin, Danish West Indian officers, slave owners, overseers, and slave traders used impressive amounts of representational resources in turning men and women into non-gendered numbers in bonds, mortgage deeds, probates, taxations lists, and the like. Indeed, this was probably the most common way of depicting the enslaved in the Danish West Indies.[61] It had its literary attendant in descriptions that turned enslaved people into parts of the West Indian landscape, such as Reimert Haagensen's celebration of the "beautiful sight" of "slaves, standing side by side on a piece of land," holing in almost complete symmetry and order.[62] These slaves were neither male nor female, but rather figurative signs in a productive landscape.

Specific ideological work was needed to turn African women into such productive signs. As in other Atlantic slave societies, tropes of exceptionally strong African women circulated in the Danish West Indies. Descriptions of these strong, yet fictional women emerged in the narratives of travelers and planters, and in the administrative reports of the Danish colonial state; they promoted the claim that the differences between African men and women were minimal. Consequently, such tales were, as Jennifer Morgan has argued in relation to the Anglophone Atlantic, an important ideological corollary to the concentration of women in fieldwork. In the 1740s, an unknown writer, presumably associated with the planter Johan Lorentz Carstens, remarked that Africans were "thick, fat and flabby, and in those characteristics there is no difference between males and females, except that the female negroes have large, long breasts […]."[63] These women could give birth without pain and therefore their reproduction did not diminish their ability to perform hard work in the cane fields; in their productive capacity they were similar to their male counterparts. It was this female figure that allowed slave owners, as Morgan also notes, to imagine African women as a twofold source of capital. Both their children and their labor could potentially be realized through market transactions.[64]

The web of ideas and practices that established Atlantic racial slavery weighed heavily on enslaved people's working and family lives, but they did not face only these pressures. Competing gender models from the old worlds of Africa and Europe were also at play in the Danish West Indies. The female peddlers that crowded the Sunday markets in the Danish West Indies were a sight foreign to most observers who frequently commented thereon.[65] Here African economic divisions between men and women appear to have gained the upper hand in the encounter between Africans and Europeans in the islands. More important for the limited social advancement accessible to enslaved people, however, was the transfer of elements from a European labor tradition to the Caribbean. This tradition enabled some enslaved men to climb their way up in the plantation hierarchy. European masters and their descendants associated masculinity with craft, training, and the ability to command; consequently, there were more ways to get out of the cane fields for enslaved men than for women. The authority enjoyed by slave drivers was reserved for men in the Danish West Indies and the power, delegated by masters, to punish often lay in the hands of these men.[66] Some enslaved men were also trained to become craftsmen; they took up positions such as distillers, boilers, coachmen, guards, herders, and valets.[67] Since many of these skills were necessary for the efficient production of sugar, they were highly prestigious, and the men who possessed them were compensated with better provisions and more free time, among other benefits. In comparison to slave men, the range of occupations available to enslaved women was limited, and the tasks they performed were less prestigious. Enslaved women could move out of the field by becoming domestics, working as washerwomen, seamstresses, cooks and maids. Altogether hard labor in the cane fields dominated the working lives of the majority of slaves, yet old world ideas about manly authority and womanly service, and the gendering of professions that these ideas undergirded, may have shaped the hopes and dreams of enslaved men and women alike.[68]

Racializing Gender

Intersecting with the pressures responsible for altering, and often marginalizing, the gendered practices among enslaved men and women, Atlantic travelogues, literature, and art, teemed with fantasies about the intractable and overpowering sexuality of Africans and their descendants.[69] Not surprisingly, colonial agents in the Danish West Indies appropriated such ideas. Members of the Danish West Indian administration, including the islands' judges, worried that life in the West Indies turned their known gender order upside down. This was not only because Africans', allegedly, freewheeling sexuality was a challenge to Christian life. It was also because they reckoned African sexuality to be a force that fostered a fierce resistance to masterly authority. In 1802, Government Councilor, future governor general, Adrian Benjamin Bentzon claimed that the slave man demanded "to seek out over the entire island as many wives as he pleases, and force in this matter will not only prove useless, but, perhaps especially among the Africans, might result in the most fatal occurrences."[70] In 1774, Judge Hellvad believed that he had detected one such fatal occurrence. He argued that the enslaved cooper John had set fire to his master's sugar cane because one wife had been taken away from him and another wife had been ordered to perform fieldwork.[71] With considerations such as these, Danish West Indian colonial officers established African sexuality as a particularly tense domain that was best left undisturbed since interference in the conjugal and sexual lives of slaves could prove ruinous to the social order of slavery.

In contrast, missionaries in the Danish West Indies believed that their ability to change Africans' conjugal lives was a measure of missionary success and therefore this was a subject that could not be ignored. The Moravian missionaries, who had established themselves in the Danish West Indies in 1732, saw African sexuality as a key obstacle to their mission. Mission inspector Oldendorp believed that the "negroes are […] particularly inclined to carnal lust and are keenly carrying on with it."[72] The Lutheran Pastor Torkild Lund expressed a similar view when he reported to his superiors in Copenhagen in 1788. Lund focused exclusively on the marital lives of his flock of 163 Africans and Afro-Caribbeans.[73] According to Lund, most were unfaithful and had shifting partners. In an attempt to mend this conjugal disorder, Lund introduced a non-legal marriage ritual, perhaps inspired by similar rituals developed by the Moravians, in order to accommodate his Christian ideals to West Indian slavery.[74] Time and again Lund admonished members of his congregation to commit to long-term monogamous relationships; time and again he compelled them to hold hands and pledge fidelity. Repeatedly, according to him, they did not keep their promises. In Lund's world, African and Afro-Caribbean men and women were driven by strong, sinful desires to entertain connections with the other sex.[75]

The allegedly powerful sexuality of Africans, which white West Indians imagined, proved both tempting and attractive. In the 1740s, the writer associated with Johan Carstens praised domestic slave women for their noble dispositions. They were "well-behaved, modest and of a willing disposition," indeed, these women were supposedly so willing to please that they had "seduced most of our young European men to have common physical intercourse."[76] Together with the daily practices of cooking, cleaning, washing, and caring that brought some enslaved women close to their superiors, these descriptions of enslaved women's licentious natures framed the sexual encounters — from rape, assault, and enforced intimacy to negotiated partnerships — between enslaved women and white West Indians.

For a few women, often termed *husholdersker* (i.e., housekeepers) in official Danish records, their relationships to their owners or other white men resulted in promotion or even freedom. Indeed, of the slaves manumitted in the town of Christiansted in the period from 1780 to 1812, 55 percent were children, 14 percent were adult men, and the remaining 45 percent were women.[77] Maria Elizabeth Yard was one such housekeeper. Born in the 1780s, probably the child of an enslaved African woman and a white father, she acquired her freedom in 1800 and went on to establish herself as a successful businesswoman and a slave owner herself. By 1804, she resided in Fisher Street in Christiansted town with Johannes W. Mouritzen, judge in Christiansted Police Court and Christiansted Lower Court from 1806-1824. Their relationship continued until he died in 1839, leaving her both real estate and a significant pension.[78]

The tropes of the African woman as sexually attractive, easily available, or, alternatively, brutish, and hardworking were central elements of the racial ideology that legitimized Atlantic slavery. These tropes, in one way or the other, focused on the body as a site of productive, reproductive, and sexual deviance, yet they were often contradictory and pointed in opposite interpretative directions. Thus, for instance, the idea of the promiscuous African was sometimes used to explain why enslaved people in the Danish West Indies were unable to reproduce. Hans West, school teacher in St. Croix and notary public in Christiansted Lower Court, assertively argued that the "common animal mingling [between slaves] must interfere with procreation" in the late eighteenth century.[79] At other times, the figure of the hard-working woman in the field was associated with ease of reproduction. Reimert Haagensen, in the mid-eighteenth century, argued that enslaved women were "tough by nature and used to hardship, they do not consider it much to give birth to a child. There are many, therefore, who are up and about in one or two days." These women, Haagensen advertised, were "altogether quite fruitful, many of them giving birth to twins and sometimes even to triplets."[80] The inconsistencies and variations that marked racial thinking in the Danish West Indies made for a plastic ideological universe that backed the practice of the more or less violent interracial relationships while also undergirding the expropriation of women's childbearing abilities and the use of women in fieldwork. Therefore, rather than confronting a wholesome and smooth ideological universe, Africans and their descendants confronted a web of intersecting ideas that — as we will see — could be mobilized, ignored, negated or appropriated by them and their judges as best they could.

Christian Gender Ideals

Parallel to the ideas about gender that enslaved Africans brought to the West Indies from their diverse homelands, to the degendering practices linked to fieldwork and to the discursive racialization of Africans' gender and sexuality, the Danish West Indies also witnessed the development of a powerful image of Christian slaves. This image emerged through the success of the Moravian mission that, as mentioned, began its activities in the islands in 1732.[81] The Moravians initially encountered fierce resistance from planters, primarily, mission inspector Oldendorp related, because they believed that enslaved women, once converted, would "no longer let themselves be taken advantage of to do impermissible and godless things."[82] However, these obstacles were overcome. By the 1760s many of the African helpers and elders within the Moravian Church were highly placed on their plantations, occupying positions as drivers and craftsmen or as housekeepers.[83] The Moravian missionaries had also integrated into plantation society. They owned Bethlehem Estate from 1765 to 1806 and possessed no fewer than 151 slaves in 1825, a number that placed them among the larger slave owners in the Danish West Indies. Soon, succeeding governors general and other high-ranking officers in the Danish West Indian colonial administration supported the Moravians and came to believe that some enslaved men and women could be truly Christian, modest, and chaste.[84]

The figure of the Christian slave woman had a particular place in Moravian thinking. The Brethren claimed that equality in spirit could exist between masters and slaves. They argued that Christianity could reform slaves, forwarding as one of their favorite examples the figure of the chaste slave woman resisting the promiscuous attempts of her white master.[85] One of the most celebrated Moravian converts was the free woman of color Rebecca who married the Moravian missionary Matthäus Freundlich in 1738.[86] This marriage was a singular event, but enslaved and free African and Afro-Caribbean women were appointed as helpers and elders within the Church and used as exemplars of dedicated Christian living by the missionaries. For instance, Benigna was described as a "very dependable and faithful worker among the widows," while Jonathan and Barbara "constituted an example of the powerful impact of evangelical grace on the hearts of the most evil people, such as they were before their conversion."[87] Alone and as the wives of male helpers, women emerged in the Moravian canon as icons of faith. They shouldered the responsibility of reaching out to other women, and, judging from the fact that women constituted the largest group of baptized Moravians, women helpers were diligent in spreading the gospel among enslaved women in St. Croix.[88]

In contrast to the highflying travelogues and tedious administrative reports about African promiscuity, the dream of a Christian community of slaves was made readily available to enslaved men and women in the Danish West Indies. The small Danish Lutheran congregation was primarily active in the towns of Christiansted and Frederiksted, and, although Pastor Lund primarily saw promiscuity among Africans and their descendants, he was also able to report on the transformative power of his faith. The Christian slave couple Maria Magdalena Fridrik and Johannes Wied was held out as an example. According to Lund, Johannes wrote love letters to Maria Magdalena with "admirable decency and pleasantry."[89] Meanwhile, in the countryside, the Moravian Brethren reached out to a large proportion of the enslaved population from two, and as of 1805 three, blossoming mission stations in St. Croix.[90] Friedensthal, the oldest station, saw some 5,000 slaves baptized in the years from 1760 to 1799, and since the congregation also included those not yet ready for baptism, the station may have established contact with around 25 percent of the enslaved population in St. Croix by the turn of the century.[91]

Many slaves, whether or not they had actually adopted Christianity, had the chance to learn about Christian teachings through these thorough missionizing activities. In weekly prayer meetings and conversations between teachers and proselytes, the Moravian missionaries made a detailed knowledge of Christian notions of morality and marriage available to those who could and cared to listen to their teachings. According to missionaries, slaves would reform their housing, clothing, eating habits and marital lives when they adopted Christianity. Wife and husband would sleep in a room apart, they would cover their naked bodies, and they would eat together instead of separately. Christianity, it was claimed, ensured a stable marital life and decreased promiscuity among slaves and between slaves and their masters.[92]

Enslaved Africans and Afro-Caribbeans encountered Christian gender ideals through their meetings with island missionaries and Danish West Indian judges, among others. These ideals were changing in the late eighteenth and nineteenth centuries. In Lutheran political thinking, marriage and household were viewed as central pillars of the state. Social order was established through ties of fatherly authority that stretched from God the father, through the king, to the master of a household and his underlings. Women were subordinate and complementary members of the household, with responsibilities revolving around the proper running of the house, including the handicrafts and trade that generated additional income.[93] However, in the late eighteenth and nineteenth centuries, new ideas emerged. Now loving sentiment, rather than God-given hierarchy, was imagined as the glue that held families together and engendered social cohesion.[94]

In Denmark-Norway, men and women of middling rank, particularly in Copenhagen, participated in the development of ideas about respectable living that emerged in Northwest Europe during the second part of the eighteenth century. So-called patriotic societies, such as *The Sisterly Philanthropic Society* established in 1790, were often modeled on British and German precedents. Members were encouraged to take upon themselves responsibility for the development and progress of society and its members. Women of middling rank were expected to withdraw from public life and devote themselves to their husbands and children, providing loving homes that catered to the needs of all family members. Danish educational literature was dominated by themes such as diligence, deference, sexual propriety, and piety. Private girls' schools mushroomed in Copenhagen, offering a curriculum that combined Christian instruction with academic courses and household training.[95] It is not surprising that one of the first Danish anti-slavery pieces, authored by Peder Paludan, a well-known Danish pastor, was entitled *Letter to the Ladies on the West Indian Islands* (1784) and called on white women to better the treatment of slaves and spread Christianity among them. Women, Paludan believed, were more sensitive to the plight of slaves than men.[96]

The new ideal of womanhood that circulated among educated and commercial groups in Denmark did not leave men untouched. In seventeenth- and early eighteenth-century Denmark, religiously motivated legislation portrayed women as subjects who could actively seduce men.[97] In the late eighteenth century, however, the legal debate turned away from ideas of female promiscuity and focused on

Frederiksted town, watercolor by Frederik von Scholten, 1837. In the foreground the artist is seated with his sketchbook, assisted by a young boy, perhaps his valet, and an older servant. Frederiksted is in the background. The well ordered landscape of La Grange plantation is presented as nearly empty, except for the minuscule figures of a row of field laborers cutting cane. Not counting infants, 230 adults and older children lived at La Grange in 1837. They are almost entirely absent from this watercolor. Instead, the cane fields appear to be productive all by themselves (courtesy of *Museet for Søfart*, the Maritime Museum of Denmark).*

*   86.64-86.65. Reviderede Regnskaber, Vestindiske Regnskaber, Matrikler for St. Croix, 1837-1836, La Grange, 103.

helping mothers of illegitimate children. Single mothers were seen, at this point, as naturally inclined to care for and love their children. To help mothers, fathers were made legally responsible for paying alimony.[98] Indeed, the middling set of ideas that circulated in Copenhagen, echoing similar ideas in the larger Atlantic world, contained the claim that the threat to white Danish women's sexual purity came from men's desire rather than from unrestrained passions hidden within the female body.[99]

Enslaved men and woman had ample opportunity to acquaint themselves with this new muddle of ideas about Christian respectability. The Moravian Brethren remained the most important church in the Danish West Indies during the eighteenth century, but, in the nineteenth century, other churches, among them the Roman Catholic, Anglican and Dutch Reformed, also established thriving congregations in the Danish West Indies.[100] Together these congregations had baptized approximately 66 percent of the plantation slaves in St. Croix in 1804, and thirty years later, in 1835, they had reached out to 99 percent of the enslaved population of St. Croix.[101] As also suggested by the parties in the conflict at Hermon Hill in 1828, Christianity became an important narrative resource for enslaved Africans and Afro-Caribbeans, although it never stood uncontested.[102]

The Potential for Reform

When Thomas and Limmerich clashed in 1828, ideas about sexuality, family, and female and male authority and behavior had become increasingly important to slaves and judges alike, albeit for different reasons. In 1792, the Danish Crown ordered the abolition of the Danish transatlantic slave trade by January 1, 1803. Up to and after abolition, slaves' reproductive potential became a central concern for those involved in the debate about abolition. The metropolitan commission with the somewhat misleading name *The Committee for the Better Organization of the Slave Trade in the West Indies and on the Coast of Guinea*, which carried through the proposal to abolish the slave trade, began its analysis by stating that the Danish slave trade was not profitable for the Crown. Yet Denmark's West Indian colonies were lucrative, and enslaved labor was necessary for the continuing harvest of the gains. For the committee, therefore, abolition became a question of whether the enslaved population could be made to reproduce itself. The ten years leading up to 1803 would ensure that a sufficient number of enslaved women were imported, after which reproduction would become a question of whether enslaved men and women could be made to live in monogamous Christian families.[103]

Contemporary observers agreed that population growth in the Danish West Indies was negative. According to the committee, the problem was caused by the unequal sex ratios on sugar estates, the harsh conditions endured by pregnant enslaved women, mothers, and infants, and, not least, the unstable conjugal relationships among slaves. These circumstances could, however, be changed: the committee recommended the Christian instruction of all slaves and the strengthening and protection of marriages. Abolition of the transatlantic slave trade was possible, the committee believed, if debauchery was done away with and if marriages and morals were strengthened in order to encourage family life among slaves. It was a vision that drew on the long Moravian missionary tradition, which had shown that Africans and their descendants could indeed be transformed into respectable Christian men and women.[104]

The chief architect behind the abolition edict of 1792, Finance Minister Count Ernst Schimmelmann and his family owned large sugar estates in the Danish West Indies, and he received confirmation from his local West Indian staff that slavery seriously interfered with respectable gender conventions. In 1796, his estate managers, Charles Vanderbourg and François de La Porte, lamented to Schimmelmann that women slaves were obliged to do men's work. Women could only be removed from the cane fields, they believed, if more slaves were purchased through the transatlantic trade. This was the sole solution, if sugar production was to be organized "according to the ordinary rules of humanity."[105] In the minds of these estate managers, the degendering pressures that characterized fieldwork in the Danish West Indies was absolutely destructive to the very humanity of enslaved men and women.

The abolition edict did not meet with immediate resistance from planters and colonial authorities in the Danish West Indies. In response, Governor General Ernst Frederik Walterstorff considered how planters could be encouraged to establish hospitals and nurseries and how enslaved women could be convinced to provide better care for their children — a string of suggestions that were obviously based on the premise that infant mortality was due to African women's lack of motherly care rather than to sugar agriculture and slavery.[106] Walterstorff agreed with metropolitan authorities that Christian marriages would decrease the practice of polygyny and remove what he saw as the unrestrained rule of passions among enslaved men and women. Christianity had the potential, according to Walterstorff, to offset the main causes of negative population growth. Although the West Indian Government was less confident about the reform that Christianity could bring about, it also believed that Christianity could promote what it considered to be decent behavior among the enslaved population.[107] In the West

Indies, as in Copenhagen, the goal of these plans was to promote the ability of the enslaved population to reproduce itself.

But as the time for the ban of the slave trade in 1803 grew closer, planters and powerful colonial officials, among them Governor General Walterstorff, launched a campaign against abolition that fed on the old Atlantic idea that the supposedly beastly promiscuity of Africans was the reason that the enslaved could not reproduce themselves. In a shrill discourse directed at metropolitan authorities, this group now forwarded the claim that slaves' alleged lascivious habits diminished their reproductive capacities. Colonial officials admitted that the triad of Christianity, sexual propriety, and marriage could promote reproduction, but maintained that in their estimation, slaves' natural promiscuity made them unfit for reproduction. Indeed, in 1792, planter and Chief of the Burgher Militia, future governor general, Major Peter Lotharius Oxholm claimed that enslaved women induced abortions "only in order to indulge their unrestrained passions, without being hindered by children," a claim repeated by several governors general.[108] There was no hope for reform. Enslaved men and women could not escape their nature and therefore they would never be able to keep up their numbers. Abolition would cause the collapse of Danish West Indian sugar production.

The anti-abolitionists gained the support of the Danish ruler Crown Prince Frederik (de facto regent as of 1784 and King Frederik VI from 1808-1839). But *The Committee for the Better Organization of the Slave Trade in the West Indies and on the Coast of Guinea* managed to delay a final decision by requesting additional information. Questionnaires, designed to cast light on the marital habits and living conditions of enslaved men and women on sugar estates, were sent to the West Indies, and the West Indian Government was ordered to carry out an investigation.[109] Time passed and, by 1807, the British abolition of the transatlantic trade in enslaved Africans settled the dispute. The abolition of the Danish transatlantic slave trade was allowed to stand.[110] After more than a decade of continuous delays and negotiations, Christiansted's judges, the slave owners and overseers, and the enslaved men and women who answered the questionnaires about their intimate lives, could not doubt that reproduction, and, therefore, the sexual and marital relationship of enslaved men and women, was at the center of the absolutist metropolitan administration's attention.

Abolition became a fact in the Danish West Indies in the early nineteenth century. It prompted the Danish West Indian administration to slowly reconfigure its role in relation to slaves and masters. Government Councilor Bentzon succinctly argued that the West Indian Government had "to make slavery easier on the slave and safer for the planter."[111] The Danish West Indian authorities could no longer simply collect taxes, secure their mercantile interests and create the best conditions for sugar production and plantation owners. The colonial state had to insert itself, its juridical apparatus and regulatory practices, between masters and slaves in order to uphold the stable reproduction of the labor force and the continued production of sugar.[112]

During the eighteenth and nineteenth centuries, Atlantic, European, and African gender regimes met in the courts of Christiansted. For enslaved men and women this meant that they had to find their way between the gender ideologies and roles they knew from their various West Africans homelands, the Christian, middle class household ideals that were propagated by missionaries and colonial administrators in the Danish West Indies, and the Atlantic racial ideologies that legitimized their enslavement by figuring them as physically, sexually, and morally deviant. This was never easy, but abolition brought a further tension to the gender troubles experienced by enslaved Africans and Afro-Caribbeans in St. Croix. For judges, abolition meant that their long tradition of ignoring slaves' gendered concerns became even harder to uphold. For enslaved men and women abolition combined with a harder work regime, and continuing high mortality resulted in further pressure on the fragile domestic order they had established during the eighteenth century. It was against this background that, in 1828, the men and women on Hermon Hill fought about their conjugal relationships and about the traditions to be drawn upon in establishing the nature of masculine authority. In the Danish West Indies, death charged life, and in this brittle atmosphere enslaved men and women began to voice their ideas about authority, sexuality, and family. In the courts of Christiansted, they encountered judges who had become almost as interested in these issues as they were.

Detail of the court book containing the testimony of the enslaved man George, 1804.
A week after the trial against George began on August 3, 1804, he gave the statement, translated on the next page, in Christiansted Lower Court. During his statement, he quoted the threat of the driver Jimmy against Grace.

CHAPTER 2

Representing Slave Voices

In July 1804, the enslaved man George appeared before Christiansted Police Court and explained why he had attempted suicide. He did so by sharing a story about his troubled marital life with Judge Hans Cramer Winding and Court Scribe Johan Ludvig Rosenstand Goiske. Scribe Goiske noted that

> the negro George appeared before the court. He explained that he is born on the coast [i.e. of Guinea], does not know his age, is not baptized and does not confess to any religion. He has been in this country for approximately 20 years. His explanation from the preliminary interrogations was read to him, and he acknowledged it as correct, adding that the driver had told him "that if you will give me a prize then I will get you your wife back, but if she is given to you without my permission, then I will flog her daily. This I can do and nobody shall protest, as our master is in his house, and I will seek opportunity when the overseer is not present" […] The indignation aroused by this and by the driver Jimmy hindering his wife from returning to him and also wanting to cart-whip him for no fault of his own drove him to the wretched act [of stabbing himself with a knife in the stomach]. He explains that he could not help it. His wretched condition at the moment when he learned that he was so near an undeserved mistreatment made him wish that he was dead rather than alive.[113]

More than a year had passed since the Danish transatlantic slave trade had been formally abolished, and colonial authorities and planters were still debating whether conditions on estates were conducive to married life and reproduction. Intentionally or not, George contributed to this debate as he explained the difficulties he faced maintaining his common law marriage.

The transcription of George's deposition, in which he powerfully described his failing male authority, illustrates that Christiansted Police Court and Christiansted Lower Court allowed slaves to explain their actions and invested the representational resources necessary to conserve their explanations; even when their statements were not a close echo of the concerns with slave crime formulated in slave legislation. Yet George's recorded testimony, which is anything but unique, does not reveal under what conditions slaves' statements were made in Christiansted's courts, and, consequently, how trial prose can be read as containing self-portraits and stories formulated by enslaved men and women.[114] Indeed, George's words-in-writing are less transparent than they might appear, and they were certainly not a verbatim reflection of what George said during the court session.

When enslaved men and women entered Christiansted's courts they faced rigid and formal procedures designed to ensure the supposedly efficient and fair working of justice. Danish West Indian legal procedures shaped what slaves said and how their statements were transformed into written records. Procedures framed the inquisitorial techniques judges used and formed the thematic content and narrative structures of slaves' answers. Legal protocol was restrictive both in form and substance. Yet it also ensured that enslaved men and women were included in the process of litigation through their formal roles as defendants, witnesses, and informal plaintiffs and in their substantial capacities as men and women; hence George was not merely represented as a slave, but also as a man. The inclusive, yet restrictive, elements of Danish West Indian legal culture turned gendered ideas and practices into a shared, yet disputed, common ground through which enslaved Africans and Afro-Caribbeans spoke, sometimes as best they could, sometimes against their will, and at other times not at all, to Danish West Indian judges.

Danish West Indian legal procedures were established to ensure justice, as it was understood by the royal administration in the West Indies and in Denmark, and it was tightly linked to legal writing; to turning the vaporous words uttered by enslaved people into stable signs on paper, carrying legal validity. Such stabilization also occurred in the trial against George, charged with attempted suicide in Christiansted Lower Court in 1804. During ten court sessions, from July to September 1804, Court Scribe Goiske entered the statements of seven slaves, their master, and their overseer on eleven sheets of the folio-sized court book authorized by Governor General Balthazar Frederik Mühlenfels.

As noted, the question about what trial records represent is much discussed among historians of Atlantic slavery, yet all agree that it only makes sense to think about slave voices if the enslaved were involved with some degree of volition in the fashioning of the prose at hand.[115] Enslaved men and women needed a narrative space in which they could craft their stories, and such space often, but not always, existed in Christiansted Police Court and Lower Court in the eighteenth and nineteenth centuries. Slaves' appearances before Christiansted's courts were ordinary events, and slaves were embraced, with restrictions, by ordinary legal actices. To capture how such curbed inclusion shaped the statements enslaved people made in court, the conditions that simultaneously enabled *and* constrained slave speech and its preservation in the court books of Christiansted jurisdiction in St. Croix need to be mapped.

The Danish Atlantic Legal System

In the Danish West Indies, enslaved people were tried in ordinary courts that were part of a hierarchical Danish Atlantic legal system. In 1754-55, when the Danish state took over the Danish West Indian islands from the Danish West India and Guinea Company, the Danish West Indian courts were instructed by royal decree in an *Ordinance on Justice and Police* to operate as their Danish counterparts.[116] Unlike British Caribbean slave societies, the Danish West Indies, therefore, had no slave courts designed specifically to deal with slave crime.[117] Danish West Indian slaves were tried by the same judges and in the same courts as free West Indians. The judge, or magistrate, that slaves were most likely to meet was the *byfoged*. The office of the *byfoged* included posts such as judge in the lower court and police court as well as the position of chief of police. This meant that, at the low end of the Danish Atlantic legal system, enslaved people would need to communicate their version of events to the *byfoged* who monopolized, so to speak, state legal power at this level of the system. Other legal decision-makers, judges in instances of appeal, the governor general, and the absolutist king, only became relevant to enslaved people at a later stage of the legal process.

In the eighteenth and nineteenth centuries, there was one police court in each of the four jurisdictions of the Danish West Indies. These courts prosecuted crimes against public order and performed investigations into more serious crimes that, subsequently, might be prosecuted in ordinary courts.[118] The ordinary courts consisted of a lower court, one in each jurisdiction, and a West Indian Upper Court (until 1804 St. Croix and St. Thomas including St. John each had their own upper courts). The ordinary courts had the authority to try both civil and criminal cases. From the lower court verdicts against slaves could move to the West Indian Upper Court and to the Supreme Court in Copenhagen. Most often it was the acting governor general who would decide if a slave case was to be moved from the police court to the lower court or appealed from the lower court to the West Indian Upper Court, and from the Upper Court to the Supreme Court.[119]

Figure A: Danish Atlantic Legal Institutions in St. Croix and Copenhagen, 1755-1848

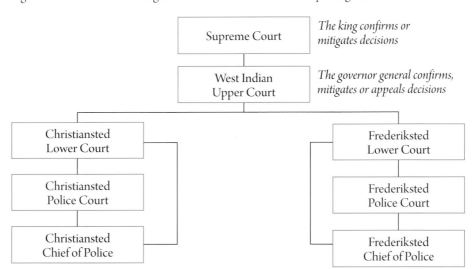

In the hierarchical Danish Atlantic legal system, writing was a key element of the legal process. Judges and scribes meticulously drew up volume after volume of court protocols containing the transcripts of proceedings and verdicts. Writing was central because the lowest level of judicial authority was connected to the very highest level. It was the transcripts of proceedings in Christiansted Police Court, Christiansted Lower Court, and the West Indian Upper Court, as well as the written deliberation in the Supreme Court, that allowed judges and other legal authorities to communicate. Trial transcripts enabled appeal courts to evaluate decisions made at lower levels and allowed West Indian governors to exercise their duty of supervising the police courts. For instance, Judge Lars Wiel sent a clerk with the court book to Governor General Ulrich Wilhelm von Roepstorff to receive instructions on how to proceed during a trial in Christiansted Police Court against James Scott, accused by his slave woman, Johanne Maria, of killing her baby in 1772. The clerk returned with the order that the public prosecutor was to prosecute Scott in the lower court.[120] In this way court records made it possible for governors and kings to intervene in legal processes by using their prerogatives to confirm, appeal, and mitigate verdicts. Links were established and maintained by the court scribes who meticulously documented the proceedings. This propensity for textual representation meant that Danish West Indian slaves were tried in a setting wherein the transformation of oral testimonies into written depositions was common practice.

Indeed, the statements made by enslaved Africans and Afro-Caribbeans were inserted into the circulation of documents that linked distinct legal institutions and grounded legal decisions much more often than transcripts of statements made by other court participants in the Danish West Indies. This was partly because the vast majority of slave trials were based on criminal law, often slave legislation, and criminal trials were often up for appeal, but it was also because enslaved people did not and, for the most part, could not, participate in disputes by delivering written complaints and depositions to the courts. The only way to gather and preserve their knowledge about the episodes in dispute was to record their statements, and this happened either in the police court or in the lower court. Higher ranking legal officers who needed to acquaint themselves with legal disputes involving slaves in the jurisdiction of Christiansted could read the transcripts of the interrogations made in Christiansted Police Court and Lower Court.[121]

Inquisitorial Procedures

In criminal trials, enslaved Africans and Afro-Caribbeans, like everyone else, were put through inquisitorial examinations that gave them the opportunity to present themselves to Christiansted's judges. The inquisitorial procedure placed the questions and answers exchanged between judges on the one hand and witnesses, plaintiffs, and defendants on the other, at the center of the legal process, and allowed judges to intervene more actively in court proceedings. Inquisition had emerged as a way to achieve a more efficient process in criminal trials in Denmark during the first part of the eighteenth century and was brought to the Danish West Indies in 1755. In contrast to most civil suits that involved the lengthy exchange of documents between litigants, the inquisitorial procedure allowed judges to make their own enquiries and to establish knowledge about a case independent of the parties involved.[122]

Danish West Indian slave law provided ample space for slaves to appear as defendants before the Danish West Indian courts. The picture, however, was much more bleak when it came to slaves' ability to act as witnesses and plaintiffs. Neither of the two main slave codes issued for the Danish West Indies — the slave code decreed by Governor Philip Gardelin in 1733 and the royal slave code of 1755, crafted in Copenhagen as a close copy of the French *Code noir* of 1685 — could be used as strong legal guidelines.[123] The former code did not receive royal confirmation, and the latter code was not proclaimed in the Danish Indies, only emerging as a legislative reference point during the early nine century.[124] Neither of the codes, therefore, constituted a solid legal foundation for the prosecution of slaves.

Nevertheless, the codes contained some indication as to how the colonial courts were to handle the question of slaves' positions as witnesses and plaintiffs. The 1755 slave code contained a drastic restriction of slaves' legal abilities, prohibiting them from acting as plaintiffs and legal witnesses. Yet the code also allowed judges to use slave testimonies as a "means of obtaining further knowledge about the case" at hand.[125] The widely cited 1733 code was less harsh in this respect. It stipulated that a slave could be punished upon the testimony of a "white or a Christian who knows the meaning of an oath"[126] Strictly speaking, this rule merely contained a procedure for weighing court statements against each other. Neither of the two slave codes, however, prohibited judges from questioning slaves as subjects with information relevant to legal disputes. Although formally prohibited from oath taking, slaves were allowed to speak *as if* they were witnesses in the Danish West Indian courts. Not until October 1830 did this change. At that point, a royal ordinance allowed Christian slaves of "good moral" character to provide sworn testimony.[127]

During the eighteenth and nineteenth centuries, slave legislation and Danish procedural traditions provided juridical backing to Christiansted's judges when they tried slaves as defendants and questioned them as witnesses. The same possibilities were not available to enslaved men and women who wished to act as plaintiffs. The 1755 slave code explicitly prohibited slaves from acting as plaintiffs, and the 1733 code's elevation of one persons oath as sufficient proof against a slave, in principle, disqualified any complaint a slave could have had against a free, white or Christian person. Yet small fissures in the legislative landscape suggested the possibility of slaves acting as plaintiffs.[128] In 1771, Governor General von Roepstorff and the West Indian Government were instructed by the metropolitan government to warn and, if necessary, prosecute those masters who mistreated their slaves.[129] These instructions raised the possibility that enslaved people could enter the Danish West Indian courtrooms as victims of abuse represented by legal officers of the Danish colonial state.

Narrative Framing in Slave Legislation

Whereas the institutional set-up and the procedural rules of the Danish West Indian courts enabled enslaved Africans and Afro-Caribbeans to speak as defendants and witnesses, slave law established a restrictive narrative structure against which slaves had to craft their stories. Substantial slave law in the Danish West Indies consisted of West Indian *plakater,* i.e., placards issued in the West Indies, royal ordinances formulated in Denmark, and *The Danish Law* (*Danske Lov*), a comprehensive law compilation issued in 1683 and the foundation of Danish metropolitan jurisprudence in the eighteenth and the early nineteenth centuries.[130] Of these legislative acts, the Gardelin slave code of 1733 provided the most important reference point. Similar to slave laws in the wider Atlantic world, the Gardelin code established the slave as a criminal subject who acted out of a hodgepodge of dangerous emotions and inabilities. It consistently linked skin color and servitude, describing bondspeople as "negroes" who were "evil," "disloyal," "disobedient," "threatening," "proud," "obstinate," "stupid," "blind," and capable of "insolence" and "excesses;" in the code the only acceptable alternative was for slaves to be "submissive."[131]

So, Danish West Indian slave law chiseled out the many crimes slaves could commit and supplied judges with a pool of derogative adjectives through which they could understand enslaved peoples' depositions. At times, enslaved men and women attempted to appropriate some of these terms to craft a defense. This was possibly what Christopher did in 1802. He had deserted his position as a carpenter's apprentice without returning to his master. In Christiansted Police Court, Christopher explained that he believed that he was not "obliged to return" before his tenure expired since he would then return "as a bad carpenter."[132] Christopher may have attempted to provide a new interpretation of the rules of apprenticeship, but he may also have been playing on the stereotypes codified in slave law, pretending that he had not known better and had been just as ignorant as Danish West Indian slave laws asserted that slaves were.

The thematic content of Danish West Indian slave law was open to partial appropriation by enslaved Africans and their descendants, but the law also constrained slaves by its descriptive gaps, and these were hard to overcome. The consistent use, in slave legislation, of the term "negro" to describe both men and women, marginalized gender as a social principle that judges should consider in slave trials, while it also pushed slaves' diverse African backgrounds out of legal view. The result was a slave figure with no biography caught, so to speak, in the limited time frame provided by the criminal acts described in legislation.[133] Indeed, in the approximately seventy-five West Indian placards concerning slaves, issued between 1755 and 1803, only two divided slaves by their sex, and none of these were used by Christiansted Lower Court judges.[134] This absence of the gendered identity of legal subjects was characteristic of slave legislation. In contrast, free blacks and free people of color were described in Danish West Indian placards as men and women, and gender specific punishments were designed for members of this group.[135]

Well aware that they were supporting a policy that stood in stark contrast to metropolitan norms, authorities in Copenhagen actively supported the removal of gender as a category with legal implications for women of African descent in the West Indies. In Denmark, cases concerning illicit sexuality emerged when a parish minister informed the local judge that he had baptized an illegitimate child. The judge would then take action against the parents, prosecuting their illegitimate sexual behavior and securing alimony to the mother.[136] This practice was also used in the Danish West Indies in the 1770s and 1780s where around forty enslaved women claimed alimony, although they do not appear to have faced charges for fornication. In 1784, however, West Indians judges were instructed by royal ordinance to not hear cases concerning adultery that involved black women and women of color. The ordinance prohibited clergymen from enquiring about the fathers of children born to women of African descent, and it proscribed that clergymen who knew the identity of such fathers were not to inform legal authorities. Danish West Indian judges therefore faced no pressure to prosecute illicit interracial relationships, and mothers of African descent were unable to claim support for their children.[137] In conclusion, the ordinance stated that it was not to be made public, as its articles would offend the sensibilities of the king's metropolitan subjects.[138]

Coming to Court

The first step in a trial against enslaved people in Christiansted jurisdiction in St. Croix was often an interrogation in the police court. Such interrogations occasionally drew large crowds into the courtroom. This, for instance, happened in 1773 in the trial against Johnto, accused of murdering her mistress with poison. Johnto denied the charge. Yet Judge Christian Hellvad, echoing the Gardelin slave code, believed that her denial was caused by what he viewed as her "stubbornness." It was, Hellvad thought, related to the fact that the "courthouse was full of people."[139] Mostly, however, court proceedings appear to have been dominated by professional legal experts. During sessions in the police court, the judge, the notary public, and at least two police officers were present. In Christiansted Lower Court, the number of legal officers increased. Enslaved defendants met the prosecutor, who was often the *advocatus regius*, that is, the public prosecutor. From the 1770s onward, enslaved defendants were represented by defense attorneys, and from the 1810s, lay jurymen participated in trials concerning capital offenses, although neither defense nor jurymen played a significant role.[140] The examination of slaves was in the hands of Christiansted Lower Court judges and they were assisted by notaries who acted as translators. These were the men who orchestrated the trials. They made sure that oaths were taken and that material evidence was presented. They also saw to it that slave defendants were brought from Fort Christiansværn in Christiansted, where they were imprisoned during the trial, and unchained before questioning.[141]

Thus, enslaved Africans and Afro-Caribbeans in the Danish West Indian courts met Danish and Danish-speaking white West Indian judges, the *byfogeder*. These judges served in courts that operated according to Danish legal traditions, with Danish as the language of law and transcription.[142] Many judges were recruited from Denmark; others came from the Danish West Indies. Irrespective of their birthplace, many were rooted in or had links to Copenhagen's emerging, educated, middling ranks and were linked by ties of patronage to the Danish-Norwegian absolutist regime. Many were married — some had married into important plantation families — and most were slave owners. Judge Christian Juul, for instance, who served in Christiansted in the 1760s, lived on Queen's Street with one, sometimes two, adult slaves as well as a few enslaved adolescents and children. In 1763, he attempted to enter the plantation business with the purchase of an estate in the district of Prince Quarter — in the eastern part of St. Croix — as well as its enslaved population, consisting of about forty adults in addition to some children. However, his plantation business was not successful. In 1764, he rented the property out, and the following year he appears to have sold it.[143] Some of his successors were more successful. Judge Alexander Cooper, born in St. Croix, and presiding in Christiansted's court in 1779 and 1780, owned two estates with his brother.[144] Likewise Judge Winding, son of a Danish parish minister, who served as police court and lower court judge in Christiansted for more than ten years around 1800 owned Cassava Garden and about sixty slaves in the Queens Quarter district.[145]

The judges serving in Christiansted's courts from the mid-eighteenth to the mid-nineteenth century had legal training. They held law degrees from Copenhagen University; either they were *candidatus juris* or they were *examinatus juris*, a degree obtainable by private students.[146] So these men were educated and well read, trained in law, and served by royal appointment. Engelbrecht Hesselberg, for instance, judge and court scribe in Christiansted in the 1750s and 1760s, was author of one of the first systematic expositions of Danish jurisprudence, the four-volume work *Juridical Lectures*, published in 1753-55, that became a standard reference work for lower court justices in Denmark in the eighteenth century.[147]

Like Hesselberg, Edvard Colbjørnsen, judge in St. Croix Upper Court in the late eighteenth century, was closely connected to metropolitan legal expertise. Both his brothers, Jacob E. Colbjørnsen and Christian Colbjørnsen, occupied powerful positions in the Danish legal infrastructure, the former holding the chair in law at Copenhagen University and the latter serving as Attorney General. Additionally, both were connected in various capacities to the Supreme Court.[148] Indeed, the judges of Christiansted jurisdiction in St. Croix were part of a transatlantic legal community that had its center in Copenhagen, with the Supreme Court, the Danish Chancellery and the absolutist king.

When slaves came to Christiansted Police Court and Lower Court to participate in interrogations, they encountered judges who included them in a standard division of legal subjects into plaintiffs, defendants, and witnesses. This division reflected the assumed contradictory interests of each party to a trial and ensured that the knowledge each brought to the courtroom would be contained in separate textual entries. Judges obtained the division when they interrogated plaintiffs, defendants and witnesses individually, and court scribes furthered it when they took down the statements of slaves one at a time. The formal division of statements was also guaranteed by physically separating those participants who were expected to give corresponding testimony, thus ensuring that one would not influence the other.[149] Hence, in 1764, acting Judge Søren Bagge noted that three slaves had "unanimously, though they were interrogated separately" declared that the enslaved man Mingo had played all night at a dance. On the basis of these and others depositions Bagge acquitted Mingo, who was accused of assisting a runaway woman.[150]

Although the slave codes of 1733 and 1755 restricted slaves' ability to appear as witnesses, enslaved men and women frequently appeared as subjects who could operate as (if they were) witnesses in Christiansted Police Court and Lower Court. In the former, slaves acted as witnesses in more than one-fifth of all trials conducted. They testified in trials against other slaves, but also in trials against free West Indians of all races.[151] The legislative restrictions in the 1733 and 1755 slave codes, did not, in other words, exclude slaves from appearing in Christiansted Lower Court and Police Court to provide information about the events examined by the courts during proceedings.

The ban on slave plaintiffs also became less effective during the late eighteenth and the nineteenth centuries, despite a strong Atlantic tradition supporting this particular legal disability.[152] Enslaved Africans and Afro-Caribbeans began to walk to Christiansted to complain about their owners and overseers to the chief of police or to the governor general. They described maltreatment, lack of provisions, overwork, and undue interference in their daily lives. Often slaves were dismissed and given a flogging because of their so-called "ungrounded complaints." Nonetheless, from 1785 onwards, no less than ninety-five trials and investigations in Christiansted Police Court and Lower Court began because enslaved men and women complained.[153] Also, enslaved men and women achieved legal representation when their owner or a third party brought charges to the court on their behalf,[154] and, similarly, the governor general or the West Indian Government ordered prosecution on behalf of injured slaves based on rumors and complaints.[155] Yet enslaved complainants were few when compared to the many enslaved Africans and Afro-Caribbeans who appeared in Christiansted Police Court and Lower Court as defendants in criminal trials.

Despite the inclusive formalities that were practiced in Christiansted's courts, the prosecution of slaves was characterized by a highly selective mobilization of legislation. Again and again, Danish West Indian judges ignored metropolitan legislation against various forms of illicit sexuality. The slave defendant was elaborately described in slave legislation, and it is not surprising that slaves entered Christiansted Police Court and Lower Court as defendants. Yet enslaved men and women did not appear in Christiansted's courts facing charges on account of their intimate lives. The royal slave code of 1755, which contained a vision of a formalized marital life among slaves and aimed at eradicating illicit sexuality, was never mobilized by judges to further this vision. The same happened to *The Danish Law*'s articles criminalizing extramarital sexuality. Lower court judges commonly invoked this comprehensive law compilation's section on crime when handling crimes that enslaved people had committed against each other, such as assault and murder, acts that were not covered in slave legislation. Yet *The Danish Law*'s section on crime also contained extensive provisions against adultery and fornication that were ignored by Christiansted's judges. No bondsmen or -women were prosecuted for these crimes, although they were explicitly prohibited both by Danish legislation and by the slave code of 1755. In contrast, a number of slaves were accused of murder, murderous assault, and assault on other slaves, although substantial slave legislation did not contain provisions against such acts.[156]

The narrative framing of slave trials that resulted from the ways in which Christiansted's judges selected from the legislation available to them changed little during the eighteenth and nineteenth centuries. This was mainly because the legislation informing slave trials remained more or less static. Enslaved men and women met the same charges and similar questions during the entire period from the mid-eighteenth to the mid-nineteenth century (see Figures B and C below). So, for instance, judges continued to question enslaved defendants about the duration of their marooning, because they needed this information in order to determine the correct sentence. Likewise, they questioned slaves about when and how they stole, because this knowledge was necessary to determine what punishment was relevant according to the law.[157]

The legislative framework, and hence the types of charges enslaved defendants faced, remained more or less the same during the eighteenth and nineteenth centuries. Yet the abolition of the transatlantic slave trade, and the growing concern among elite planters and colonial officers with the productive and reproductive potential of enslaved men and women, did affect the prosecution of slaves in Christiansted's courts. The new political order, described concisely by Government Councilor Adrian Bentzon, when he argued that the Danish West Indian Government should ensure a new balance between enslaved laborers and their owners, turned judges' eyes toward the bodies of slaves whose strength and health needed protection. So, Christiansted's judges moved crimes, such as marooning and disobedience, downward in the legal system from the lower court to the police court, and thence from the police court to the discretionary decision of the chief of police. Here punishments were less harsh and formal rules less strictly enforced. This reshuffling resulted in a significant decrease in the number of charges raised in Christiansted Lower Court by the late eighteenth century; a similar decrease occurred in the charges investigated by Christiansted Police Court in the 1820s (see Figure D).

There were other signs that the changing political environment of the nineteenth century informed prosecution in Christiansted jurisdiction. An increasing number of trials emerged concerning the treatment and maltreatment of slaves. Whereas there was merely one such case in the mid-eighteenth century, there were more than a hundred in the late eighteenth and the nineteenth centuries.[158] Even more suggestive of the need to preserve the labor force, the number of charges for suicide and self-mutilation among slaves grew significantly in Christiansted Lower Court during the early nineteenth century. George, with whom, this chapter began, was questioned because he had attempted suicide, an act viewed by Christiansted's judges as a severe threat to the stability of the West Indian colonies. Indeed, when another enslaved man, Thomas, was convicted for cutting off his left hand in 1801, Judge Winding argued that this was a crime against the Danish colonial state. According to Winding, the state protected slave rights and in return the enslaved were obliged to submit to the authority of their owners.[159] Likewise, in 1812, Judge Mouritzen described grand marronage as high treason because it deprived the colony of slaves and would "undermine its prosperity and shake its foundation."[160] Without slaves, Mouritzen argued, the viability of Danish colonial presence in the West Indies was at serious risk.

Figure B: Charges against Slaves in Christiansted Lower Court, 1756-1848

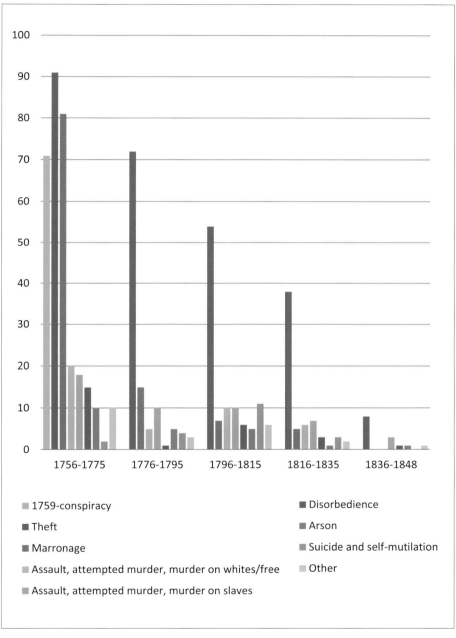

38.6.1-32. Christiansted Byfoged, Domprotokoller, 1756-1848; note that a defendant could face several charges at once.

Figure C: Charges against Slaves in Christiansted Police Court, 1756-1841

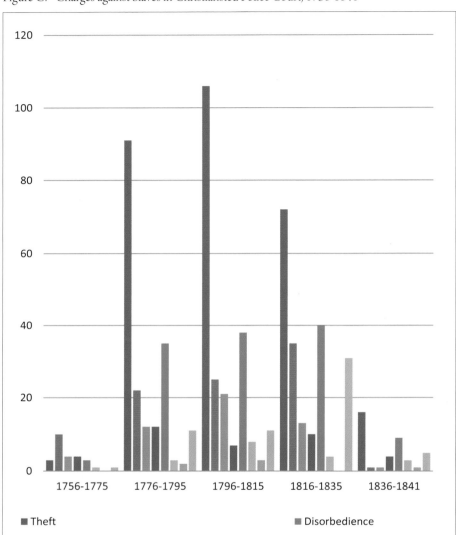

38.9.1-24. Christiansted Byfoged, Politiretsprotokoller, 1756-1841; note that a defendant could face several charges at once.

Figure D: Slave Trials, Christiansted Police Court, 1756-1841, and Christiansted Lower Court, 1756-1848

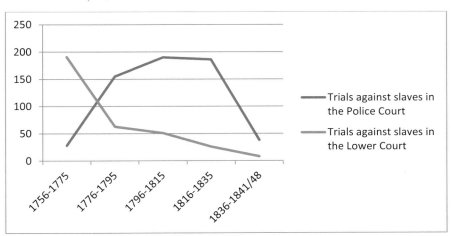

38.9.1-24. Christiansted Byfoged, Politiretsprotokoller, 1756-1841 & 38.6.1-32. Christiansted byfoged, Domprotokoller, 1756-1848.

Unfolding the Slave Figure

Whereas slave legislation and the charges drawn from it viewed slaves in terms of their bondage, judges and scribes worked with more elaborate, though still crude, portraits of the enslaved people they interrogated. Christiansted's judges made a standard series of observations in order to establish slaves' identities when they were first introduced to the court. As in George's case, the courts recorded the name, birthplace, religion, age, skin color, sex, and owner of the enslaved questioned. For the most part these classifications were adopted from ordinary interrogative practice and were similar to those used by judges to describe white West Indians. Such labeling was an indispensable feature of legal procedure because of the hierarchical links between the courts in the Danish Atlantic empire. Transcripts of interrogations had to be sufficiently detailed so that the governors general and the judges in the West Indian Upper Court and the Supreme Court could distinguish between the many people speaking to them through the trial records.

While slave legislation pushed slaves' gendered identities out of view, procedural practices brought them back into the courtroom. For slaves, this inclusion in ordinary practices diminished the reductive effect that legislation had on their ability to frame the dialogue with Danish West Indian judges. The legislation referred to a slave figure without biographical fixpoints, exclusively defined by subjugation, yet in courtroom practice, enslaved men and women were described as subjects with some, albeit not many, social characteristics. As the trial against the "negro George" in 1804 illustrates, these labels shaped the possibilities enslaved people had of speaking as individual men and women rather than purely as slaves. It was as an African man with a long history in the West Indies that George spoke of the "indignation" he felt when the driver interfered in his intimate life. Even the most widespread terms to denote slave status in trial records, "negro" and "negress," which collapsed slavery and race, also reproduced the social fact that slaves, like everybody else, could be divided into men and women. In contrast to legislation that consistently described enslaved men and women as "negroes," judges and scribes in Christiansted always noted the sex of slaves. Slave status did not lose importance, but it intersected with other identity markers to shape the ways in which enslaved men and women could appear in court.[161]

The reintroduction of gender categories, signaled by the scribal practice of classifying enslaved Africans as either "negroes" or "negresses," went hand in hand with the use of other social markers used in scribal practice. However, as with the gendered categories, enslaved men and women had little say in how court scribes labeled them. Scribes used set formulae with their own repetitive inertias. Skin color, like gender, was a matter of observation rather than inquiry and family history. Scribes laconically noted that enslaved men and women "did not know" their age. They reduced the diverse origins of enslaved Africans to a generic birthplace by noting that slaves were born in "Africa," "Guinea," and on "the Coast."[162] The many national appellations — Mandingo, Bambara, Amina, Watyi, Igbo, Kalabari, Mokko, Kongo and Loango, among others — by which enslaved Africans identified themselves in the West Indies and used to establish ties of belonging as well as to describe differences among themselves were removed from legal transcripts. The same happened to Africans' and Afro-Caribbeans' religious beliefs which were concealed under the standard phrase: "no religion."[163] So, while enslaved people in court had a sex, they were either men or women, Christiansted's judges did not see them as subjects with religion, meaningful origins, or a personal history that could enlighten the court and inform the proceedings.

The only element of this labeling that slaves appear to have been able to influence was the description of their faith. When judges asked about Christian belief, mechanical formulae gave way to the nuances of slaves' own statements. In 1782, the enslaved man Petrus stressed his adherence to the Christian faith by emphasizing that he was "baptized" and had been "to communion."[164] Daniel, in 1791, stated that he was not baptized, but he added that he had received Christian instruction from a Danish Lutheran mission priest. After thus stressing his links to Christian expertise, Daniel continued his statement by explaining that he had absented himself from his owner, Custom Officer Claus Schonning, not on account of being involved in theft, but because he visited "a negress in the countryside with whom he kept together."[165] Similar nuances surfaced in 1802 when one enslaved woman stated that "her Christian name is Juliane, but she goes under the name Aurelia on the plantation [… and] she confesses to the Moravian Church."[166] These enslaved men and women, and many more, outlined their personal histories of conversion. Their engagement with Christianity probably involved them in the broader meaning of Christianity as a sign of monogamous sexuality and respectable behavior as propagandized by Moravians, Lutherans and other churchmen in the Danish West Indies. In legal terms, however, Christianity was associated with trustworthiness and truth.

Declarations of Christian faith may have persuaded Christiansted's judges that these enslaved Africans and Afro-Caribbeans were somewhat more trustworthy than the slave figures established in slave legislation, yet it was not an option available to all. In 1802, the enslaved man Peter could only state that he had received instructions from the Moravians but was not yet baptized.[167] Indeed, more reluctant responses were also possible, as in 1797 when Baa stated that he "did not confess to any church, though he had been in the Church of the Moravian Brethren three times, but then abandoned it as he did not feel comfortable afterwards."[168] Nevertheless, the idea that Christianity transformed slaves — as the Moravians and other churchmen widely promoted, and which elite members of the Danish West Indian administration adopted — entered the courtroom through the regular unfolding of procedural formality. It gave enslaved men and women a narrow avenue through which to expand their narrative repertoire. As more and more enslaved men and women joined Christian congregations during the nineteenth century, it would, however, take more than the declaration of baptism to establish a Christian persona before the courts of Christiansted.[169]

Dinner party at custom officer Claus Schonning's and wife, 1796, watercolor by H.G. Beenfeldt. This depiction of a dinner party gives an impression of the different positions enslaved had within European households. The woman of color, to the left, wears jewelry and is well dressed. She stands close behind her mistress, ready to serve and presumably such intimacy enabled her to acquaint herself with the ways in which white West Indians hoped their slaves would behave and speak. The enslaved man wears less expensive clothing, indicating a less powerful position in the household. Though unnamed, this man may have been the enslaved man, Daniel, who visited his common law wife in 1791 (private collection, courtesy of *Nationalmuseet*, National Museum of Denmark, photo by Roberto Fortuna).

Commandeur Munthe von Morgenstierne.
Fair Grabroun.   Obesförmynder Tismand.
ved Truppene.   En Opvartende Malalinde.
cht.

Interrogating Slaves

During proceedings, the initial, rough presentation of trial participants allowed Christiansted's judges to determine what ritual to follow in order to secure the truth of their depositions. All free Christian inhabitants, men and women, Europeans, Africans, and their descendants, confirmed their statements by oaths when required to do so. Oath taking was a simple procedure. When the Christian freedman Johannes Gottlob appeared in Christiansted Police Court in 1781, the court instructed him to "take his oath" and "with raised fingers [he] restated that his statement was the truth in every respect."[170] Christiansted's judges could understand this ritual with the description of an oath from *The Danish Law* in mind. The raised thumb signified God the Father, the forefinger God the Son, and the middle finger God the Holy Spirit.[171] Consequently, oath taking linked Christianity to truth in the Danish West Indian courts.

Before 1830, slaves were not allowed to swear before God and the court that they told the truth. Nonetheless, Christiansted's judges met slaves with rituals that impressed upon them their obligation to tell the truth. Court scribes registered this practice through the standard phrase: "admonished to tell the truth."[172] This wording was identical to the one used to describe oath taking, suggesting that many slaves were cautioned about their obligation to speak honestly in much the same ways as free West Indians.[173] Yet the answers available to slaves and free persons were not similar. For free West Indians, the oath was the answer to a truth-admonition, for slaves, responding was more complicated. In 1800, the enslaved man Christian, who was called upon to testify in a case between two white men, began his statement by "solemnly promising that as he expected to receive the sacrament worthy of Jesus Christ, he would say nothing but the truth."[174] Yet most of the enslaved men and women, who attempted to respond to the admonition to speak the truth, did so through their courtroom stories. Some included the word "truth" in their statements; some attempted to craft a persuasive story. Others could not or would not play this truth game.[175]

The pressure on slaves to speak in ways that judges believed to be honest could increase as the trial progressed, particularly in the eighteenth century. During incarceration in Fort Christiansværn, ministers would visit enslaved defendants to urge them to speak the truth.[176] Inside the courtroom, some enslaved people, in addition to being confronted with simple admonitions, were more seriously admonished to tell the truth. Although the phrase "a serious admonition" was not used in the police court case against Johnto, the woman accused of poisoning her mistress in 1773, threats escalated during her trial as Judge Hellvad attempted to secure what he believed to be a true deposition. The "hangman" was called in to "scare" Johnto's daughter and "bring her to a true confession," and the interrogation of Johnto was moved from Hellvad's private residence to Fort Christiansværn "in order to see if said negress Johnto more easily could be brought to give a confession in a place like the fort." Later Johnto was tortured heavily, but without result. She maintained her denial.[177]

Indeed, the progression, in some trials, from simple admonitions, which judges sometimes described as "gentle," to serious admonitions, and from serious admonitions to torture suggests that the expression "a serious admonition" described flogging, if not the intimidation initially faced by Johnto and her daughter. In 1780, Louisa was "seriously admonished to tell the truth," and when that did not produce the desired confession she was subjected to thumbscrews, which, similarly, failed to change her statement.[178] Likewise, in 1784, Dublin received both "gentle and serious admonitions," but none convinced him to change his statement.[179] As Danish West Indian administrators did not view flogging as torture, they may have adopted the term "serious" to describe its use during interrogations.

In addition to the simple and serious admonitions, the latter a wording that may have been a euphemism for flogging, the courts of Christiansted also employed torture against slaves whom judges believed spoke falsely or were unwilling to speak. This was a practice supported by the Gardelin slave code of 1733, which allowed courts to have slaves flogged if there was a suspicion against them.[180] During the interrogations conducted by Lower Court Judge Hesselberg in 1759-60, following the discovery of what colonial authorities and planters believed to be a conspiracy to revolt, several suspects were tortured.[181] Yet when tensions were less high, during the ordinary and everyday proceedings of Christiansted's courts, torture was not generally practiced; this is likely because Danish West Indian judges relied on Danish procedural traditions wherein torture was rare.[182] Hence Christiansted Lower Court scribes noted the use of torture in seven verdicts of the 339 trials conducted against slaves in the court from 1756 to 1848, and, additionally, torture was noted in six of the 597 slave trials conducted in Christiansted Police Court from 1756 to 1841.[183] Indeed, one of the main Danish West Indian legal experts, State Councilor, future governor general, Wilhelm Anton Lindemann believed that it would be impossible to introduce military procedure, including torture, in slave trials, because Danish West Indian judges were so "accustomed to the civil procedure" that they were unwilling to change their habits.[184]

Despite its rarity, the use of torture signified the importance attributed to slave speech within the Danish West Indian legal institutions. Torture was used to force slaves to speak because slave depositions were the basis upon which justice could be enacted.[185] Far from silence, therefore, the point of torture was to produce speech. When Christiansted's judges ordered torture, they hoped that slaves would either begin to speak or speak differently about the incidents in dispute. However, this was not exactly the result of torture within the courtrooms in Christiansted. Torture was applied when a slave had already given a first statement. Thumbscrews or, what scribes termed, Barbadian gloves (a device with short, thick sticks that were interpolated between the defendants' fingers and tightened with a string), would be tightened once or twice but often to no effect. Most of the victims did not change their explanations substantially. In 1782, for instance, the slave Jørgen was whipped with fifty lashes for three successive days to extract a confession, but he did not confess; similarly, in 1779, Qvashy was tortured, but did not admit to having handled stolen goods.[186] Flogging was used up until the early nineteenth century, while screws and gloves went out of use in the 1780s.[187] Hence, in 1795, when Police Judge Winding asked Governor General Ernst Frederik von Walterstorff for permission to torture an uncooperative slave, he received a negative reply.[188] In his verdict Winding concluded that the use of torture during legal interrogations of slaves was no longer practiced in the Danish West Indies.[189]

More than anything else, Christiansted's judges used their questions to establish the depositions they wanted to hear. During interrogations, judges' attention swiftly turned from one issue to another — as happened to Sally whose story began this book. Sally, who came to court with a complaint about maltreatment, eventually faced a charge of attempted murder of her common law husband. Like Sally, the enslaved man George, whose conflicts with the driver Jimmy had driven him to suicide, also experienced a rapid shift of attention. During George's trial, Judge Winding began to question the driver Jimmy intensely about his involvement with the alleged obeahman Plato; at this point Winding was apparently less concerned with George's destruction of his own body than with Jimmy's possible misuse of his authority as a driver. Sweeping interrogations thus allowed judges to expand their net and incriminate slaves for any number of the many, many crimes described in slave law; and, if evidence for more serious crimes could not be established, the common crime of marooning often came in handy.[190] This all-encompassing interrogative practice made it particularly important to keep good records, even during police court proceedings, since police court judges could never know whether the testimonies delivered would later function as written evidence in Christiansted Lower Court and the appeal courts.[191]

When slaves were charged with crimes against other slaves the judges' questions were often precise, unemotional, and factual, but when slaves were charged with crimes against whites, they were met with insistent intimidation and leading questions designed to make them admit their guilt.[192] Thus Raina, accused of poisoning her master in 1774, was interrogated on five separate occasions, each time for hours. She was bombarded with long and convoluted questions that presumed her guilt. Public Prosecutor Balling, for instance, asked her,

> if she would not confess, now, that she both knew for what purpose the exhibited
> and previously mentioned powder was used or was to be used, and that she had
> put some of it in the cup, as explained, in order to kill her master?

Balling was convinced that Raina was lying. He asked Judge Hellvad to inform Raina that "other means," probably a reference to torture, would be used if she did not give a truthful explanation. Despite these terrifying and stubborn attempts at extracting a confession, Raina stuck to her initial account and insisted that she added powder to her master's wine whey because "old negroes" told her that it would "soften" his heart towards her.[193]

Fear and uncertainty shaped and constrained the testimonies enslaved men and women gave when they appeared before Christiansted Police Court and Lower Court. Enslaved defendants and slaves whose owners were on trial for mal-treatment, were imprisoned in Fort Christiansværn, sometimes for long periods, and at risk of being assaulted by Danish soldiers or isolated in the so-called black hole, a particularly foul place of detention found in the basement of the fort.[194] Enslaved people had good reason to fear both the judge and his officers.[195] As mentioned above, the judge in the police court and the lower court also held the office as chief of police and was closely associated with the daily floggings of en-slaved men and women at the public whipping post outside Fort Christiansværn as well as the frequent mutilations and executions at the gallows. Likewise, police officers, who were present during interrogations in the police court, patrolled Christiansted town with whips and dogs and may have carried these into the courtroom. Instruments of torture were readily at hand, and, if not in the court-room, stored nearby in Fort Christiansværn. Faced with these terrifying condi-tions, some slaves presumably attempted to craft persuasive stories while others may not have believed that it mattered what they said, and others still probably did not know what to say in their defense in the Danish West Indian courts.[196]

Although Christiansted's judges expertly employed their judicial knowhow to shape slave testimony, they were less prone to accept such measures when used by slaves' white superiors; perhaps because they suspected that owners were able to pressure, scare, and hurt their enslaved men and women to a degree that would

View of the harbor area in Christiansted, St. Croix, watercolor by H.G. Beenfeldt, 1815. Fort Christiansværn is shown in the back. Here enslaved defendants and occasionally also witnesses were kept during proceedings. The slim dark pole, left of the gate, is possibly the so-called *justitsstøtte*, literally the 'pole of justice', that is, the town whipping post (courtesy of *Rigsarkivet*, the Danish National Archives).

destabilize juridical authority. Indeed, enslaved men and women occasionally made it clear that their ability to speak in court was shaped by the violence and abuse they faced from their masters. This was, for instance, the main thrust of the statement of the enslaved man Jack in 1824. His demotion from foreman at the mill to fieldworker, he argued, was his master's way of punishing him for his previous court appearance during which he had testified to the illegal handling of produce on his master's estate.[197] More important for the judges, however, were the pressures exerted before trial proceedings. In 1766, the enslaved woman Catharina was acquitted because the slave girl who witnessed against her had been flogged, and, in 1783, the trial against the enslaved woman Rachel for poisoning her owner did not move from Christiansted Police Court to the Lower Court, perhaps because Rachel recounted that her confession was obtained when her owner flogged and tortured her.[198]

Despite the heavy constraints imposed on enslaved people by their masters, judges continuously upheld their ability to give testimony. Whereas some white Caribbeans interpreted slave legislation to the effect that slaves were prohibited from appearing as witnesses, judges consistently called on slaves to present themselves at court. In 1800, one Mr. Rohde, for instance, argued that allowing the testimonies of slaves was against Danish West Indian law. Nevertheless, Judge Winding found it "most proper" to hear what two slave witnesses had to say.[199] Slaves were allowed, and on rare occasions even forced, to answer the questions they were asked. Their answers provoked new questions and this exchange between slaves on the one hand and judges, notaries public, and prosecutors on the other turned the proceedings in Christiansted Police Court and Lower Court into a peculiar, broken, distorted, sometimes even violently enforced dialogue, but a dialogue nonetheless.[200]

Assembling as many depositions as possible, creating a polyphony of voices, was a fundamental part of legal proceedings in the Danish West Indies during the eighteenth and nineteenth centuries. Although many questions were shaped by slave law, and were designed to clarify whether slaves had committed specific acts (did you run away, did you steal, did you assault, did you stay out after dark and so on), the many social markers, particularly gender, by which slaves were introduced to the court established a constricted narrative space that could be filled with concerns beyond those given by legislation. Some enslaved men and women — as we will see in the chapters that follow — both used this space and attempted to enlarge it. They crafted stories that did not square with the figure of the degendered slave dominant in slave legislation. Debating the many, competing gendered ideals and practices present in the Danish West Indies, these men and women emphasized that they ought to be understood as gendered subjects, as men and women with specific desires, motives, and customs.

Words on Paper

For enslaved people's legal utterances to be represented rather than altogether distorted, to become ink on paper rather than transient words without permanence, Danish West Indian court scribes had to insert slaves' depositions into the court books in a manner that ensured that such written entries corresponded to what slaves said. Since the Danish transcriptions were not verbatim, the many words uttered by court participants had to be translated, summarized, and transcribed. If the judges of Christiansted Police and Lower Court wanted to alter slaves' statements, it was as words were inserted into the trial protocol that they had their chance. Yet this was not exactly what happened. Although the transformation of oral statements into written text summarized slaves' depositions, it did not entirely alter them.

Christiansted's scribes summarized hours of speaking into a few handwritten pages.[201] To do so, they reused phrases and established narrative coherence within each deposition. These measures allowed them to ignore the idiosyncratic oral formulations of court participants and decide immediately what to include and exclude. Scribes would leave out similar depositions or fuse similar testimonies into a single deposition that would then be attributed to many witnesses.[202] Moreover, they often excluded the questions posed by judges and prosecutors.[203] Together these techniques gave scribes a fast hand and enabled the Danish West Indian courts to base decisions on the preserved statements of all those questioned.

In the cosmopolitan Danish West Indian world, translation was a necessary precondition for the recording of court testimonies. The majority of those who appeared before Christiansted Lower Court and Police Court did not speak Danish, but the administrative language in the Danish West Indies was Danish and court books were kept in Danish. This meant that translation was essential to the legal process and that it was a routine task of Christiansted's judges, scribes, and notaries public.[204] Translation took place during proceedings rather than afterwards, leaving little room for later editing and alteration. In Christiansted Lower Court, the enslaved man John Danesen, for instance, heard Notary Public Christian Müller "read" to him "in English" the Danish transcript of a statement he had made previously in Christiansted Police Court. For this to happen, Müller translated a Danish text into spoken English on the spot during the court session.[205] In this way, legal officers would translate from Danish to English and *vice versa;* oral statements were rendered in written Danish only to be turned back into spoken English in later sessions when defendants were confronted with what they had said previously.

Enslaved Africans had to speak a European or a creolized European language to be understood by Christiansted Police Court and Lower Court. Most slaves spoke English or English-Creole when they were interrogated. Many would have had just as varied and nuanced a language as the Danish judges and scribes for whom English was also a foreign language. Indeed, during the eighteenth century, Danish, German and, to a lesser degree, French was spoken in Denmark, whereas knowledge of English was relatively rare. Interrogations were also conducted in Creole, or *kreolsk* — a term that probably referred to the Dutch-Creole, which had emerged on St. Thomas as Dutch settlers established themselves on the island in the late seventeenth century — and was used by the Moravians and the Danish Lutheran mission. In 1802, Christiansted Police Court thus questioned six slaves in "Creole." They complained that their master punished them because they did not speak "English to him."[206] In addition to these languages, a few slaves were recorded as speaking French or Danish; such as Adolph Ulrich, born on the "Coast of Guinea," who explained himself in Danish in 1800.[207]

In contrast to Africans and Afro-Caribbeans who mastered the languages of Christiansted's courts, newly arrived Africans had extremely limited possibilities for using the representative space created by the procedures of the Danish West Indian courts.[208] Unlike gender, which awkwardly brought together men and women despite their skin color, African origins and languages rigidly separated Christiansted judges from enslaved Africans. When, in 1780, Christiansted Police Court called on the enslaved woman Bellinda to act as witness, Scribe Christian Ewald noted that Bellinda "explained that she had recently come here to the country" and could not "without great difficulty explain herself in Creole or the other languages used here." Notary Müller declared that he could also not understand her, and she was dismissed from court.[209] Whereas speakers of European languages and Creoles were translated into Danish, such services were not provided for those who spoke an African language. They were simply not represented.

Witnesses such as Bellinda, without sufficient fluency in the languages of the Danish West Indian courts, were dismissed. However, enslaved African defendants who could not explain themselves were in a worse situation still. In 1795, a defense attorney argued that the enslaved defendant Cudjoe ought to be excused because he could only explain himself in the "Coast-language."[210] Judge Winding did not agree. He believed that Cudjoe was simply uncooperative and decided that what he saw as Cudjoe's rude behavior during the interrogation was grounds for an arbitrary sentence.[211] Governor General Walterstorff concurred, and Cudjoe received one hundred lashes at the whipping post in Christiansted town.[212] Language barriers also hit the two newly arrived African women, Sarah and Present, when they were charged in Christiansted Police Court in 1802 with assault of their overseer. During the trial, Present managed to explain that she had nothing to do with the assault. Sarah spoke a language that was altogether incomprehensible to the court and her statement was not taken.[213] The court sentenced both women to be sold away from the Danish West Indies; Governor General Walterstorff agreed, adding that Sarah should be allowed to bring her child with her.[214]

There is very little evidence in existence that can give us an idea of the kind of language enslaved Africans and Afro-Caribbeans used in court. Yet observers of Danish West Indian society noted that some slaves had sophisticated storytelling skills that were not restricted to language alone but actually involved the whole body as an instrument of narration. Mission inspector Oldendorp described how the Africans he met engaged their audience. They show, Oldendorp wrote, "with their hands how the event unfolded; they get up and imitate the movements which occurred in the story, and they animate the narrative in many ways, also with their tone of voice and pronunciation."[215] Court scribes and judges seldom noted that slaves used movement and intonation to shape their depositions; indeed, this rich tradition of narration almost never entered the trial transcripts.[216]

Most enslaved Africans came from societies that developed and stored knowledge in oral performances. In the West Indies they met Danish legal officers accustomed to a literate elite culture. The result of this meeting was probably that trial transcripts had a stricter time progression and clearer lines of causality than slaves' spoken statements actually contained. The unique statement of the enslaved woman Sibell, made in Barbados in 1799, may provide a glimpse of how Africans spoke in the Danish West Indian courts during the eighteenth and nineteenth centuries. In her story, Sibell related that she was captured in Africa; she explained that her "Budder in Law come in, and take me up and say he going to carry me to see his udder wife, he take and carry, carry, carry, carry, carry me all night and day, all night and day 'way from my Country."[217] Although elements of Sibell's language may have been exaggerated to show her flawed English, her story also contains features that related to a tradition of oral performance. Repetitions were used to stress important points and coherence was achieved by the use of copulative conjunctives, particularly "and." In contrast, the trial transcripts circulating in the Danish West Indian legal system were saturated by subordinating conjunctions, such as "so," "then," "because," "therefore," and "for which reason."[218] These terms linked events, establishing that one event led to the other, and, therefore, were central to the establishment of a coherent plot that identified culprits and explained how slaves had prepared and executed their offenses.

The many slave depositions about fear illustrate what happened when slaves' stories were written down in Christiansted's courts. Throughout the eighteenth and nineteenth centuries, court scribes noted that slaves ran away "because" they were afraid.[219] The causality that suffused the transcripts emerged because judges wanted to identify acts and motives. They wanted to know what had been done, who had done it, and why. So, instead of being a diffuse emotion that shaped enslaved peoples' interaction with masters, fear was streamlined in the trial prose. It was reduced to a feeling that erupted at a given moment and explained a specific action. Yet it was not Christiansted's judges and court scribes who imposed this feeling on slaves; enslaved men and women referred to fear to explain their behavior. Thus, the transcription of slave depositions sharpened the causal links already present in the warped dialogue between judges and slaves; it did not, however, remove the narrative substance of slaves' court statements altogether.

With few exceptions, enslaved Africans and Afro-Caribbeans did not participate with written complaints and depositions as did free West Indians involved in litigation in Christiansted's courts. Therefore, slaves depended on court scribes' ability and willingness to accurately render what they said in writing. *The Danish Law* stipulated that transcriptions should take place "immediately in court," and court scribes appear to have followed this instruction in Christiansted's courts.[220] Often, slaves were asked to confirm that their statements, as recorded by the scribe, were correct. Many transcripts included references to the progression of the court session. Scribes would note when court participants arrived and left.[221] Judges "read" statements made by one court participant to another, who had spoken earlier in the same session. These readings were possible because scribes wrote while the court was in session. In 1781, during one session in Christiansted Police Court, acting Judge Ewald questioned one John Benners and later in the same session he "read" Benners' statement to the enslaved defendant Pallas.[222] Likewise, Daniel, on trial for threats of arson in 1804, had the testimony of another slave, Clinton, "read" to him.[223] Twenty years later, this scribal practice was still in place. When a group of slaves complained to Judge Mouritzen in 1822, he began by hearing a few spokespeople, and then he had their statement "read" to the whole group.[224] Transcription, like translation, occurred quickly after the spoken statements, ensuring, of course, that scribes had court statements clear in their minds when they recorded the interrogation transcripts.

The transformation of slaves' statements, which took place when they were translated and transcribed, meant that some episodes and forms of causality were given little weight in the records of interrogation; it did not, however, always imply that they were altogether excluded. In 1779, for instance, Christiansted Police Court questioned Thomas Nugent in a trial against the slave Lembrecht, accused of poisoning his master. Scribe Ewald had to correct himself several times as he transcribed Nugent's statement. According to Nugent, Ewald wrote, Lembrecht "had put ~~poison~~, something in a dish of cabbage in order to ~~kill~~ make the overseer *Soft*."[225] Ewald did not impose a predetermined interpretation on Nugent's statement, though he was certainly tempted to do so. The moment in the legal process when judges decided guilt and punishment was postponed, and, before verdicts were written up, there was still some space for statements that did not altogether correspond to the preconceived ideas of the judges and scribes.

The formal procedures in the Danish West Indian courts created a constrained space for the emergence of slave voices and gave enslaved men and women limited opportunities to present their view of the events in dispute. Court scribes presented slaves by noting a number of social markers. Taken together these markers represented an opening up of the harshly reductive and abstract slave figure present in slave legislation. Yet in contrast to, for instance, descriptions of religion and birthplace, which placed Africans in a position that few white West Indians would ever assume (i.e., as subjects born in Africa without Christian faith), gender categories pointed to the possibility that white West Indians could have something in common with the Africans they enslaved.

The textual slave voices emerging from court records were neither completely free nor completely estranged and determined. They surfaced in the meeting of slave legislation, formal procedures, and, as we will see, the narrative contributions of enslaved men and women. The sheer ordinariness of the legal procedures that surrounded enslaved Africans and Afro-Caribbeans meant that they met interrogative and scribal practices similar to those used in conjunction with other court participants; these practices aimed at preserving legal depositions, including those made by slaves. The formal division of legal subjects meant that judges questioned slaves one at the time, and scribes recorded their statements in separate textual units. It also meant that the trial prose generated in the Danish West Indian courts did not have a single, stabilizing author, a kind of 'master judge' that endowed the interrogative records with coherence and pre-settled the question of guilt. Instead, authorship was unevenly divided between judges, scribes, and slaves and, therefore, many enslaved men and women must be understood as co-authors, if sometimes reluctant authors, of the trial statements produced by Christiansted's courts. Slaves' stories were streamlined and abbreviated, but during this phase of the legal process, Christiansted's judges and scribes did not wholly remove those elements of a statement that did not correspond to their own perception of a case.

Indeed, the representative practices of Christiansted's courts, purely formal, created a particular site in which Atlantic racial slavery fused with Danish judicial traditions and allowed slaves to engage in an unequal dialogue with Danish West Indian judges. In this meeting, ideas about femininity and masculinity became an important narrative stage set because Danish West Indian judges considered enslaved people as gendered, that is, as men and women with behaviors, capacities, and desires that corresponded to their sex. Despite the reductions performed by slave legislation, ordinary legal procedures turned slaves into men and women and this inclusion created a possibility, a tenuous common ground for presumed understandings, deep misunderstandings, and outright distortions. It was on this slippery foundation that enslaved African and Afro-Caribbean men and women began to craft narratives that focused on how men and women, African as well as European, behaved, misbehaved and ought to behave in the Danish West Indies.

CHAPTER 3

Sexual Violence and
Legitimate Authority

In December 1829, the enslaved girl Cecilie appeared before Christiansted Police Court. She told Police Judge Frederiksen that her overseer had forced her to have "sexual intercourse" with him. Cecilie's experience was not exceptional for enslaved women in the Caribbean slave societies, but it was unusual for the Danish West Indian courts to hear a claim like hers.[226] Danish West Indian judges had used all of their creative legal skills to exclude such claims from the courts during the eighteenth century. They had effectively ignored those elements of slave law and metropolitan legislation that could have brought cases of sexual abuse and violence to their courts. Indeed, they were so effective that court book after court book was penned containing only the faintest traces of such experiences. Yet it was no mere coincidence that Cecilie's claim appeared in court in the 1820s.[227]

Cecilie's position of speech, what she said and the conditions that enabled her to craft her testimony, was shaped by a specific historical conjuncture whereby enslaved Africans and Afro-Caribbeans represented themselves as respectable, Christian men and women and used these self-portraits to contest the authority of their masters. Enslaved peoples' narrative inventions emerged in the stiff legislative arenas of Christiansted, where procedure and legislation stood almost unchanged until amelioration in the 1830s. Yet these narratives also emerged in a world of rapid change. Abolition of the transatlantic slave trade in the early nineteenth century, reconfigured the world of slaves and judges alike. In the Danish West Indies colonial officers had been engaged in debates about enslaved peoples' potential for reform, the nature of their sexuality, and their gendered behavior since the late eighteenth century. Indeed, the nature of gendered relationships among the enslaved population had become absolutely central to official concerns about the future of sugar production in the Caribbean.

Abolition further amplified the impact of the appalling mortality rates on the lives of enslaved Africans and their descendants. Yet in the nineteenth century, more and more enslaved men and women had families and existed as parts of wider social networks that stretched across St. Croix and beyond. Enslaved people looked to the world around them. Evangelical missionaries and abolitionists in Britain and other European states criticized slavery as immoral and economically inefficient.[228] In Saint -Domingue, slaves fought to revolutionize the political order, and revolts and uprisings ran like wildfire through the British Caribbean.[229] Enslaved Africans and Afro-Caribbeans in the Danish West Indies were not isolated from these events. Some slaves read abolitionist literature, such as a young man named Adam who had taught himself to read and write and enjoyed the antique Aesopian fable of the wolf and the dog that celebrates the freedom of the wolf over and against the bondage of the dog.[230] Others used their knowledge of wider Atlantic conditions when they ran away to, in the eighteenth century, Puerto Rico and, increasingly in the nineteenth century, to other Caribbean and North American destinations.[231]

In the late eighteenth century and during the nineteenth century, enslaved people developed ever more forceful narratives about themselves as Christian men and women in the courts of Christiansted jurisdiction in St. Croix. Slaves exploited the opportunity for self-representation provided by the formal legal procedures to emphasize that they were faithful spouses, caring parents, and responsible workers. Against this backdrop of Christian, gendered subjectivity, slaves raised an increasingly sharp critique of their superiors, whether white or of color. They began, among other things, to accuse both white masters and masters of color of improper sexual conduct, assault, and rape. The self-portraits slaves crafted — even in the many court sessions wherein sexual violence was not at issue — allowed some enslaved women, like Cecilie, to present the sexual violence they encountered as criminal acts. Slaves insisted that they had to be heard and understood as men and women rather than as slaves and this allowed them to introduce the tabooed theme of interracial sexual violence in Christiansted's courts.[232]

Unfinished Stories

In contrast to Cecilie's straightforward assertion of her overseer's sexual misconduct, most slave testimonies of the eighteenth century were vague and equivocal when violent sexual encounters between Europeans and Africans were at stake. During the eighteenth century, enslaved Africans and Afro-Caribbeans relied on hinting at rather than explicitly stating their own respectable behavior and their superiors' lack thereof. The portraits and self-portraits contained in slaves' testimonies were established by a variety of indirect descriptions and detours. Slaves crafted stories that relied on juxtapositions and quotations that supported their case rather than on explicit evaluations of the behavior of their superiors and opponents in court. These stories were often fragmented and inchoate, leaving ample room for interpretation and conjecture.

Whereas weak undercurrents in the Danish West Indian court books at times suggest sexual misconduct, such hints were not translated into explicit legal claims during proceedings in the eighteenth century. For instance, the statement made by a white witness that an estate manager had tried to persuade a slave woman to commit "fornication" was not pursued by Judge Cooper in 1780, nor was the description of a white distiller's brutal attack on a slave woman, who reproached him for uncovering her breasts, examined by Judge Winding in 1804.[233] Indeed, hints of the exercise of sexual power and coercion were so subtle as to be nearly invisible. Such was the case in 1772, when Police Judge Wiel investigated the death of an enslaved infant. In court, Johanne Maria, the enslaved mother of the deceased baby girl, initially declared that she did not "dare speak" as she was afraid of her master and his "negro wife" Sophia with whom he had several "mulatto" children. Eventually Johanne Maria overcame her fear and told Judge Wiel that her master had killed her baby and punished her harshly while she was pregnant.[234]

Despite her detailed account, however, Maria Johanne did not explain why her master had punished her so harshly. As a result her statement was loose and fragmented, lacking narrative coherence. However, the trial script in Maria Johanne's case contained vague traces of the motives that might have caused Maria Johanne's owner to abuse her and kill the baby. In court, Maria Johanne's infant girl was recorded as a "mulatto." This made Judge Wiel inquire about the father of the child. Maria Johanne claimed that the father was a black plantation slave, and Sophia explained that since Maria Johanne was "of a reddish kind, her children all look as mulattos when newborn." Nevertheless, the baby's status as a "mulatto" and Maria Johanne's fear of her master left the specter of a white father in a household where interracial sexuality was already practiced; there was a hint that Maria Johanne's master might be the father. Judge Wiel, however, did not pursue the issue. Indeed, such traces of interracial sexuality seem to have turned judges into very reluctant inquisitors. When Police Judge Brown investigated the death of a baby "who appeared to be a mulatto or mustice," rumored to have been born to the enslaved "negress" Polly in 1792, he never even questioned her. Although a large crowd of Afro-Caribbeans had gathered to protest and the corpse of an infant had been found half-eaten in a street in Christiansted, Brown accepted Polly's owner's claim that she was still pregnant. Against a background of interracial sexuality, the case was not pursued in Christiansted Lower Court.[235]

Not even a long association with the Moravian Brethren, whose mission, as mentioned, enjoyed wide support from the Danish colonial administration, enabled enslaved people to make overt claims about the improper sexual intentions of white West Indians, although it probably helped them to ease their way around some of the censoring pressures of Christiansted's courts. When the enslaved man Petrus appeared in Christiansted Police Court in 1782, he was, apparently, well aware of how to speak as a Christian, and he crafted a story about female decency and male temperance that enabled him to hint at, but not overtly claim, that a white man had misbehaved. Petrus lived and worked as a cooper on Princesse, a large estate owned by the Schimmelmann family at the time, and, previously, by the royal house. Here, Moravians had long been active and taught slaves to speak in a language of pietistic, unctuous, and passionate Christian devotion. Twenty years earlier, in 1762, the woman Mari Magdalene, also enslaved on Princesse, had sent her greetings to the Moravian community in Bethlehem, Pennsylvania, in a letter full of Christian imagery and sentiment. Petrus relied on this tradition when he stood in court.[236]

The case in which Petrus testified concerned a white man named Robert Jones, and was brought to the court by the inspector at Princesse. In court, Petrus presented Police Judge Ewald with a story about a group of enslaved men and women who had been on their way back from a Moravian sermon when they met Jones. According to Petrus, Jones told the women slaves to ride with him, an offer they refused. In response, Jones threatened to shoot them and they ran away. At that moment, Jones took his gun, warning Petrus that he would blast him to pieces if he did not catch one of the women. Petrus responded that he could only bring a woman if Jones let go of him. Instead of accepting this reasonable proposal, Jones rewarded Petrus with several strokes of a stick.[237]

Petrus did not explicitly state what Jones' intentions were, if he knew them. He did not, for instance, explain why the women ran away instead of obeying Jones' command and accepting a, seemingly, easy ride to the estate. Instead, Petrus implicitly measured the behavior of Christian men and women against a white man who lost his temper and had immoral intentions. The enslaved women modestly refused Jones' offer and Petrus acted with calmness and respect. It was the indirect comparison, rather than any overt accusations, that allowed Petrus to hint at Jones' lecherous and irascible behavior.

The case against Jones never went further than Christiansted Police Court. The estate inspector decided not to pursue the complaint, perhaps because he knew that there were other charges against Jones who was also accused of assault and smuggling. Yet the estate inspector may also have been aware that Petrus' charge was difficult to uphold. Although Moravian ideas about the outstanding chastity of a few Christian slave women could be mobilized to back Petrus' testimony, the racialized tropes about African women's unremitting sexual desires as well as the censorship exercised by Christiansted's judges made it hard to pursue a complaint against white men for their sexual misconduct against and abuse of enslaved women.

The interrogative reluctance of the Danish West Indian courts was thematized in 1787 by Governor of St. Thomas and member of the Moravian Church, later governor general, Thomas Malleville who lamented that evidential rules made it difficult to prosecute white men for sexual coercion and violence. To illustrate his point Malleville related a "true story" about an overseer who wanted to have illicit intercourse with a "Christian" slave woman. Therefore, he had accused the woman's husband of assault. It was, Malleville argued, only by personally convincing the overseer to drop the case that he had saved the life of an innocent enslaved man. In his story, Malleville described the enslaved male protagonist as a "husband," a "man," a "negro-man," and a "negro."[238] Some of these terms echoed the categories established through racial slavery, others pointed to a representational space wherein enslaved men emerged in their capacities as men and husbands rather than simply as slaves. As men and women, the enslaved could, Malleville pointed out, be the victims of gross sexual misconduct.[239]

Despite such lamentations, Christiansted's judges were doing their best to exclude depositions in which enslaved Africans and Afro-Caribbeans spoke of sexual intimidation and abuse from white West Indians. However, they seldom relied on the provision in the slave code of 1733 that allowed slaves to be convicted on the basis of a single sworn statement. Instead, they failed to follow the leads provided by enslaved men and women and attempted to solve such cases out of court. So, for instance, the statement made by the slave Acra in Christiansted Police Court in 1783 about the relationship between his wife and a white man was not pursued in the subsequent trial in Christiansted Lower Court and was not mentioned by Judge Brown in his verdict against Acra.[240] In 1810, Police Judge Giellerup likewise seemed unconcerned when the enslaved man Cuffy stated that his manager was jealous of him and had him flogged. The manager, Cuffy related, "kept together" with Cuffy's wife, mother of his two children. This was why Cuffy had gone all the way to the British island of Nevis to stay with his sister. Instead of following Cuffy's lead, however, Judge Giellerup concentrated on discovering who had provided Cuffy with a false travel pass.[241] In this way, Cuffy's claim, like

Acra's, remained buried at a low level of the Danish Atlantic legal system. It never became the starting point of sustained judicial concern and inquiry.

The enslaved man Barnes also faced the sophisticated exclusions performed by Christiansted's judges. In 1815, Barnes complained to Judge Mouritzen, in his capacity as chief of police in Christiansted, that the overseer on La Reine Estate "had taken his wife" away from him, destroyed the fence he had built around his house, and prohibited him from "coming in […] his house."[242] Mouritzen acknowledged that the overseer "had intercourse with Barnes' wife" and that this was a "great crime," yet it was not, he argued, "easy to prove." An out of court settlement was the best solution to the complaint, and, therefore, Barnes' claim never reached the courts of Christiansted.[243]

In contrast to their treatment of enslaved peoples' complaints about white misbehavior, Christiansted's judges were eager to let their imaginations run free when they thought about slaves' sexual preferences and desires; to do so they relied on and reproduced the malleable ideology of the allegedly deviant and forceful sexual energies contained in African bodies that circulated in the Danish West Indies. For instance, when Christiansted's judges ventured to understand why enslaved women sought to poison their masters, they imagined that slave women's desires were so strong that they drove them to poison those superiors who interfered in their intimate affairs. When Raina — whom we met in the previous chapter — was accused of poisoning her master in 1774, Judge Hellvad asked if she had not done so out of "resentment" because the white man she fancied had been dismissed from the estate. In a similar way, Judge Brown pursued the idea that Rachel, accused of poisoning her master in 1783, had done so because her master had prohibited her from staying with her husband. In both cases, the enslaved women denied the charge.[244]

Descriptions, juxtapositions, and quotations rather than open critique characterized slave depositions in Christiansted's courts in the eighteenth century even when sexual violence was not at stake. In contrast to the 48 slaves of Princesse Estate, who collectively complained about their "hard" treatment in 1822, most enslaved people in the eighteenth century apparently refrained from the use of adjectives and adverbs when they presented their cases.[245] Such as in 1780, when two enslaved women, Louisa and Nanny, were accused of poisoning the milk of their powerful mistress Madame Schimmelmann, wife of Heinrich Ludvig Schimmelmann, administrator of the Schimmelmann family's large estates and later governor general, and cousin to Count Ernst Schimmelmann, who, as mentioned above, was the mastermind of Danish abolition.[246] If proven true, this charge would cost them their lives. Louisa and Nanny, therefore, had good reason to craft a credible account in Christiansted Police Court. They both did so by comparing their own respectful behavior to the ill-tempered nature of their owners. Neither, however, directly characterized their mistress or her behavior. Adjectives were absent from their defense.

In Christiansted Police Court, Louisa contrasted her own behavior with that of Madam Schimmelmann and thereby established her mistress as hot tempered and vengeful. While unbaptized, Louisa told Judge Cooper that she "frequented the Church of the Brethren." She related that when she protested her innocence, her mistress had replied, "I will teach you to confess." Louisa then described how, on hearing this threat, she had fallen to her knees and attempted to persuade her mistress that she was, in fact, telling the truth. Her mistress had refused to listen. Louisa substantiated her own innocence by quoting the words of a Danish woman servant who claimed that their mistress always complained about the milk. What Louisa did not say directly was that Madam Schimmelmann was of a hasty, passionate disposition and could have turned bad milk into poisoned milk without much reflection. Judge Cooper ultimately subjected Louisa to thumbscrews, but she did not confess. Her case never moved to Christiansted Lower Court. Most likely she was flogged at the public whipping post on the order of Governor General Peter Clausen.[247]

Nanny, Louisa's presumed accomplice, was a washerwoman at the Schimmelmann estate. She was born on the Dutch island of St. Martin and baptized in the Roman Catholic Church. At the time of her interrogation, she belonged to the Moravian congregation in St. Croix. She had given birth to five children, of which only a daughter, Quasiba, lived. From this fragmentary biography it seems safe to suggest that she worked in close proximity to white West Indians and that she was not terribly young. Through the Moravian mission she had access to a strong network of Christian Africans and Afro-Caribbeans. She might even have been literate in the written Dutch-Creole developed by Moravian missionaries and Lutheran pastors, and she would have had some knowledge of Christian teachings acquired, perhaps, by reading the Dutch-Creole hymnal or the prayer book, both of which had been published by 1770.[248]

Like Louisa, Nanny portrayed herself as peaceful and servile when describing her owners' harsh treatment. She related that she had been punished several times by her owners, and, although it "hurt" she "had to suffer this" because her owners had ordered it. Nanny denied the charges against her, declaring that if this was her "last moment then she could with truth confirm" that she had done nothing to cause harm.[249] Nanny may have used her knowledge of the Christian rituals concerning death, repentance, and confession, figuratively turning her own death into a sign of trustworthiness. In any case, her words emphatically underscored her own innocence and echoed the way in which Danish West Indian judges, based on *The Danish Law* of 1683, would have understood the connection between death and veracity.[250] Like those before her, Nanny described the events that led to her trial, but she did not characterize her adversaries and she did not evaluate their actions.

During the trial, Prosecutor Balling attempted to undermine Nanny's self-portrait as a truthful Christian woman. He interrogated prisoners from Fort Christiansværn, where Nanny was imprisoned, as well as Nanny's daughter to show that Nanny had forged her defense. Finally, he called on two enslaved men and questioned them about Nanny's marital life. He asked if it was not true that Nanny had two husbands and if these had not quarreled over her. Both men denied this and explained that Nanny had one husband who belonged to another slave owner. Such questions were, presumably, asked to establish Nanny's character before the court. If she could be shown to be a promiscuous troublemaker, rather than a continent, Christian woman, the presumption against her for poisoning her mistress would be stronger.

Nanny was imprisoned for eight months before her case was finally resolved in Christiansted Lower Court. Her forceful denial had undermined the suspicion of poisoning. During interrogations, however, she had admitted to being a runaway. For this crime she was sentenced to 150 lashes, branding, and transportation.[251] However, State Councilor Lindemann and — now also, Nanny's master — Heinrich Schimmelmann believed the sentence was too harsh. On Schimmelmann's intercession, Governor General Clausen agreed to mitigate the sentence. Nanny was to receive the amount of lashes stipulated and then be delivered to her owner who would cover the trial expenses.[252] Although Louise and Nanny at no point during their trial explicitly argued that their owners were mistaken, their servile Christian depositions undermined the charge of poisoning. Nevertheless, they did not escape harsh punishments.

Respectable Men and Women

As the nineteenth century began, slaves' marital relationships, reproductive capacities, and moral potentials became a central concern for both Danish metropolitan and colonial authorities.[253] At the same time, enslaved men and women presented stories in Christiansted Police Court and Lower Court depicting themselves as moral agents, concerned spouses and parents, and responsible and compliant workers. Slaves argued that they were capable of sentiment, moderation, and restraint, in contrast to their superiors. In these stories, enslaved men and women suggested that they should be defined as gendered subjects and, in turn, what their relations to their masters should be. Still relying on the narrative tricks and subtleties — description, quotation, and juxtaposition — they had employed in the eighteenth century, enslaved people now voiced an increasingly explicit critique of authority; and they tied this critique to Christian ideals of manly and womanly behavior.

As they wove these narratives, the enslaved appropriated a concern with the relations between race, status, and gender that circulated among elite colonial officers and judges in Christiansted. In 1764, Judge Juul, for instance, argued that the slave Qvako deserved the "milder" punishment of having his right hand cut off for his assault on two white men. Qvako, Judge Juul argued, only attacked the men because of the behavior of one Santanelle, a white female pub owner or guest, who had persuaded him to assist her only to accuse him of theft afterwards. It was, Juul believed, a "truth" grounded in experience that the "disgraceful conduct that often occurs at these liquor houses […] by such people as this woman Santanelle," encouraged "negroes" to behave in ways they should not. People like Santanelle first "made themselves equal with the negroes" only to complain loudly when they thought themselves offended. This behavior eroded social distinctions. Since white skin was not always a guarantee of orderly social conduct, Qvako could look forward to dismemberment rather than a death penalty. This distinction likely made little difference to Qvako. His owner was compensated with 170 rix-dollars, the sum normally awarded to owners of slaves who were sentenced to death.[254]

Enslaved men and women played with the idea that respectable conduct rather than skin color ought to define social relations in various ways. Often they simply reminded their superiors of the patchwork of ideas — informing Judge Juul's verdict in 1764 — that equated whiteness with respectability. In their depositions, enslaved men and women linked whiteness and, by association, authority to a bundle of traits that, among other things, included Christian faith, the ability to contain anger, show mercy and sentiment, work diligently, respect social hierarchies, speak and dress modestly, and, not least, care for family and spouse. The competing claims to respectability that shaped the encounters between enslaved people and their superiors stand out in a police court trial from 1840 involving the enslaved woman Regina from Rattan Estate. Her manager had imprisoned Regina for two weeks in the sick-house. In court she argued that the manager did not behave as white men ought. He was rash, unkind, and disrespectful. She related that the incident began when the manager came riding up to her calling her *good living* which she certainly did not like. She did not answer him before he had called her by her name Regina [… She] says that he came riding so close to her that the horse nearly stepped on her feet. Then, she said that, indeed, he ought to remember that he was a white man and not behave as a negro and let the horse step on her [… She] says that it is true that the assistant manager […] has spoken to her about asking the manager for mercy on her behalf. To this she answered that it would be useless because the manager had said that he knew how to punish and torment her [… S]he said to the manager that she did not know why he kept her imprisoned and punished her. If she deserved punishment, he did best by sending her to the town or '*to the Judge*', which he answered that he would not do.

In her disposition, Regina painted a portrait of a white manager who spoke un-kindly, used undue threats and violence, showed no mercy, and ignored colonial authorities, and she claimed that such behavior was improper for a man of his color. The manager denied Regina's charges. He argued that he had not "wanted to punish her for her rudeness" but considered imprisonment "as the mildest way of getting her to admit her wrongdoings," which, among others, concerned her unwillingness to work. He had only wanted her to ask for "forgiveness." At stake was his position as a respectable male slave manager and hers as a servile slave woman.[255]

Similar wordplays linking racial identity and authority took place in a somber case from 1815 concerning the enslaved at St. John Estate. Rumors about the estate manager's possible murder of an enslaved woman, his maltreatment of another, and a threatening drum dance around his house surfaced during the inter-rogation. Yet Judge Mouritzen focused on the possible challenge to the manager's racial status and authority voiced by three enslaved women. During the trial, a family of enslaved women of color claimed that their manager treated them like beasts while a white witness asserted that the women had claimed that the man-ager "was not a white man" and abused him by calling him a "beast". The estate's owner had arrived from Antigua and the women, a mother and her two daughters, had taken it upon themselves to prepare the master-house for his arrival. They had, as they explained, done so out of their own "free will." They were "pleased" that their master came. Yet their actions upset their manager who had not given any orders regarding such preparation. During the trial one daughter explained that the manager had threatened to put her in the bilboes. Hearing this threat, her sister had interceded by yelling "for God's sake let my sister be and do not treat her like a beast." In this way, the women relied on the authority of the Christian

God, their manager's questionable racial status, and their self-portraits as good-natured and servile, to discredit his authority; indeed, by treating one of them as a beast he came close to being bestial himself.[256]

During the nineteenth century, the ties between legitimate authority and racialized ideals of virtuous womanhood and responsible manliness became stronger in the stories slaves crafted in Christiansted's courts. The critique voiced by slaves, most of whom were born in Africa, from La Reine Estate in 1821 was based on exactly this link. According to the overseer, La Reine's slaves had behaved disobediently by collectively preventing the punishment of the enslaved woman Helena. The incident began because a free woman of color, Nancy Rollin, alleged that Helena had attacked her. The overseer ordered Helena punished, and a large group of slaves intervened. Helena told Judge Mouritzen that she was innocent: "she had neither beaten nor touched Nancy Rollin," adding that if she were to meet Rollin "alone some place, then she would beat her up." According to Helena, Rollin had vilified their mistress by claiming that she carried herself indecently in England. Thus, Helena claimed that her behavior was justified by Rollin's crude expatiations. Other slaves backed Helena's deposition. They testified that they wanted Rollin to leave because she abused their mistress by calling her a "whore" and a "bitch."[257]

La Reine's slaves challenged the overseer's right to castigate Helena by pointing out that he was protecting an indecent and morally suspect woman. Rollin had not shown due respect for her white mistress, had inappropriately involved herself in the management of the estate, and had used dirty words. Therefore, she had no right to assume authority over them. Rollin's many faults enabled the enslaved to challenge their overseer when he supported her. Yet the depositions made by La Reine's slaves did not help them much. They had complained about Nancy Rollin before. Their first complaint had been deemed ungrounded and they had been released without punishment. Judge Mouritzen, who as noted was in an intimate relationship with the slave owner Maria Yard, a free woman of color, was not convinced by their critique. After their second complaint, La Reine's slaves were heavily whipped and sentenced to work in chains on the estate.[258]

Parallel to the claims that white West Indians ought to behave with restraint and respect toward their slaves, enslaved men and women also attempted to dissociate authority from racial status altogether. They argued that their upbringing, training, and physical stature, rather than racial enslavement, should determine social hierarchies, duties, and rights. In the nineteenth century, Christiansted's courts began to conduct proceedings in order to determine if slaves, particularly women, were domestics or field hands.[259] When the enslaved woman Judith Lydia argued such a case in 1816, she wove a tapestry in which she figured herself as a caring but frail Christian mother while she portrayed her owner as hard and unchristian. In court, she pointed out that her owner had declared that he wanted to use her as a seamstress when he bought her. When her skills did not satisfy him, she asked to be sold. He refused and, instead, set her to fieldwork in chains. This, Judith Lydia stated, she could not "endure since she has had several children and is weak!." She was not "meant" for work in the cane fields. Adding to this portrait of her owner, Judith Lydia related that he showed little concern for her as a mother. He had forbidden her children to visit her during the trial and once he flogged her when she asked permission to have her youngest child baptized. In this way, Lydia Judith attempted to establish herself as a caring, Christian, and, therefore, trustworthy woman before the court.[260]

The trial against Luke Codwise, accused of the maltreatment of the enslaved woman Peggy in 1803, also illustrates how ideas about respectable womanhood were used to support enslaved peoples' claims. Peggy's case went all the way to the Supreme Court by which she was freed in 1804.[261] The trial began because Peggy complained to Governor General Mühlenfels. Peggy was an extraordinary woman and possessed, at least when judged by the interrogation script, remarkable rhetorical skills. She was twenty-six years old, a member of the Danish Lutheran congregation, and in a common law marriage to a free man of color when she appeared in court. Peggy portrayed herself as an obedient house servant, willing to obey the commands of her masters, but, obviously, incapable and afraid of performing work that lay outside the realms of her womanly expertise. Peggy began her statement by emphasizing that she had been occupied with housework since her early childhood, noting that her work placed her within the womanly sphere of the home. After she was ordered to Codwise's estate, she learned that she was to be chained to a "field negro and work in this way in the field." She "was afraid of this work which was entirely new and strange to her," and, therefore, she ran away to hide with her common law husband, Nicolas Righton.

It was with this self-portrait as her backdrop that Peggy claimed that she had been unjustly punished. She explained that Madam Codwise harbored unfounded suspicions against her and mistakenly believed that she spread rumors about an amorous relationship between Madam Codwise's sister and stepfather. Such direct criticism constituted a significant development of the narrative possibilities open to slaves in Christiansted's courts. Peggy had suggested to her mistress that she should bring her before the court. In response, Madam Codwise stated that she would rather "torment her to death slowly."[262] Given that Peggy had been heavily cart-whipped, the Codwise couple were well on their way to reaching precisely this goal. Nonetheless, and in contrast to Nanny and Louisa in the 1780s, Peggy was able to speak openly about what she considered her mistress' faulty conclusions.

Although Peggy's self-portrait may appear to be no more than an accurate description of her life, it was much more than that. She claimed that she should have been treated as a female servant and a respectable woman. This claim refigured the narrative field within which her case was discussed. The interrogation came to center on Peggy's womanly qualities rather than on servitude and slavish obedience. Peggy's owners related that Peggy claimed she could be the "*maitresse*" of any married white man she chose. They argued that it was indecent claims like these that justified their harsh treatment of her.[263] Other witnesses, however, believed that Peggy's impertinence was a result of her female sex. The object of her gossip, the clergyman Neiles, argued that Peggy was a "passionate woman." It was "passion more than evil that had made her set aside the deference she owed her master."[264] All parties, irrespective of their stand on Peggy's treatment, attempted to explain what kind of woman Peggy was.[265]

The claim that respectable womanhood was as important as, if not more important than, slave status also structured the deposition of the enslaved woman Polly of Sight plantation. In 1802, Polly's husband, Cork, was accused of the attempted murder of the estate overseer. In Christiansted Police Court, Polly used her position as wife and mother as the backdrop against which she narrated the incident.[266] She told Judge Winding that she and Cork lived in a common law marriage and had three children. Explaining the incident that brought Cork to court, Polly related that Cork brandished a knife while the overseer punished him. Afraid that Cork would hurt himself, Polly asked him to give her his knife, which he did "willingly." From this point, Polly went on to explain that she was "convinced" that Cork had no intention of harming his overseer. In Polly's deposition, it was her marital relationship that gave her the authority to speak with certainty about Cork's peaceful intentions. The overseer had initially called on Polly to testify. When he heard her deposition, he changed his opinion and argued that she was unreliable not because she was enslaved but because she was Cork's wife.

Cork's case was sent to Governor General Walterstorff who ordered him back to the estate without punishment.[267] The exact reasons for the governor's decision are unclear, but Polly's testimony may provide part of the answer. When Polly, without being prompted by a specific question, told Judge Winding that she had three children she was providing more than factual information. In the discussions about slave reproduction and demography that informed government policies in the nineteenth century, fertility and respectability were closely linked.

In conjunction with this debate, Polly may be understood to have said that she was respectable, and, accordingly, trustworthy. Polly's statement, like Peggy's, placed slaves' gendered subjectivity at the center of the legal encounter between slaves and their opponents. Her deposition echoed the statement of another enslaved woman who complained in 1805 that her son was treated harshly by his overseer, "although" he was "neither lecherous nor negligent" and fulfilled his "duties."[268] In these stories, slaves postulated that prudent sexuality and diligent work habits were characteristics that should entitle them to fair treatment.[269]

The interpretation of Polly's statement as a conscious claim to respectable womanhood may seem hyperbolic. Yet if we look at how Judge Winding and many other Danish West Indian officials commonly perceived enslaved women, it becomes clear that, for them, enslaved mothers distinguished themselves by the simple fact of motherhood. In their whimsical fantasies, Christiansted's judges, as we have seen, envisioned African women as incapable of maternal love. Accordingly, Judge Winding, a few years earlier, in 1799, argued that enslaved women had neither natural decency nor shame. Slave women, he believed, killed their newborns because of "the constraint, the trouble and the bad sleep that follows for a female slave who hatches a slave for her master."[270] It is no surprise that the expectations of white women were entirely different. In 1824, Judge Frederiksen argued that white women's "duties as mothers were so holy" that nothing could excuse them if they did not take care of their offspring. Negligence was a sign of "unnatural indifference" for white women whereas it was the inevitable result of black women's overwhelming sexual desire.[271] It was against these racialized perceptions of motherhood and sexuality that Polly's children and marital union became significant markers of a respectable Christian way of life.

The emphasis on children and partnership became stronger in slave depositions in the nineteenth century. In 1840, the enslaved couple Judith and John, like Polly and Cork before them, structured their depositions with reference to their status as a caring Christian couple with children. John, owned by the Moravians, had complained to Judge Frederiksen that the manager on Montpellier Estate had forbidden him from coming to the plantation where Judith lived. The trouble emerged because the manager had castigated their son. In court, John emphasized his respect for managerial and church authority while maintaining his fatherly distress. He related that he brought his son back when he ran away, and acknowledged the instructions of his owners, the Brethren, who told him to be "good-natured." Although the manager had initially forgiven John's son, he was later flogged and imprisoned. The incident "hurt" John and he asked the manager why he had ignored him when he "pleadingly begged" for his son.

Judith supported John in court by describing their relationship. She related that she had lived for many years in marriage with John. They had seven children of which five were alive. John had been in the "best agreement" with previous managers and overseers, and the couple had disciplined their children themselves when they misbehaved. Nevertheless, the manager had told her that John was not to come to the estate; she "should leave him and take another man." She had answered "that she could not leave John and take some other man since they had lived together for so long and had several children together."[272]

Judge Frederiksen listened to Judith with some sympathy. He acknowledged that the manager had gone too far. He ought to have recognized that Judith "wanted and needed John's help;" yet he had eagerly tried to separate a couple "who as a seldom example among the negroes [has] kept together continually for so many years" and had hindered "a father from seeing and coming to his children." Governor General Peter von Scholten agreed with Judge Frederiksen. He fined the manager and warned him not to repeat such treatment of Montpellier's slaves.[273]

Although most enslaved men and women achieved no legal advantages by representing themselves as respectable men and women, many bondspeople claimed this identity for themselves in the Danish West Indian courts. They argued that only qualities such as decent and monogamous sexual behavior, parental love, sentiment and temperance, working diligence, and social deference could justify power. This shared narrative emerged in the stable legislative environment of the Gardelin slave code of 1733. Herein, there were no slave rights, only sketchy caricatures of allegedly devious slaves. In the early nineteenth century, therefore, slaves could not make claims on the basis of legal rights. Instead, they had to make claims on the basis of who they were through self-portraits that depicted them as both different from and more than mere slaves.

Refined Stories

As enslaved West Indians refined their stories about themselves as moral agents, they built a rostrum from which they addressed the faults of their superiors. And, as they tied legitimate authority to Christian propriety, they opened up the legally taboo area of white men's sexual abuse and coercion of enslaved women and men. Thus, the development of narrative techniques and self-portraits went hand in hand with an expansion of the field of legal inquiry. Some enslaved women, particularly, began to publicly narrate their violent encounters with owners, managers, overseers, and acquaintances. The courtrooms of Christiansted did not

Montpellier & Two Friends, watercolor by Frederik von Scholten, 1846.
Order and calmness characterize this drawing of Montpellier. Enslaved workers are altogether
absent. A man on horseback (perhaps a man of color) and a four wheeled carriage with a black
coachman and a white passenger leisurely approach the estates. As an ideological statement
about the nature of West Indian society, the drawing operates by ignoring the
conflicts and violence that shaped life for enslaved men and women in the
islands (courtesy of *Museet for Søfart*, the Maritime Museum of Denmark).

overflow with stories of sexual abuse and violence, but where there had been almost complete silence during the eighteenth century, new stories of sexual malfeasance began to trickle into the annals of the Danish Atlantic legal regime in the nineteenth century.[274]

During the eighteenth century, sexual violence was, as noted above, no more than an implicit possibility in the depositions made by slaves in Christiansted's courts. Although enslaved men spoke of the threat they felt from white superiors who "took" their women, of male competition, and jealousy, they did not speak of sexual abuse. In 1760, for instance, the enslaved man London explained that Cudjoe, one of the suspected leaders of the alleged conspiracy to take over St. Croix in 1759, was motivated by male pride and jealousy. According to London, Cudjoe suspected that a certain Charles Dackly wanted to "take [his] wife" from him. Cudjoe had sworn that he would rather kill his competitor or die himself than let this happen. In response, London wondered if Cudjoe "dared lay hand on a white, particularly as it was possible that the white had had her [the wife] before Cudjoe." London's deposition may very well have been a painful invention since torture was used during the conspiracy trials in Christiansted Lower Court in 1759. Yet his story resembled those of other enslaved men who appeared in less dramatic proceedings during the eighteenth century.[275]

In contrast to London's eighteenth-century deposition, enslaved men and women began to thematize sexual violence in Christiansted's courts and in other encounters with legal officers during the nineteenth century.[276] In 1805, the enslaved woman Juliette complained to Police Judge Winding that her overseer had chained, flogged, and imprisoned her because she refused to "come to him and sleep with him." This was an accusation that, apparently, could not remain unanswered, and the estate owner, defending his employee, declared that the overseer was a "very respectable man who would not compel any of the negresses of the plantation to have intercourse with him."[277] The enslaved workers on Slob Estate also referred to sexually motivated violence when they testified that their overseer had killed the enslaved woman Mary because she was about to leave him for another man. Likewise, the enslaved woman Marie explained that her white partner, who accused her of infidelity, had stabbed her with a knife.[278] Together enslaved men and women pushed the judges of Christiansted to listen to their stories of sexual abuse and violence against enslaved girls, women, and, more rarely, men.

It took courage and persistence for enslaved Africans and Afro-Caribbeans to forward claims about their superiors' sexual assaults. In 1793, the young enslaved man Francis, owned by a Mr. Bradshaw, had his ear cut off by Philip McKenna, overseer at Hermon Hill Estate, when McKenna discovered Francis and the slave woman Margrethe having sex in his house. Explaining the incident in Christiansted Police Court, Francis merely stated that McKenna had cut off his ear, but denied knowing who Margrethe "kept together with." St. Croix, the slave who had assisted McKenna in mutilating Francis, denied having knowledge about the incident and Margrethe refused to admit to having a relationship with McKenna.[279] During the interrogations in the police court none of the slaves admitted that Francis had been the victim of McKenna's claim to sexual power.

The slaves' stories, however, changed when Governor General Walterstorff ordered them to be detained in Fort Christiansværn for their own protection. In Christiansted Lower Court, Margrethe and St. Croix now related that they had been threatened by McKenna to lie about the incident. Margrethe admitted that she regularly "slept in the house with McKenna," she related that McKenna had said to Francis "I shall cut off your ears because you sleep in the house of a white man," and she argued that McKenna's actions were inspired by jealousy. Margrethe's mother corroborated her portrayal of McKenna as a violent and indecent man. She stated that McKenna also had a relationship with another slave woman with whom he had a "mulatto child."[280] In the verdict, Judge Winding saw evidence of "considerable strength" in these testimonies, but, nevertheless, he allowed McKenna to prove his innocence by oath.[281] This was a rare and inelegant choice. Winding, like the other judges in Christiansted's courts, normally preferred to assemble as much evidence as possible in slave trials. In this case, however, in which an enslaved man claimed that an overseer was overly interested in his sexual life, Winding relied on the one-oath rule, supplied by the slave code of 1733, to put an end to the legal representation of enslaved people's voices.

Enslaved Africans and Afro-Caribbeans introduced sexual violence as a theme in Christiansted's courts either by complaining about rape or by pointing to their superiors' violent transgressions in trials raised on other grounds. Some of the earliest slave depositions mentioning sexual violence emerged in trials wherein the enslaved had the support of their owners. This was the case for the enslaved woman Francky in 1788. In Christiansted Police Court, she was charged with theft and assault on one Andre Merscir, a French assistant baker, but she turned the charge upside down by accusing Merscir of attempted rape. Francky enjoyed the patronage of her owner, Royal Warehouse Manager Grutzmann who emphasized her special servile qualities and her female modesty by describing her as "a quiet and calm negress who always stayed at home." She had served him with "exceptional loyalty and willingness" and had no "dealings with whites or coloreds or had shown any such inclinations."[282]

With this fine description as her starting point, Francky crafted her defense against Merscir. She told Judge Brown that she had gone to the bakehouse to buy flour. There she encountered Merscir who immediately

> grabbed her and pawed her, which she would not suffer, but the plaintiff grabbed her and pulled her into a little room close by the sitting room. Here there was a bed upon which he wanted to force her. She in no way wanted this and then he grabbed her and wrestled with her until she fell on the floor.

She did her utmost to escape, but he continued to pull her back into the little chamber "to sleep with" him. When he saw that he could not "have his will with her, he took a *sikkefælle*" (i.e., a whip very similar to a cart-whip) and hit her. Finally, she escaped. In court she showed her torn dress as evidence of their struggle and called upon three slave women to support her deposition.[283]

Enslaved women, like Francky, who were attacked by men other than their owners, managers, and overseers, described these horrid encounters as resulting from chance meetings in public places: at the market, in common yards, or on paths in the cane fields.[284] In contrast, the sexual abuse of enslaved women and girls by their immediate superiors was often the result of longer periods of intimidation, threats, and abuse. The trial against Count Lucas de Bretton Sr. in 1807 amply illustrates the devious pressures that owners could bring to bear on their enslaved women, but it also illustrates how enslaved men and women could use their newfound narratives of respectability to counter their owners in court.

In the trial against Count Lucas de Bretton, each party forwarded claims about their own respectability and their adversary's lack thereof. The trial began because de Bretton had mistreated his young slave woman Anna Catherina. She had been displaced from her position as domestic servant and sent to the fields, imprisoned, chained, cart-whipped, stripped of clothing, suffocated, shaved, and burned. At the trial, the de Bretton couple argued that this treatment was due to Anna Catherina's stubborn misbehavior. She had, they claimed, scalded their daughter, infested her with lice, lied, and been impertinent. Moreover, she had failed to beg for mercy, which, they claimed, would have been granted had she merely asked for it.

Against this account, in which the de Bretton couple figured themselves as merciful slave owners, Anna Catherina, her mother, and her grandmother crafted a story of respectable Christian womanhood. In court, Anna Catherina stated that she had refused her owner's many advances and asserted that she had neither "neglected her work nor been impertinent." To corroborate her account, she called on her mother and grandmother. These two women, one enslaved and the other free, both Christians, stated that Anna Catherina was neither "impertinent nor rude;" they had heard nothing "bad" about her. Both stated that the Count had approached them on several occasions to persuade Anna Catherina to come to him. In their depositions, they emphasized Anna Catherina's emotional distress and related how the young woman came "crying" to them again and again because she feared her masters' punishments. Anna Catherina's mother described how, one Sunday after service in the Danish Lutheran Church, she had found her daughter in tears and sheltered her until the next morning, adding further weight to the description of her motherly care and Christian way of life. The mother also explained that when she attempted to resolve the problem by informing the Countess about her husband's lewd intentions, the noble woman replied by taking God's name in vain and urging Anna Catherina to sleep with the Count "for God's sake." In these testimonies, the de Bretton couple emerged as lacking in sentiment and reason, they were hard, uncompassionate, and insensible. All three women plainly characterized the de Brettons' treatment of Anna Catherina as "hard."[285]

A narrative battle about Christian respectability similar to that of the de Bretton trial also characterized the trial against one Mr. Davis, manager at the Boetzberg Estate, for the rape of the young enslaved woman Cecilie in 1829. Cecilie, with whom this chapter began, had been in the bilboes for three weeks and had been flogged, starved, and stripped naked by her superiors. In court, Cecilie related that the manager had tried to have sexual intercourse with her but she had managed to flee. Eventually, however, he had gotten his will despite her opposition. During one of these attempts, Cecilie's mistress had heard her husband and interrupted his rape attempt. Yet this had only caused Madam Davis to strip and flog her. In court, Cecilie's father Nelson, who was born in Africa, supported her. He stated that his "Christian name was Adam" and noted that he and his wife had Cecilie baptized in the Anglican Church just after her birth. He did not believe Cecilie to be "a bad subject" and argued that, if that had been the case, the manager would surely not have employed her in the house for the last two years. When she ran away, Nelson argued, it was a sign of emotional distress: she was "afraid." She had "asked for mercy," but Madam Davis had been unwilling to grant it. Together, Cecilie and her father conjured up the image of a servile, Christian, enslaved woman suffering from her owners' rash and irresponsible slave management.

In contrast, the Davis couple depicted themselves as hurt and distressed by a slave whom they had treated with parental discipline. Cecilie received such heavy punishment, they related, because she constantly ran away, was negligent, and "a bad subject." Mr. Davis found it "terrible" to be met with her charges and "solemnly" maintained that they were untrue. Madam Davis, however, needed to explain away her own involvement in Cecilie's punishment. First, she noted that her husband "generally did not allow her to punish any of the estate slaves" and had stopped her flogging of Cecilie. Then she explained that she had only wanted to castigate Cecilie as she did her own children, and, therefore, did not think of it as a "hard" punishment. After nine years of marriage she had no reason to believe the allegations against her husband and stressed that if they were true then she would "surely have left him."[286] In this way, Davis and his wife attempted to counter the accusations that Cecilie voiced by making the claim that they were respectable slave managers.

The narrative of Christian respectability that enslaved men and women developed during the nineteenth century expanded their possibilities for legal representation, but some experiences were not easily translated into this narrative frame. Christianity, in its Danish West Indian version, put heavy demands on enslaved men and women. Anger and rage, as well as compromise and pragmatism, were not valued Christian qualities. Enslaved men and women, therefore, would at times have to bend over backwards to reconcile their experiences and actual behavior to their courtroom stories. Such was the case for the enslaved couple Ancilla and Cornelius. In 1820, Cornelius was charged with arson in Christiansted Police Court. Court Scribe Bille took down the following depositions during the trial:

> The negro Cornelius was brought forward, unchained. He is born here, estimated to be 26 years old, a member of the English Church [i.e., the Anglican Church] where he is baptized William. He explained that he lives together with the negro woman Ancilla, belonging to the Old Bethlehem Plantation. He explained that he missed her in the evening of the 17th last. After he had looked for her, he was informed that she was at the Assistant Overseer Rain's. He went to his [Rain's] door, knocked, and asked for her. The deponent became very indignant when Rain would not open the door and denied that she was there. He thought, though, that he had to accept the assistant overseer's denial. And with the intention to light his candle, he took some fire under the rum-distillery […]. On the way to his house he lost it. Although he sought to put it out with his foot, the fire got so much out of hand, because of the strong wind, that he could not stop it. Whereupon he had to shout for help, but the negroes who came could not stop the fire, hence the whole bagasse house burned down. During the fire and when Assistant Overseer Rain arrived, the deponent saw that Ancilla came out of said Rain's room above

the boiling house. Then the deponent grabbed her and reproached her for her disgraceful behavior, particularly because Rain also keeps together with her sister. At first Ancilla denied it, though she later begged the deponent to forgive her and promised not to do it again. — Dismissed.

The negro girl Ancilla appeared. She is born here, estimated to be 14 years old, a member of the English Church, where she is baptized Elisabeth. She explained that she had kept together with Cornelius belonging to the plantation New Beth-lehem, since the previous November or so. She explained that in the afternoon of the 17th this month, Assistant Overseer Rain sent the negro boy Daniel, who is part of the small negro gang, to the deponent, in order [to ensure] that she would come to him in the evening. The deponent at first refused, but Rain threatened to flog her if she did not come. For this reason she was led to go to him in the evening. During her stay there she heard her husband Cornelius coming and knocking on the door. He asked Rain if she was there, which Rain denied. When, shortly afterwards, the fire broke out, the deponent went from Rain's room to the place of the fire. Here her husband grabbed her by the arm in order to go home. He also reproached her for her behavior, whereupon she begged him to forgive her and promised not to do it again. — Dismissed.

Samuel Rain appeared. He is assistant overseer at the plantation Bethlehem that belongs to Peter de Wint. He is born here, 27 years old, a member of the English Church. He explained that, yes, indeed on the evening of the 17th this month, when the negro driver Daniel came to him to receive instructions for the next day's work, he sent him to Ancilla [to ensure] that she would come to him that same evening. She did this voluntarily without being threatened with a flogging by the deponent [Rain]. When Ancilla had come to the deponent's room, he asked her if it was really true that Cornelius was her husband as he was such an imprudent negro. Ancilla answered no. She would not have anything to do with Cornelius or had ever had. Around this time, between 10 and 11, someone knocked on the deponent's door. And the deponent heard Cornelius shouting: Ancilla, you better come out of that attic. Right afterwards he said: Mr. Rain you do better in letting Ancilla go, otherwise something will happen tonight. Whereupon the deponent sent his boy to Cornelius to tell him that he better go away and that Ancilla was not there. The deponent said this because he knew Cornelius as an impertinent and impudent negro. Around 12 o'clock his boy woke him up and told him that the bagasse house was on fire. It burned down in spite of the efforts made. The deponent's suspicion immediately fell on Cornelius. — Dismissed.[287]

As the trial transcript shows, Cornelius admitted that he started the fire. He also, however, suggested that he was innocent, at least in a moral sense. Cornelius and Ancilla effectively managed to turn Judge Mouritzen's attention away from the fire toward Rain's conduct. Although the trial could have ended when Cornelius admitted that he started the fire, Cornelius, Ancilla, and Rain all spoke about Rain's possible sexual impropriety. Nevertheless, the trial transcript convinced Governor General Bentzon that Cornelius should receive seventy-five lashes at the public whipping post in Christiansted.[288]

The depositions made by Cornelius and Ancilla introduced them as a Christian couple whose relationship had been endangered by a white overseer. Both Cornelius and Ancilla presented themselves with double names. In addition to their slave names, they also noted their baptismal names, Elisabeth and William, when they gave testimony in court. In Cornelius' testimony we hear how he "missed" Ancilla and went searching for her only to realize that she was in Rain's room. While it upset him, he had to accept the authority of the overseer. Indeed, within the narrative Cornelius developed in court, he could not act on any possible anger he might have felt. Cornelius spoke, not as a slave, but as the Christian man, William. In this persona, he had to accept social hierarchies, put aside pride, and resist opposition. Yet he did have legitimate authority over his wife, Ancilla, and in court he argued that she had disgraced herself by being in a room with Rain. As her husband he took it upon himself to reproach her.

Ancilla and Cornelius crafted similar depositions, but there was one important difference. Ancilla told Judge Mouritzen that Rain had threatened her with a beating. She was not in Rain's room by choice but because she feared the physical punishment he could administer if she did not come to him. Ancilla spoke explicitly about the threats she had received and her motives for entering Rain's room. She was frightened, not promiscuous. Yet Ancilla concluded her deposition with a description of herself begging her husband for forgiveness. Ancilla's awkward ending, in which she accepted her part in an act that was not volitional, may be related to the specific Christian ideals about enslaved women that circulated in the Danish islands. Despite being a member of the Anglican Church, Ancilla was part of a world wherein Moravian missionaries, for almost one hundred years, had developed a strong, albeit peculiar, martyrology in which those slave women who, like Anna Catherina, suffered heavy punishments instead of succumbing to the sexual advances of their white masters were praised. Although Ancilla did not disclose what she did in Rain's room, her actions — in so far as they can be considered as such — were illegitimate within the narrative of Christian respectability on which she and her husband relied, and, therefore, she had to ask her husband to forgive her.

Detail of Mary's Fancy with slaves working in the fields, St. Croix, oil painting by unknown artist, possibly Fritz Melbye, c. 1840. This painting depicts an overseer with a whip in his left hand in conversation with an enslaved fieldworker. Behind the overseer, another white man on horseback, possibly the owner or the manager, observes the scene. The beating that Ancilla feared would probably have been carried out with a long-thonged whip as the one carried by the overseer on Mary's Fancy (courtesy of *Museet for Søfart*, the Maritime Museum of Denmark).

Unsurprisingly, Rain sought to counter Cornelius' and Ancilla's statements. He asserted that Ancilla came to him voluntarily and added that he had not encroached on a pre-existing relationship. This argument allowed Rain to portray Cornelius as an impertinent slave rather than as an upset husband. Rain's claim was, it seems, a common way for white men to explain their relations with enslaved women. In 1800, the enslaved man Andreas assaulted Police Officer de Windt when he found de Windt in the house of the woman he asserted was his wife. In his defense, de Windt explained that the woman had told him that she had nothing to do with Andreas.[289] While only fragmented evidence exists, claims like these, suggest that white West Indians argued that their sexual power was morally defensible when enslaved women could be portrayed as voluntary partners. It was an argument that could be smoothly intertwined with the much more detailed descriptions of African women's sexual deviance and appetite as found in the many genres of Atlantic writing, from travel literature to administrative tracts, that undergirded racial slavery in the Caribbean.

As the theme of sexual violence was explored by enslaved men and women in the courts of Christiansted, their depositions began to reflect communal discussions about how to deal with these transgressions. Ancilla and Cornelius established a narrative plot that made Ancilla partly responsible for the episode, perhaps by drawing on Moravian ideals of submission to secular authority, whereas other enslaved men and women in their depositions lay the blame on white men. When rape accusations were made, family members and friends were consulted prior to the complaints, and parents sometimes made the initial accusation. This was often, but not always, because the victims were very young. Cecilie, with whom we began, appeared in court in 1829, because her father, the enslaved man Nelson, had complained to Police Judge Frederiksen. Nelson, Cecilie's mother, Madlene, and one David Martin, a mason and a free man of color, had all discussed the manager's rape of Cecilie before the complaint was made. Likewise, in 1841, Sophina discussed the rape of her daughter with her brother-in-law and the estate nurse before she walked to Christiansted town to complain to Governor General von Scholten.[290]

Discussions among relatives of the injured girls and women may explain why they put forward similar stories. When Cecilie was interrogated, she explained that one night the manager had "sexual intercourse" with her, and when she wanted to scream he covered her mouth. He had tried another time but without success because of her noise. Margrethe likewise related that her manager had "sexual intercourse" with her two nights in a row, even though she resisted and screamed. Both girls included descriptions of their resistance in their trial depositions. Women and girls likewise related that they had their clothes torn and showed physical wounds in court, important elements in a rape charge within Danish jurisprudence.[291] None of the rape victims, however, claimed that they had been so terrified that they had not known what to do; all had resisted, screamed, and yelled. Indeed, these girls and women, in collaboration with family members and friends, appear to have tweaked their stories to accord with the legal definition of rape that West Indian judges would recognize from Danish legislation and legal practice.

Respectable portraiture dominated the legal testimonies of enslaved men and women who complained about sexual abuse and violence. Yet this was only one of the possible responses to the abuse of sexual power that circulated among enslaved Africans and Afro-Caribbeans in St. Croix. This became clear in the murder trial against the three enslaved men, Christopher, Adam, and Henry of Golden Grove Estate in 1832. They were sentenced to death for their brutal killing of the estate manager Peter Mackin. During the trial, Christopher stated that "he did not believe that there had been anything evil in what they had done."[292] Asked about the reasons for their "hatred," Christopher explained that he believed that the manager had "sexual intercourse" with his wife. Henry added that Mackin "ran after the young negresses on the plantation, the wives' of the negro men, their sisters and families, and either [he] went after them in the negro houses or had them brought by the watchmen at night." Other slaves who argued that the manager was "too bad" repeated this argument.[293] Peter Mackin had crossed a line, he was not merely bad, but "too bad," and this was the reason they decided to act.

The themes of servility, sentiment, composure, and Christianity that ran through many slave depositions were absent from the trial prose in this murder trial. The slaves at Golden Grove voiced a clear-cut condemnation of their manager's sexual transgressions, and they had not gone to the Danish West Indian authorities with their grievances. Instead, they determined to solve their problem independently. During long and convoluted interrogations, enslaved people told a legal commission that they had tried to get rid of their manager five times. Initially, they had sought the assistance of an "old negro," "born on the Coast of Guinea" who performed divination and magic. Most of the enslaved involved had pitched in to pay for his obeah services. The purpose of these performances, it appears, was to "get manager Mackin off the estate" rather than to kill him.[294] When spiritual manipulation proved ineffective in ridding them of their manager, many slaves from Golden Grove were asked, and agreed, to assist in assaulting and killing Mackin. The depositions made by the slaves at Golden Grove Estate indicate that Christian respectability was not the only narrative approach employed to counter sexual violence among slaves in the Danish West Indies. African-Atlantic ideals and practices, in this case expressed as the use of obeah, were also employed to deal with violence and abuse. However, the Danish West Indian courts seldom represented such African-Atlantic responses to sexual coercion.

A profound shift in narrative substance and form had taken place. In the eighteenth century, some enslaved Africans and Afro-Caribbeans hinted at and subtly described the faults, mistakes, and ill-use of their superiors in Christiansted's courts. As the nineteenth century progressed, slaves expanded their narrative repertoire, both in form and in substance. Pointing to their identity as respectable men and women, enslaved people crafted stories in which their subjugation did not define who they were. In their status as slaves, Africans and Afro-Caribbeans could not easily oppose their masters, but as servile, diligent, Christian men and women with ample capacities for sentiment and composure, they could make the claim that such conduct was a requisite for the exercise of legitimate authority. Appropriating Christian gender ideals, slaves began to criticize their owners, managers, and overseers. In the courts of Christiansted, they named and condemned some of the violent sexual advances they experienced. They added evaluation to description, adjectives and adverbs to comparisons and juxtapositions, and moved from implicit critique to explicit condemnation.

As the nineteenth century progressed, divergent views on how to conceptualize sexual violence emerged in the stories enslaved people crafted within Christiansted's courts. At the same time that slaves' involvement in a long Danish West Indian tradition of Christian respectability gave them a strong language in which to speak about sexual violence, it also made certain narrative expressions impossible. In the 1820s, Cornelius and Ancilla did their best to erase any signs of anger from their depositions. Ancilla was not angry — at least, not in her court statement. She spoke about herself as a Christian woman who had made a mistake. She should have refused her overseer's orders despite the flogging she would have received for disobeying. Yet other slaves chose to focus on more clear-cut condemnations of sexual violence. This was the stance taken by those enslaved women and girls who had the support of their friends and relatives; and some, like those at Golden Grove, found that African-Atlantic spiritual practices rather than Christianity comprised the best response to those superiors who violently transgressed sexual boundaries.

Enslaved peoples' courtroom stories strongly suggest that, among themselves, on estates and in towns, slaves tied legitimate authority to ideals about moral and sexual propriety. They discussed whether and when superiors had gone too far and how to deal with such transgressors; they also debated, and sometimes disagreed, as to the correct interpretation of the behavior of the women who had been harassed. Enslaved Africans and Afro-Caribbeans may not always have adhered to the self-portraits they crafted in court. But, as they insisted that they were to be defined through their gendered identity rather than by their slave status, they moved from tacit critiques to open and multifaceted condemnations of the sexual aggression exercised by their superiors in the Danish West Indies.

CHAPTER 4

African-Atlantic Domestic Troubles

In 1831, enslaved men and women from Jerusalem Estate appeared before Christiansted Police Court and unveiled a story of infidelity, animosity, and spiritual conflict. The immediate cause for the police court investigation was the death of one of the slaves of Jerusalem Estate, the enslaved man George, who fell into a deep well when the cover skidded off. Rumor had it that the cover had been tampered with. As proceedings progressed, it turned out that George was not the target of this hostility; his death was an accident. The real target, some enslaved people related, was Nicholas, and the culprit was Michael. Their conflict revolved around Antoinette, the wife of Michael and the former wife of Nicholas. Whether true or not, the tense relationship between Nicholas, Michael, and Antoinette became the basis of rumors about a fierce conflict between the two men. Michael admitted that he and Nicholas were at "loggerheads because of Antoinette" whom "Nicky would not let him keep alone." Nicholas likewise recognized their vexed relationship.

During the proceedings, the overseer at Jerusalem explained that Antoinette had admitted that Michael had gone to one George at Peter's Rest Estate and gotten "obeah in order to harm" Nicholas. Questioning George, the overseer learned that Nicholas had likewise tried to harness supernatural power to his advantage. He had visited a slave at Cane Garden Estate who was also an "obeah man." During the proceedings, the protagonists of this triangle denied obeah charges, but enslaved witnesses supported the overseer's account. They believed that Michael and Nicholas had turned to African-Atlantic spiritual experts in order to resolve their domestic conflict. Acting Judge Hoffman notified Governor General von Scholten about the accusations of malignant strife, and he resolved that there was no need for further investigation. Instead, the overseer was warned to pay more attention to plantation equipment in the future.[295]

The trial involving the enslaved people of Jerusalem Estate testifies to the presence of a debate about marriage and adultery among enslaved men and women in the Danish West Indies; a debate saturated with references to African-Atlantic spiritual power. Additionally, however, the trial prose underscores the fact that the representational practices of Christiansted's courts seldom allowed enslaved people to precisely detail the forms, contents, and ideological backgrounds of their marital practices and ideals. Did these enslaved men and women understand their intimate affairs, their troubles and fortunes, as a result of their relationship to a spirit world, or was the invocation of spirit power of a more perfunctory nature? It is difficult to say on the basis of the court book containing the statements in the trial against the slaves of Jerusalem Estate.

Danish West Indian government officers, slave masters, and overseers seldom recognized that the marital lives of enslaved men and women were shaped by specific cultural customs and horizons. When, for instance, Lower Court Judge Mouritzen examined the nature of slave unions in 1819 by questioning a number of white West Indians, one witness responded that "menfolk and women leave each other without qualms and ceremonies." Another witness explained that when a slave couple had lived together for a longer period, a break-up would only occur after major disagreements. Even in such well-established relationships, however, no form of "ceremony" conditioned divorce, according to this witness.[296] In these statements, slave unions emerged as lacking institutional order; they were chaotic and promiscuous. As we have seen, such ideas about the nature of slave unions were far from new in the Danish West Indies. They reiterated the larger narrative of the stereotypically loose sexuality of African men and women that had circulated in the Atlantic world for centuries.

For the enslaved men and women involved in trials about domestic violence, marriage appears to have been at the center of their lives. Indeed, marriage was so important that it was worth fighting and, occasionally, killing for. Whereas no enslaved people were charged with crimes against other family members in Christiansted Lower Court and Police Court in the eighteenth and nineteenth centuries, a number of enslaved men were charged with the assault or murder of their wives. In the trials that followed, men and women talked about their unions with a diction that demonstrated emotional commitment, economic cooperation and dependence as well as obligation and formality. Their stories did not support the idea put forward by whites in the Danish West Indies that divorce was easy or informal for bondsmen and -women.[297] While these trials emerged out of exceptional events — such as murder, assault, and self-mutilation — the conceptualization of marital life that structured slaves' court testimony was less exceptional. Enslaved men and women crafted stories that were shaped by ideas about acceptable marital behavior, adultery and divorce; some of these ideas drew their force from African-Atlantic marital and legal traditions.

Natural Marriages

When enslaved men and women appeared in Christiansted's courts to recount stories about their domestic conflicts, they had to narrate them against strong representational barriers. Judges characterized the slave union as a "natural marriage" and this notion situated slaves' marriages in a legal no-man's land between the legal pact and the illicit liaison. Whether Danish West Indian judges found inspiration for this idea in the British American common law traditions or in Danish scholarship on natural law is not entirely clear. However, as learned men holding degrees from Copenhagen University, they would have been acquainted with the most important Danish introduction to natural law by the enlightenment thinker Ludvig Holberg. Here, Holberg described the "*matrimonium amazonium*" as a union whose purpose was procreation. Such matrimony was characterized by the absence of a binding pact and a lack of male dominion.[298] The genealogy of the notion of the natural marriage aside, the term allowed judges to disregard Danish marriage regulations when they evaluated slave behavior.[299] Literally, the concept of the natural marriage was absent from Danish legislation; by using it, judges placed marriage among enslaved men and women outside the confines of positive law.

Judges chose the concept of the natural marriage with care. Had they wanted, they could have pointed to the, allegedly, illicit nature of slave unions by characterizing them as "concubinage." This was the term used by Danish Lutheran missionaries active in the West Indies and by royal authorities in Copenhagen.[300] Judges could also have adopted a term like the "*cassare* marriage" used in the Danish slave trading stations along the Gold Coast. Then they would have recognized that African marriage customs were, at least partly, legitimate.[301] But the idea of the natural marriage served a purpose. It excluded enslaved men and women from being subject to relevant legislation concerning marriage and adultery, while simultaneously establishing that their unions had a customary nature that allowed judges to speculate about the motives that drove slaves to act in particular ways.[302]

Indeed, the entire vocabulary used to describe slaves' intimate lives worked to corroborate the legal displacement of their unions. Enslaved Africans and Afro-Caribbean were described in a language that removed them from notions of both legitimate and illicit sexuality. Accordingly, terms connoting unlawful sexuality such as "whore" and "bitch" were rare in trials concerning enslaved Africans and Afro-Caribbeans.[303] Such expressions emerged, instead, in cases involving free West Indians, of both European and African descent. Thus, the free woman of color, Flora, alleged that her husband beat her and abused her as a "whore and rascal" because he suspected her of infidelity in 1774. In 1806, Pricilla Renadus, also a free woman of color, complained that the overseer at Betsy's Jewel Estate had wanted her "as his concubine."[304] Similarly, the "free negro" Martin Friderick charged his "free negress" wife Fridericha with "adultery," because she had given "birth to a mulatto child instead of a negro child" in 1807.[305] Such vocabulary, which connoted illicit sexuality, was also used in trials involving whites. In 1821, the sister of the white woman Johanne Adams declared that Johanne "had fallen into bad company and led a licentious life, despite all warning."[306] Likewise, when Susanna Hartford and Thomas Dipnall, both white, were accused of adultery in 1769, Judge Sevel found it appropriate to describe her as a "loose woman" and him as "indecent."[307] Such loaded words were seldom, however, applied to enslaved people within the representational economy of the Danish West Indian courts; probably because judges did not believe that enslaved men and women were guided by moral codes that could be transgressed in the first place.

Along the same lines, judges avoided describing enslaved spouses in terms denoting legality and formality. Free spouses in the Danish West Indies, no matter their racial status, were described as *hustru,* referring to a woman who had gone through a Christian marriage ceremony, *ægtehustru,* a legally married wife, and *ægtemand,* a legally married husband.[308] For the majority of slaves, however, these terms were unavailable.[309] Instead, judges and scribes used the Danish words *mand* and *kone* to describe the male and female partner in a slave union. These were generic terms for *man* and *woman,* but they could also describe a husband and wife. Imprecise and open to multiple meanings, such terms allowed judges to disregard legislation concerning unlawful marital behavior when they adjudicated in slave trials.[310]

Enslaved Africans and Afro-Caribbeans who spoke English or English-Creole in court probably referred to their partners as 'wife' and 'man', and these terms were then translated into the Danish words *kone* and *mand.*[311] Slaves may have told judges that they "kept together with"[312] or "lived with"[313] each other "as wife and husband."[314] This terminology was not, however, in itself capable of endowing slaves' relationships with legal validity; and judges did not mobilize any legislative rules against those enslaved women (and men) who were accused by their spouses or former spouses of infidelity and adultery. Instead, Danish West Indian judges developed a sophisticated vocabulary that excluded slaves from legal prosecution and protection while at the same time acknowledging their conjugal practices. It was a conceptual fiction that left Danish judges free to interpret slaves' domestic troubles as they saw fit. More concretely, it meant that judges understood slaves' domestic violence as crimes of passion caused by fits of "jealousy" that emerged because of the unceremonious and informal nature of their conjugal customs and sexuality.[315]

Shared Ideals, Missing Contexts

Danish West Indian judges represented unions between enslaved men and women with a vocabulary that made it difficult for slaves to present their relationships as legitimate. More than merely instituting verbal distortions, this representational practice contributed to the effacement of the African-Atlantic traditions that guided enslaved men and women in their marital lives. Although few enslaved men and women gave depositions illustrating the role that African-Atlantic traditions played in shaping the emotional and domestic expectations of enslaved spouses, the representational procedures of the Danish West Indian courts often resulted in a complete erasure of the specific ideological contexts in which slaves formulated their ideals. Thus, when Jaque attacked his wife in 1768 and thereby endangered her life, he explained that he had done so "because he believed that she did not care for him."[316] Emotional bonding, "care," emerged as an ideal in Jaque's testimony. If he had other grounds on which he justified his violent actions, they were not disclosed during his trial.

Nonetheless, and despite strong legal erasures, enslaved men and women were able to outline the contours of their domestic expectations and practices. In deposition after deposition, enslaved men and women turned their most valuable material objects, their houses and clothing, into symbolic markers of their unions.[317] When conflicts emerged, doors were locked, houses were burned, food stood untended, dinners were not cooked, and clothing was removed or destroyed. In 1783, the enslaved man Acra, convicted of the murder of his wife Markitta, structured his defense around these themes.[318] In contrast, Acra's biography never became part of the trial. He was born in Africa, perhaps as his name suggests on the Gold Coast in the area around or inland from the Danish slave trading station, Fort Christiansborg, where the inland state of Accra together with the coastal towns of Dutch Accra and English Accra were involved in the transatlantic slave trade. Once in the Danish West Indies, Acra had risen from field laborer to the position of sugar-boiler and rum-distiller. However, Acra's Atlantic trajectory and the ways in which it might have informed his experiences of domestic life in the Danish West Indies were not elaborated on in the trial against him.[319]

During the trial against Acra, Judge Brown, ostensibly, established that jealousy was the main motive for the crime. Brown did so by focusing exclusively on the relationship between Markitta and the slave Anthony. Many slave witnesses testified that Acra and Markitta had quarreled prior to the murder. After the murder, witnesses learned that Markitta had left Acra in favor of Anthony. According to one enslaved witness, Acra had disclosed that he was very "jealous."[320] Acra's master quoted him as saying: "Master, I could not help it, my wife was herself the cause of it."[321] Anthony confirmed that for three days "he had kept together" with Markitta.[322] These were some of the testimonies that allowed Judge Brown to view Acra's crime as an act of jealousy. It seemed to be a clear cut case.

Although Acra's defense was incoherent, even contradictory, his statements in Christiansted Police Court and Lower Court suggest that there was an alternative story to the one told by most witnesses during the trial. Acra began his statement by noting that he "had a wife," namely Markitta, and was "very fond of her."[323] However, she occasionally visited a white man. Acra explained that he had used a series of corrective measures to prevent his wife's infidelity. Without effect, he had criticized her in a "kind" manner. Then he petitioned his master to assist him in resurrecting his failing patriarchal control. But it was to no avail; his wife continued to visit the white man, and, in addition, she began seeing Anthony.[324] As Acra described his actions, they were not the result of a sudden outbreak of jealousy, but rather a slowly escalating response to his wife's adulterous behavior.

Acra established his wife's adultery through a story focused on domestic space, wifely duties, and fidelity. Firstly, Acra maintained that Markitta had not left his house. Although he admitted that she had been in Anthony's house during the day, he specifically stated that she was not visiting Anthony "during the night."[325] By this statement, Acra appears to have been signaling that Markitta's continued presence in their shared house meant that their relationship was still ongoing. Acra also emphasized that Markitta had failed to perform her wifely duties. Although Acra offered two versions of the events that led to Markitta's death, both centered on her defiance. In the first version, he asked her "to cook for him" and she refused. In the second version, he asked her to return some of his clothing, and she refused. In both of Acra's versions, the conflict ended when Markitta ran into him, stabbing herself on his knife.[326]

Acra's statement had many ingredients. First and foremost, it was a defense of his murderous act. It also, however, contained affection and measured critique. Finally, it relied on an ideal of marriage in which wifely duties and shared domestic space were central to the continued reproduction of the marital bond. We may speculate as to why and when Acra became violent, but there is little doubt that Acra maintained that his wife had not left him; that is, he did not believe that there had been a divorce. In his deposition, Acra managed to portray Markitta's behavior as adulterous and his own violence was thereby made meaningful within the structure of his court statement.

In the later verdict, Judge Brown noted that he had in fact understood Acra's "defense," which, according to Brown, consisted in claiming that Markitta "had shown herself unfaithful and taken another man." Brown, however, did not believe that these reasons could excuse Acra's "revenge," and he declined to reflect upon them in his verdict.[327] Thus, Acra's claim about Markitta's infidelity made it into the court transcript, a sign that Acra's ideals were not entirely excluded from the representational practices of the court. It is also clear, however, that these same practices prevented Acra's ideals from being expressed with reference to a larger ideological context. He was not questioned about such a context and he did not refer to either Christian ideals or to African-Atlantic traditions when he explained himself before Judge Brown.

The importance of the house as a symbolic marker of marital status, which Acra seems to have valued, also stands out in a trial from 1819, in which the enslaved man George appeared in Christiansted Lower Court charged with the murder of Lucas. Judge Mouritzen believed that George had acted, partly, in self-defense and therefore he received an arbitrary punishment of one hundred lashes at the public whipping post, instead of capital punishment, and was handed over to his owner.[328] George was around thirty-five when he appeared in Christiansted Lower Court, a member of the Anglican Church, a cooper, and had been born in Africa. However, his African background never became an explicit element of the trial record. Judge Mouritzen did not inquire about it and George did not, it appears, refer to it. Instead, the interrogation focused on the relationship between George, Bridget, and Lucas.[329] Bridget was, depending on one's perspective, either George's wife or his former wife. Lucas was either Bridget's new husband or her illicit lover.

George and Bridget had recently divorced; at least, that was what Bridget believed. Bridget, who was born in St. Croix, told Judge Mouritzen that they had quarreled, and, therefore, she had repeatedly told George that she would no longer live with him. She had "separated" their bedstead and she considered this to be sufficient "sign and notice for George to stay away from her."[330] Moreover, she had found a new husband, the enslaved man Lucas. Bridget had enacted what she believed to be a procedure for divorce. It consisted of informing George of her decision and separating their beds. Lucas, Bridget's new husband, confirmed Bridget's statement before he died, recounting that she had told him that she had no husband "for which reason he took up with her." Bridget's account of the divorce dominated the court transcripts, and Mouritzen chose to rely on it when he set forth the grounds for the sentence.[331]

In contrast to Bridget, George told Judge Mouritzen that he had lived with Bridget in a "natural marriage" for about four years.[332] George was not convinced that Bridget had divorced him and he maintained that he did not consider "the connection between himself and Bridget as broken although they had disagreed and had been fighting." Bridget had, George recounted, taken care of his clothing and he considered her house to be his home.[333] In this way, George made it clear that he had not believed that their recent conflict was reason for Bridget to leave him.

As in the earlier trial against Acra, the house had a central place in George's statement. According the court transcript, George stated that he considered Bridget's house as his "home."[334] He felt that he could come there at will and, during their dispute, he continued to sleep there. He specified that Bridget had not moved anything but his clothes out of the house and mentioned that he had built the front door and knew the system of locks and keys. Thus, George expressed his continued relationship to Bridget in terms of access to her house. Following the same line of reasoning, but from the opposite standpoint, Bridget explained the divorce by asserting that they were no longer sharing the house and that she was no longer taking care of his clothing. She explained to Judge Mouritzen that she had moved his clothing out of her house when they divorced and that she had not slept there since.[335]

In George's deposition, Bridget's house was loaded with meaning. Access to her house was a sign of their continuing intimate relationship. George explained his suspicions against Lucas, whom he believed to be Bridget's lover, by referring to Lucas' presence in Bridget's house. George had harbored some "suspicion" when he first met Lucas in Bridget's house. This feeling was further sustained when George met Lucas there a second time.[336] They began to fight and George hit Lucas twice with a large knife, inflicting the wounds that would later become infected and cause Lucas' death.[337] The overseer on Longford Estate supported George's construction of the events wherein Bridget's behavior was described as adulterous. He claimed that Bridget had treated George badly, that Lucas was not the first man she had seen while with George, and that George had complained about her. The overseer's sympathies were fully on George's side. When he heard about the fight between George and Lucas, he slapped Bridget across the face.

Unsurprisingly, Bridget had a different version. She claimed that she had informed her overseer of their divorce, adding that she did not consider it "his business to interfere" in her choice of partner. He "had not ordered her to have

George, and thus he could not order her to keep him."[338] Bridget thus seems to have argued that neither George nor white plantation staff had any rights to impose themselves on her marital life as long as she respected certain procedures when enacting a divorce.

The house as a symbolic marker of marriage shaped most depositions about domestic conflicts made in Christiansted's courts in the eighteenth and nineteenth centuries. It was also a central element in the investigation against Tony, Cudjoe, and Marie in Christiansted Police Court in 1822. The clash between the two men emerged because of their relationship to the enslaved woman Marie. Both men considered themselves to be Marie's legitimate spouse. Tony told the court that he had "kept together" with Marie.[339] They had quarreled, and he had not seen her for some time. After their divorce, Marie lived with Cudjoe, but she left him again and re-established her relationship with Tony. Marie proved to Tony that she had divorced Cudjoe by showing him the key to her house and emphasizing that the door was locked. In Tony's version of events, Marie had made it clear that she had enacted a legitimate divorce from Cudjoe by blocking his access to her house. Tony's statement relied on the assumption that the free access that spouses enjoyed to each other's houses signaled their bond; consequently, the denial of such access constituted a legitimate divorce.[340]

Marie explained to the court that she "had sought bed with Tony for a long time" until something had come between them. Later, she had taken up with Cudjoe, but she had not been "steady with him and last week they had had a quarrel […] when she told him that she was not fond of him and would not have him any longer." Like Bridget, Marie spoke of the bed as a marker of marital status. She asserted that she had not been in a settled relationship with Cudjoe, and, although the expression "sought bed with" presumably referred to sexual intercourse, this was not in itself enough to define their relationship as marital.[341]

Cudjoe saw things differently. He told the court that Marie had left Tony and "taken up" with him. He did not recognize or accept Marie's attempt at instituting a divorce between them and still considered her to be "his wife." As in other slave depositions about domestic quarrels, Cudjoe and Marie expressed themselves in reference to domesticity. Cudjoe, for instance, recounted an episode wherein Marie had failed to light a candle for him. This seemingly minor incident aroused heated feelings. He got angry and wanted to leave, and she began a quarrel. Later, however, they were reconciled, and Cudjoe explained that thereafter they again spent time together in each other's houses. The last time he came to visit Marie, she had not been home and he could not find the key to her house. While she explained that her removal of the key was a sign of their divorce, he apparently did not understand her sign. Instead, he stated that he had worried that something had happened to her. Consequently, he went searching for her and found her with Tony, whom he then assaulted.[342]

The house — building it, sharing it, and sleeping in it — emerged as a symbol of a binding union in many slave testimonies about marital disputes. The symbolic value of the house corresponded in some measure to its material value. During the eighteenth century, enslaved people generally still constructed their own houses and enslaved men built houses for their wives.[343] Indeed, it appears that constructing and maintaining a house provided a possible means of acquiring modest material assets. Hence, in 1771, the enslaved man Nero earned 10 rix-dollars when he sold the slave house he had built for his wife. Around the turn of the century, Peter Lotharius Oxholm, who as mentioned above would later become governor general, estimated that a slave house was worth around 100 rix-dollars.[344] The value of housing also stands out in the description provided by Mary, enslaved mother and wife, of her family's house in 1840: It was of brick with a thatched roof and a wooden floor, and it contained a bed, three large straw mattresses, a table, a bench, three chairs, and two chests or wooden boxes in which she and her husband kept their clothes.[345] Valuables were kept in houses that were locked with keys and strings, and enslaved men and women used these assets to define domesticity and its borders.[346]

Like houses, clothing — access to it, tending it, and storing it — was claimed by enslaved men and women as proof of marital bonds. Enslaved men and women stored their clothes in chests and trunks and left them with their spouses.[347] Clothing, like housing, was a significant material asset. Marooning slaves could support themselves by tailoring, enslaved thieves often stole clothing, and garments were used instead of currency among enslaved people.[348] When the slave woman Sue, of Orange Grove Estate, probably a fieldworker, had her clothes stolen, she listed her losses as including: a white-and-blue striped shirt, a white apron, one checked and one blue scarf and, in addition, one white shirt and a white waistcoat belonging to her husband. Judge Mouritzen concluded that these items were worth more than 4 rix-dollars and therefore the enslaved thief was to suffer the death penalty.[349] Other slaves, although obviously few in number, had clothing of much higher value. The enslaved man Sam who lived in Christiansted town was also the victim of theft. He lost, among other things, a pair of black trousers, two dress coats, one black and two white vests, a pair of cotton stockings, and a gold brooch.[350]

But clothing was more than a matter of means. It provided social distinctions and signaled experiences. It could be used to show whether enslaved Africans had

View of Northside Quarter A, St. Croix, watercolor by unknown artist, possibly Frederik von Scholten, c. 1840. In the slave village in the foreground, houses are aligned in neat rows, whitewashed and possibly built of brick, like the house Mary described in 1840. Although brick buildings arguably improved housing conditions, they were more costly and consequently overseers, managers, and owners were often involved in their construction. In contrast, the wattle-and-daub cottages were constructed without much interference from superiors (courtesy of *Museet for Søfart*, the Maritime Museum of Denmark).

recently crossed the Atlantic Ocean and to determine status in the Danish West Indies. Moravian pictorial traditions show that the Church used clothing to signal membership through the use of white headscarves, waistcoats, and dresses, among other things. Other associations also used dress to indicate membership. Although evidence is scarce, dance societies with names such as the *Selection Society* and *The Harlequin Green Society*, headed by "directors" and "first ladies," appear to have provided enslaved men and women with the opportunity to fraternize in the nineteenth century. Here clothing also marked status; in 1814, the chairmen of such a dancing society explained that they carried silk ribbons while ordinary members wore a rose buttonhole.[351]

Detail of Mary's Fancy with the slave village, St. Croix, oil painting by unknown artist, possibly Fritz Melbye, c. 1840. In contrast to the watercolor of the Northside (on the preceding page), this painting depicts a slave village where houses appear to be irregularly distributed rather than aligned in rows. These houses appear to be wattle-and-daub constructions. This may have given enslaved men and women more choice regarding how, when and why houses were built (courtesy of *Museet for Søfart*, the Maritime Museum of Denmark).

Friedensthal in St. Croix an einem Bettage, da die Taufflinge zur Taufe in Scheitel stehet, aller Schatten senkrecht fallt, überhaupt wenig Schatten

Prayer day at Friedensthal, 1768. The print is, obviously, an idealized depiction of a Moravian church meeting. It illustrates the importance attached to clothing by the mission. All present, even children, are modestly dressed and dress is used to mark peoples' status within the church. Those who are to be baptized wear white dresses and headscarves, whereas other mission members — many still wearing

e geführt werden, 1768 zu Anfang May und zu Mittage, da die Sonne überm das Wohnhaus, zur lincken die Neger Kirche, zur rechten Neger häuser. c.g.a.o. pinx.

the white headscarves — appear in more varied clothing (Christian Georg Andreas Oldendorp, *Geschichte der Mission der evangelischen Brüder auf den caraibischen Inseln S. Thomas, S. Croix und S. Jan*, vol. II, ed. Johann Jakob Bossart, Barby 1777).

Enslaved men and women turned their material objects into symbolic capital and used them to negotiate relationships and fight out disagreements. In 1840, when John's wife for the previous ten years, Elisabeth, died, he was questioned about a quarrel they had had prior to her death. In court, John explained that Elisabeth accused him of "being connected with" another woman. He denied it, but they had a fight when Elisabeth found him in the house of her alleged rival. Apparently, Elisabeth's suspicions had been aroused because she saw her husband in the other woman's house; presumably, she took it as a sign of adulterous behavior. Similarly in 1835, John Christian gave a testimony in which a house, with closed doors, signified that his wife was seeing another man. In court, he related that he had suspected his wife Agnes of having a "connection with another man." Their immediate dispute began when she refused to accompany him home after a dance. As he returned home alone, he found the "door to their house closed," after breaking in he realized "that she had removed her trunk or chest." These acts "confirmed" his suspicions, and he was "brought into such passion that he tore the garments off their bed and set them on fire."[352] John Christian read Agnes' manipulation of material objects, their house and her trunk, as tokens of a malfunctioning union; he opted to destroy the relics of their relationship with fire.

Enslaved men and women used their clothing to establish bonds, but they also used them to signal disagreement and strife. In 1783, when the enslaved man Jesper had "gone into the negro house inhabited by his wife and found her with another man," he responded by taking "all his wife's clothes" as well as the man's trousers.[353] When Bob and his wife Phiba had a disagreement in 1794, perhaps related to her acquaintance with another man and her pregnancy (a white witness had heard Bob exclaim "I [shall] kick the baby out of her body"), he asked her to deliver him his clothes. She refused. In court, Bob admitted that he had beaten his wife after this incident.[354] A chest containing clothing was also central to the conflict between Betty and Byron, both born in Africa. In 1796, Betty explained that "she had kept together with the slave negro Byron and that she had kept his chest with clothes and money in her room." Once she removed some money, and this caused their divorce.[355]

The ways in which clothes were used as signs of marital intimacy also stand out in a trial from 1828 wherein the African John Edward, in the process of gaining his freedom, was charged with theft from his former wife, the enslaved woman Susanna. In court, John Edward explained that he had lived in "natural marriage" with Susanna, but they fell out with each other. He said that, "since he had the idea that she would take another man, he became more than angry and one night he entered her house, where he opened her chest and removed those items [of clothing] that the police had found in his house yesterday." He admitted that he had "burned" her clothing "in his passion." For John Edward, to attack Susanna's clothing and jewelry — estimated to be of more than 50 rix-dollars in value — was an obvious way of communicating his dissatisfaction and emotional distress.[356]

In their statements, slaves like Acra, George, Bridget, Cudjoe, Marie, and many more, told Christiansted's judges about marital conflicts that centered on domestic rights and duties and referred to the practical and symbolic acts that aimed at reproducing a formal marital life. Enslaved men and women established the house, the key, and the bed as well as food preparation and the care of clothing as signs through which they made sense of and argued over their intimate lives. Enslaved men could assert that their wives were adulteresses; enslaved women argued that their husbands misused authority and disrespected women's right to divorce. As these trials illustrate, enslaved people could not or chose not to explicate the normative context that undergirded these specific values and practices. Nonetheless, their use of affective language and its representation in interrogation transcripts accentuated their affinity to ideals about the importance of fidelity, the distribution of authority between spouses, and the procedures of divorce, despite the erasures of Christiansted's courts.

Many of the enslaved men and women who appeared in Christiansted's courts to debate their marital conflicts were African born, some had arrived to the Caribbean as young men and women and hence brought with them knowledge and ideals of how to sanction married life from their West African home communities. Yet this knowledge was seldom represented within the Danish Atlantic legal system. The conceptual vocabulary adopted by Danish West Indian judges, which described the slave marriage as beyond the concern of the law, being neither legal nor illegal, in combination with the barriers established by slave legislation, made enslaved people's trial prose shallow, rudimentary, and incomplete. These slave depositions did not contain 'thick' descriptions and only allow for very vague conclusions to be made regarding the narratives and ideals that guided men and women in their marital lives.[357]

The erasure of ideational depth in the depositions recorded by Christiansted's court scribes during these trials stand out in contrast to those very few enslaved men and women who adopted a Christian idiom with which to speak about their domestic quarrels. In 1779, Quashy stood accused of stabbing his wife Clarissa. The couple had received Christian instruction and was connected to a Pastor Goodchild. One day, as they concluded their Christian "reading," they began to quarrel in an "indecent" manner. According to witnesses, their dispute erupted when Quashy asked another woman to cook his dinner. When she refused,

Quashy began to abuse Clarissa as a "whore." If, he said, "you will not have me as your husband, then you shall not have any other. I will stab you to death, and I do not care that I will be hanged or that my soul goes to hell." In court, witnesses related that Clarissa "in her heart regretted" having given her husband Quashy cause to stab her. She had provoked him by "cursing him in an awful manner." Now she took all the blame upon herself. She "sincerely" begged "the almighty God to forgive her" and hoped that the authorities would pardon her husband.[358]

Perhaps Clarissa's pleadings were heard. After her death, Police Judge Cooper was instructed to proceed with a trial against Quashy in Christiansted Lower Court; yet no verdict against him was recorded in Christiansted's register of verdicts.[359] In any case, a Christian topology of heaven and hell gave Quashy and other parties to the trial an opportunity to elaborate on, and insert narratives about, who they were, their motives, and their concerns into the trial records. This was a rare option for enslaved people in the courts of Christiansted.

Shared Ideals, Emerging Contexts

The processes of distortion and effacement that shaped the taking and the recording of slave testimonies in Christiansted's courts most often instituted a thorough absence of all signs pointing to slaves' African-Atlantic cosmologies and practices. Yet such absences were not always absolute. In the trial against the slaves at Jerusalem Estate, described at the beginning of this chapter — and in a small number of other trials — enslaved men and women, either as a result of severe language difficulties or by their own volition, left traces that hint at the important role that African-Atlantic marital norms played in shaping the intimate horizons of enslaved spouses in the Danish West Indies.

In 1818, when Joe was accused and convicted of murder in Christiansted Lower Court, a sentence confirmed by the Danish West Indian Upper Court, he expressed ideals and mentioned signifiers similar to those of other enslaved men and women, but he probably thought about his predicament in an African language.[360] The accusations made against Joe were severe. He was charged with murdering the enslaved man Coffy. Additionally, he had attempted to kill his "natural marriage" wife Sophie, and, finally, he had wounded the enslaved woman Domingo [sic] because he mistook her for his wife in the dark of night.[361] Joe introduced the interpretation of his alleged crimes that came to dominate the case during the first interrogation, which took place on Mount Welcome Estate right after Coffy's death. During this interrogation, Joe explained that he harbored feelings of "jealousy" against Coffy whom he suspected of having "an intimate relationship" with Sophie.[362] Sophie and other witnesses confirmed this account, although Sophie maintained that there were no grounds for Joe's suspicions. Joe added further details during the next interrogation. He was convinced that Sophie had a "disgraceful and intimate intercourse" with Coffy and that she had "served" both men "as wife and took care of their houses."[363]

During the trial, Joe and Sophie, like so many others, explained their conflict in stories that centered on domestic obligations and space. For Joe, wifehood meant that Sophie took care of their house. His responsibility, on the other hand, was to contribute materially to the household. In court, he related that the conflict erupted one day when he returned from town where he had purchased ingredients for their evening meal and had found his wife lingering outside Coffy's house. She had left their house while the "pot with the evening meal" stood unattended on the fire.[364] For this reason he slapped her. Later, Joe changed this explanation and claimed that he had slapped Sophie because she had forgotten to lock the door to their house. In both explanations, Joe felt justified in castigating her because of her, in his view, negligent attitude towards their shared domestic life.

Joe did not, it appears, doubt that his patriarchal authority included the right to castigate his wife. Explaining his attempted murder of Sophie, he offered a straight and coherent story of how he had waited for her, hiding behind a tree, and when she returned to their house he attacked her. This story was told without evasion and with a transparent motive. The reasons for his attack on Sophie were already part of the overall structure of his account, which comprised her adulterous behavior and her failure to perform domestic duties. In contrast, Joe's explanation of why he killed Coffy was tangled and difficult to understand. Initially, Joe spoke of jealousy, but he later explained that Coffy had questioned his right to castigate his wife. They quarreled and Joe, as he claimed, had been forced to act in self-defense.[365]

Other enslaved men shared Joe's views on castigation, but enslaved women were less convinced. In 1794, Moab explained that he had given his wife some "whacks with a cane" when he learned she was seeing another man but denied that he had threatened to set the estate on fire or, for that matter, kill the "mulatto whom he had heard his wife was seeing." For Moab, it appears, wifely castigation needed no elaborate explication; it was a simple and straightforward act. Maria, whom he claimed as his wife, thought otherwise. She asserted that she was no longer his wife. They had lived for a long time in a "natural marriage," but she had left him because of his violent behavior and found a new husband.[366] The same tense conflict about enslaved men's right to castigate their wives was played out in the trial against Zuashy who beat his wife Betty in 1795. When drunk, Betty explained, Zuashy was like a "raving man," he stole her money, broke her kitchenware, and beat her. She was more than willing to leave him if only she could get back those items of her property that he held.[367]

The house had a significant place in the stories told by Joe and Sophie. Joe slapped Sophie when he discovered that she had left their shared house and was lingering outside Coffy's house. This upset her and she refused to return to their shared house. Likewise, Coffy's critique of Joe occurred when Joe slapped Sophie outside his house. Coffy may be understood as having disapproved of Joe's behavior because it encroached on the authority he exercised in the areas surrounding his house. That is, he was not necessarily voicing a general critique of domestic castigation. In these testimonies the house constituted a marker of intimacy and delineated areas of competing masculine authority. The house, in other words, was not only a material construct, but also an institution that marked the formality of a relationship.

In the trial against Joe, vague contours of an African-Atlantic context emerged not because Joe proclaimed them, but because, presumably, he formulated his ideas within an African semiotic universe. The conflict between Joe and his wife Sophie played out on Mount Welcome Estate. Yet they were both born in Africa, had arrived to the West Indies in their early twenties, and had, likely, been raised with the values of their home communities. In St. Croix, they were members of Christian congregations and might have adopted some of their views on marriage from their churches. Both of them understood marriage as entailing fidelity, female domestic work, shared domestic space, and emotional bonding. When they disagreed and argued, however, they appear to have done so in an African language. Joe's proficiency in the Creoles of St. Croix was not good. Indeed, the scribe noted that his language was "partly incomprehensible." Given their background, Joe and Sophie probably communicated in an African language during their long Caribbean relationship, and it was with this language as their conceptual tool that their conflict found its tragic end.[368]

Similarly, in the trial against Sally whose story began this book, there emerged traces of African-Atlantic domestic ideals, entangled with hints of Moravian rituals. In 1799, Sally was sentenced to death by decapitation by Christiansted Lower Court. Her sentence was mitigated and, likely, she was deported from the island.[369] Although Sally's actions were rare, she was the only enslaved woman charged with violence against her spouse in the period from the mid-eighteenth century until emancipation in 1848, her story, like most slave testimonies about domestic strife, was structured by ideas about domestic space and fidelity.

When Sally appeared in court, she and Leander had been a couple for approximately five years. Sally's tale was one of love, anger, revenge, and despair. She did not accept her husband's adultery and used intimidating and violent means to persuade him to change his behavior. For her, a polygynous marriage was illegitimate. To prevent it, she decided first to fight Leander's other wife, then to use what could be understood as a potion to reform his behavior, and, finally, to burn down his house. In court, Sally related that Leander

> was her first and only husband. However, after having lived with him for some time she learned that he had taken another wife on […] *Morgenstjene* Estate. This raised her jealousy and put her mind in such a condition that she set fire to her husband Leander's house late one evening after he had settled down to sleep […] she loved Leander and she still loves him and wished that she could live with him for as long as she lives. It was because of indignation caused by his infidelity that she had wanted to burn him. She had never wished to poison her husband Leander, but she had once in order to terrify him and deter him from the other wife taken some marl and mixed it with water. The effect of this was far from doing any harm, and she had drunk from it herself.

After the fire

> she and he for some time lived happily together [… when she again] learned that her husband Leander went astray and remained unfaithful, this [unreadable, possibly the word is flushed or heated] her heart and she had to confess that it was revengeful.

For this reason she had set fire to a cane field, and

> in anger she had told Leander that she had burned his house […] that she had done it for him, that she had fought with the wife he had taken, who was bigger and stronger than her […] that she [Sally] could leave […] but despite all this she had been unable to leave him.[370]

In Sally's deposition, her "anger" made her attack Leander's house. Like many enslaved men and women, Sally connected her emotional response to domestic space.

However, in contrast to Acra and most other enslaved men, Sally did not craft a narrative that centered on domestic duties. This may have been because such duties were less clearly defined for men than for women or because Leander, who held the position of driver on Hope Estate, was able to provide the domestic assistance Sally found appropriate. Unions were economic partnerships, and both men and women knew this. Thus, for instance, in 1800, the free woman of color Rutie ended a relationship because her enslaved partner "did not have it within his power to contribute anything to her maintenance." Therefore, she blocked his access to her house.[371] Likewise, Joseph's wife, a free woman of color, deserted him because "he had given her little or nothing."[372] And the enslaved man Billy informed a free man of color that since "he could not support the [slave] negress with whom he lived in natural marriage," he, Billy, "would take it upon himself to support the negress and her child."[373] Such economic worries, however, did not shape the conflict between Sally and Leander.

Sally blended Christian and African-Atlantic traditions in her deposition. She was not a member of any of the churches in St. Croix, but she called to the "Lord above" during her interrogation. Yet she also admitted that she had fought with Leander's other wife, mixed water and marl to "terrify" Leander, and, ultimately, turned to arson to resolve her problems. The precise nature of the marl blend made by Sally was not explored during the trial. Nonetheless, Leander and Sally, despite profound differences, agreed that it could not be reduced to turbid water; it had other effects. Leander claimed it was poison and although no one spoke of magic, Sally hinted at its powerful nature when she described how she had drunk it herself, emphasizing that it was not deadly but terrifying.

In the violent world of Danish West Indian slavery, confronted with an excruciating work regime and rampant mortality, Sally was not the first, nor the last, enslaved person to seek spiritual help from obeah experts. In the domestic conflict between Michael and Nicholas of Jerusalem Estate regarding their respective relationships to Antoinette with which this chapter began, both men appear to have consulted obeah experts. This was also the case in the conflict between Thomas and Limmerich (see Chapter 1) about the legitimacy of polygyny on Hermon Hill Estate. Indeed, Sally's account of her domestic plight echoed the depositions made in the trial against Lively who stood accused of witchcraft by the name of "obeah" in Christiansted Police Court in 1788. During the trial the enslaved woman Sholamith, baptized by the Moravian Brethren, related that Lively had offered his spiritual assistance in countering a threat from another enslaved woman who, unable to stand-up to her physically, would give Sholamith (or her daughter) "something that would make her mad so that she should wriggle on her belly like a worm and then burst with boils and ulcers."[374] Even more to the point, in 1825, rumor had it that the obeah man Qvamina had made a "doll of 4 colors" that a free woman was to put under her partner's pillow, presumably to gain some kind of power over him.[375] For these women, seeking spiritual assistance to resolve domestic conflicts was a reasonable option, as it may have been for Sally.

In addition to the potion that Sally may have concocted for Leander, other clues imply that Sally relied on African-Atlantic marital norms when she explained herself to Judge Brown. Although Sally stated that she was born on St. Eustatius, Brown initially took her to be "born on the Coast" of Africa. Brown's mistake may have been caused by the fact that Sally spoke an African language with a recently arrived enslaved woman when he first met her. Indeed, Sally's manners, linguistic skills, spiritual choices, appearance, and comportment likely suggested to Brown that she was African. If nothing else, Brown's mistake indicates that Sally may have oriented herself according to the ideals and norms brought to St. Croix by the many African nations present on the island.

Sally's husband Leander was in his early thirties when he appeared in Christiansted Lower Court. Born in Africa, he had climbed the ladder of the estate hierarchy. In 1799, he was the estate driver and a member of the Moravian congregation. In court, Leander explained that he "had taken" Sally as his wife for the sake of "*convenience.*"[376] Leander's expectation that Sally was to be a "*convenience,*" while crudely expressed, was not uncommon among enslaved men who, like many women, understood wifehood as tightly linked to service.[377] This link becomes very clear in an extraordinary case from 1807 wherein the enslaved woman Susanna complained about her owner and husband, the enslaved man Pedro. According to Susanna, Pedro, though a slave himself, had purchased her and treated her badly. Pedro, in contrast, explained that Susanna and he had long lived in a "natural marriage" and she had begged him to buy her. For some time, Pedro complained, Susanna had "served […] willingly, but lately she would not work and did nothing." When Pedro reproached her, Susanna threatened to burn down his house, and, therefore, he chained her to the door.[378] In this conflict, wifely status and slave status converged in the notion of service. Or, at least they did for Pedro who expected Susanna to work for him. In response, Susanna threatened to destroy the emblem of their union, the house.

Leander's African birth, his persistent polygyny, and his idea of wifely "*convenience*" together suggest that the tensions among enslaved men and women about the work and support they could expect from each other spanned the Atlantic Ocean and was not merely a Caribbean phenomenon. This conclusion is also suggested by the unique testimony provided by the Mandingo woman Carolina in 1805. Carolina gave her statement in Mandingo, a Mandingo boy translated it into to English, and then it was rendered into Danish in the police log. Carolina explained that

> she was a Mandingo negro, has been brought here in a ship from the coast with many more, and landed, as far as one may conclude from her gestures, on the Westend, where the capt. had put them ashore in order for them to exercise and wash them [sic]. – By walking around they came across some bushes, into which she and others went in order to relieve themselves, and an old negro had come, who had understood their language and persuaded [the] deponent and two others to follow him. – Next they ran into the bushes and hid. – And the old negro later came to the deponent and brought her to his house which was placed distantly in the field by some thicket where she was hiding when others came. – For these reasons the negro gave her food and had her work for him on his plot by planting produce etc. But as she received no clothing and the negro treated her badly, she left him to go to another place.[379]

Carolina expected clothing and support. Instead, she met bad treatment, ran away, and found a white mistress.[380] Carolina's actions and reasons were never made public; perhaps she had no other choice than to integrate into slave society; perhaps she was still living according to the ideals of her home community and could not accept the patriarchal order of the "old negro." Here, as in the trial against Sally, domestic troubles crossed the Atlantic and locked Africans and Afro-Caribbeans into contentious arguments over how they should live together.

Leander was relying on elite African polygynous traditions when he insisted on having two wives. Yet, as a member of the Moravian community, he also drew on the Brethren's traditions. In court, he stressed that his relationships to his two wives had gone on for many years. He explained that he had taken Sally as his wife "more than five years ago" and that he had taken his other wife "a long time ago." This emphasis on duration was probably intentional. For the Moravians, polygyny was considered legitimate in certain situations. Basing themselves on biblical precedents, the Brethren allowed men who had many wives before their conversion to keep them when they joined the church.[381] It was possibly this practice that Leander referred to when he specified the length of his relationships. In this way, Moravian accommodations to the Danish West Indian slave society helped Leander make the claim that his family was legitimate by Christian standards.

Judge Brown and his scribe appear to have been convinced by Leander of the legitimate nature of his family arrangements. They described Sally with the peculiar term *medhustru* (i.e., co-wife)[382] even though bigamy was strictly prohibited in Danish jurisprudence.[383] Judge Brown may have adopted the notion of the co-wife from the contemporary Danish Bible (for instance Gen. 25:6 and 2 Sam. 3:7), or it may have been Leander's own expression, adopted from Moravian biblical terminology. In any case, the presence of the term *co-wife* in the court book suggests that Leander was successfully diffusing Sally's accusations of infidelity. In Leander's version of events, he had two legitimate wives, and, consequently, his behavior was not adulterous. This was an innovative combination of Danish legal parlance, Moravian missionary teachings, and African elite traditions.

The narratives crafted by enslaved men and women to account for their domestic troubles contain subtle signs that imply that their struggles were Atlantic in scope. Enslaved Africans came from societies where slave trading put pressure on kinship, family, and marriage, and, in the West Indies, they strove to reconcile a gender order they knew with the world of racial plantation slavery. Such was the case in the trial against George who was accused of attempted suicide in 1804 (see Chapter 2). The driver Jimmy's attempts to control George's intimate life prompted his desperate actions. Both George and his former wife, Grace, had been born in Africa. It was difficult for Judge Winding to understand George, and Winding found Grace unable to give "comprehensible or coherent" answers in court.[384] Grace's new husband, the enslaved man Neptune, had recently crossed the Atlantic, presumably communicating with both Grace and George in a language learned in Africa. This, again, suggests the possibility that their controversies played out in an African semiotic universe.

The court story provided by George was built around a dispute between himself and the driver Jimmy. Their conflict arose when George wanted to reunite with his former wife Grace. Jimmy had attempted to prevent their reunion. According to George, the driver told him that

> if you will give me a prize then I will get you your wife back, but if she is given to you without my permission, then I will flog her daily. This I can do and nobody shall protest, as our master is in his house, and I will seek opportunity when the overseer is not present.[385]

For this reason, George harbored "great hatred" against the driver. Moreover, he related that "he was very annoyed that a part of the negroes on the estate mocked him" because he had lost his wife to a "new negro."[386] The ridicule George suffered led to a fight between him and his ex-wife's new husband. When Jimmy subsequently punished George, he tried to take his own life.

The ideational background of George's story remains difficult to unravel. He was not a Christian believer, had long lived with an African woman, and, possibly, they shared an African language. Moreover, he and the other enslaved men at Shoy Estate appear to have believed that newly arrived Africans were somehow less entitled to partnership and marriage. Together, these elements of George's deposition provide strong indications that George was relying on African-Atlantic conventions when he formulated his frustrations. In George's story, he described his misfortune by outlining Jimmy's interference in his marital life and the ridicule he suffered for losing her to a "new negro." George's story was structured by a series of emotions: He felt "hatred" as the result of outside interference in his personal life, "annoyance" when he was ridiculed, and a wish to "die" when Jimmy punished him unfairly.[387] His story, in other words, relied on the assumption that his ability to negotiate his marital status was central to his very existence. Without this ability, George — in his story and as attested by his suicide attempt — would rather die.

Jimmy, the other main party to the conflict, also found ideational support in African-Atlantic traditions as he attempted to maintain his position as estate driver. As the trial proceeded, Jimmy's role in George's suicide attempt became clear. Jimmy requested the help of the "sorcerer" and "wise man" Plato. Plato arrived in the Danish West Indies around 1799-1800 and had lived a good part of his adult life in Africa. In court, Plato stressed that his expertise was directly related to knowledge he had obtained in his "native country." He explained that he had been requested to perform "obeah conjurations," but emphasized that he did not consider himself an "obeah man." This was merely a name other "negroes" had given him after his arrival in the West Indies.[388] Nevertheless, Plato invoked protection for Jimmy through sticks he had cut and tied together around nails and hair and placed in Jimmy's house. In Plato's "native country," he explained, such measures "had the effect that it prevented the enemy or the *contra-part* from causing harm in battle." Now, in the West Indies, Plato used his knowledge to assist Jimmy in protecting himself. Although not directly related to Jimmy's attempts at controlling George's marital life, Plato's involvement in the case highlights the fact that African-Atlantic spiritual practices were a fertile ground upon which enslaved people attempted to organize or control their intimate affairs.

Enslaved men and women found strength and ideational ammunition in Christian and African-Atlantic spiritual powers as they sought to bring some measure of order and meaning into the unsettling and violent world of plantation slavery. As noted above, an obeah battle had taken place on Jerusalem Estate in 1831, or so enslaved witnesses believed. In 1828, enslaved people from Hermon Hill, outlined another story in which Christianity and obeah had been harnessed during the conflict between two enslaved men, Thomas and Limmerich. Further, in 1835, a similar combination of African-Atlantic and Christian cosmology was recounted in the trial against Laban in Christiansted Police Court. The enslaved man William was dead, and witnesses claimed that Laban had killed him because he thought that William had had "intercourse" with his wife Mary. During the proceedings witnesses argued that William had been the victim of a malicious, magic attack. William's sister explained that Laban had threatened to turn William, a carpenter by profession, into a fieldworker and as he pronounced this threat, he had fallen to his knees, appearing "to make the holy promise." Other witnesses stated that Laban wanted to use obeah to drive William mad while one witness related that Laban often threatened that he would make people "go to hell." In these testimonies Laban emerges as an aggressive and hot-tempered man. Many people may have wanted to remove him from the estate. Whatever their motives, however, it appears that all agreed that a narrative sequence in which victims of adultery turned to obeah was credible.[389] In these courtroom stories, African-Atlantic magic was easily blended with holy promises and hellish condemnations to influence domestic affairs.

Obeah bottle, photography by Theodor C. von Zeilau, early twentieth century. This obeah bottle appears to be adorned with — or, rather, made up of — a cross of feathers and a cross of metal or wood. As such, the bottle illustrates the creolization taking place among enslaved Cruzians and, like the testimonies of the enslaved people of Jerusalem and Hermon Hill estates, it mobilized Christian symbolism while also referring to other powers. More importantly, however, the photography underlines how the restrictive representation of African-Atlantic knowledge makes it difficult, at times impossible, to unfold the meanings attached to the bottle (courtesy of *Rigsarkivet*, The Danish National Archives).

An African-Atlantic Marital Context

Whereas most proceedings in Christiansted Lower Court and Christiansted Police Court resulted in interrogation transcripts that either excluded or rendered the ideational context in which enslaved peoples' conjugal ideals emerged barely visible, there were exceptions. Some trial records, like Sally's, George's, and Limmerich's, contained traces of the performance of African-Atlantic traditions and evidence suggesting that domestic conflicts were Atlantic in scope. Yet the freedom trial of the enslaved woman Venus, during which she explicitly narrated the African-Atlantic wedding rituals that had formalized her marriage, was exceptional.

In 1815, Venus gained freedom for herself and one of her four children in Christiansted Lower Court. During the trial she provided a short account of her life written in English. Venus informed Judge Smith that she was born along the Saloum River in Senegambia. As a young girl, she was brought to Gorée, a French, alternately British, slave trading post off the coast of Senegal. There she became the domestic slave of the wealthy Creole couple Anne Roussine and Nicolas Pépin. She lived with her owners until the arrival of the American captain John George Maddock in 1800. He fell in love with her and agreed to marry her and redeem her from slavery. The couple's wedding was conducted according to Goreéan customs. In the evening Venus was "delivered to the embraces" of the captain and the next morning the couple was

> awakened by the noise of Drums & Music [,] a sumptuous Feast was made at which were present all the Officers; all those in any Public capacity; and all persons of Note or distinction. This is the Mariage [sic] usage at Goree, to give Publicity & validity to the Ceremony.

After the wedding, Venus and John Maddock lived together at the Pépin household. During this time Venus became so fond of Maddock that she "took the resolution to come with him to St. Croix," though she demanded a "bond" that would ensure her return to Gorée and carried a "Paper […] as a Proof of Freedom" across the Atlantic. Nevertheless, Maddock sold Venus as a slave upon the couple's arrival to St. Croix. Fifteen years later, Venus used this account of her wedding and the subsequent legal agreements to successfully claim her freedom in Christiansted Lower Court. The fact that Venus obtained freedom for herself and one of her children because of this account suggests an answer as to why the formal nature of enslaved peoples' unions were so seldom represented in the courts of

Christiansted. Formality — also African-Atlantic formality — could upset the legal impediments suffered by enslaved people in the courts of Christiansted.

Venus' story was outstanding in its narrative coherence and content. Indeed, it echoed the widely popularized English tale of Inkle and Yarico in which the merchant Inkle sells his South American, alternately African, sweetheart, Yarico, into slavery.[390] Venus' story, however, was more than a piece of fiction. Her description of her marriage to Maddock reflected contemporary Goreéan practices.[391] Likewise, her first owners, Anne Roussine and Nicolas Pépin, were in fact members of the powerful and wealthy group of *habitants*, the Creole merchant community on Gorée.[392] Finally, Maddock was not a figure in a sentimental anecdote. The American captain arrived to St. Croix in 1800 only to sail on to other American destinations with a cargo of more than fifty slaves.[393]

As the story of Venus shows, Christianity — whether Moravian, Lutheran, Anglican or Roman Catholic — was only one of the traditions that allowed slaves to describe and define how they should conduct their intimate lives. In Venus' bid for freedom, Goreéan wedding practices and legal arrangements were brought to life with remarkable clarity in the courts of Christiansted. Exceptional as it was, Venus' story provides the kind of detail about her domestic life, both its emotional and legal elements, that most other enslaved men and women in the Danish West Indian courts could not give because of the limited representational possibilities available to them. In Venus' detailed story, specific customs and legal acts turned a relationship into a formal marriage. Her account — like those of other enslaved men and women — emerged in a complex Atlantic interplay between Danish West Indian plantation slavery and West African marital ideals and practices. Indeed, Venus' experiences suggest that the fracases with which enslaved couples in the Danish West Indies had to cope were part of a larger conflict, Atlantic in scope, about the implications of marriage in a time of slavery.

The depositions made by the enslaved men and women involved in domestic conflicts contain layers of meaning that are difficult to disentangle. Yet the stories crafted by these men and women allow us to sketch an admittedly flimsy picture of the shared and contested conjugal ideals and practices of enslaved men and women that persisted through the eighteenth and into the nineteenth century in the Danish West Indies. The most pronounced element of slaves' depositions was their focus on domesticity in different forms. Men and women, in different modes, attributed symbolic meaning to the house, the key, and the bed, as well as to food preparation and the maintenance of clothing. These material objects were claimed as signs that could designate a formal marriage as well as a divorce, depending on one's perspective.

The house in particular played a central role in trials concerning slave unions.[394] It emerged in slaves' courtroom stories as an important practical institution as well as a symbol of matrimony. Marie used a key to show that she had broken a relationship by locking her house, Bridget removed her husband's clothes and did not sleep in their house after the divorce, and Joe beat his wife when he found her outside the house of another man. In the 1760s, Oldendorp, as mentioned, noted that marriages between enslaved men and women involved some form of co-habitation and described practices reminiscent of housing arrangements in many West and West-Central African societies.[395] If a couple lived on the same estate, the woman would either move to the man's house or he would build a new house for them. If the couple lived on different estates, the man would build a house for his wife on her plantation and visit her after work.[396]

In addition to the provision grounds, provided to estate slaves to grow some — but rarely their entire — foodstuff, the house was among the most valuable assets belonging to Danish West Indian plantation slaves. Houses, like the provision grounds, provided enslaved people with a modicum of, admittedly fragile, privacy. People could lock their doors and at least some overseers appear to have abstained from entering without permission or prior warning.[397] Moreover, enslaved men and women may have had a significant voice in deciding with whom they would share a house. In 1804, around 28,000 enslaved people shared approximately 10,500 slave dwellings on plantations in the Danish West Indies. This number indicates that on average no more than two to three people, including children, shared a house.[398]

At first glance, the focus on domestic space, valuable assets, and women's chores described by enslaved men and women in the courts of Christiansted underline the functional element of enslaved unions. Yet these unions were much more. Although Joe (who killed Coffy and attempted to kill his wife Sophie) spoke about the conflict with his wife by referring to her domestic duties, he also used diction that directly expressed emotional distress. His statements included claims about "disgraceful intimate intercourse" that were rare in the Danish West Indian courts. He and others made marriage meaningful by referring to terms such as love, fondness, care, anger, jealousy, and revenge. The stories about marriage crafted by enslaved Africans and Afro-Caribbeans contained, in addition to their focus on domesticity, ample proof that many men and women were deeply emotionally committed to their relationships. This was in stark contrast to the notion, assumed by Christiansted's judges, that enslaved men and women had no "qualms" about leaving each other and consequently no profound attachment to their loved ones. Instead, enslaved men and women argued that emotions and functionality were two sides of the same coin and created a strong need for formal rules on how to engage in married life.

Although enslaved people stressed that notions about marital formality guided their unions, it is also evident that they faced strong representational barriers if they wanted to present themselves in the Danish West Indian courtrooms as guided by traditions that were African-Atlantic rather than European and Christian in nature. Unlike the free black woman Maria Bender whose lawyer in 1796 claimed that her husband had treated her in an "unchristian and illegal manner," enslaved Africans and Afro-Caribbeans seldom had the opportunity to provide such explicit references to the normative traditions they relied on in their marital lives.[399] And yet Venus' story, in combination with traces scattered through other slave depositions, shows that African-Atlantic legal and spiritual practices were central to slaves' understanding of their intimate lives in the eighteenth and the nineteenth centuries.

Some of the Atlantic influences that shaped domestic life for enslaved men and women came to life in the interviews recorded by Oldendorp in the 1760s. While these accounts about weddings, marriages, and adultery suggest that Africans shared ideals and traditions without much disagreement, the trials in Christiansted courts tell another story. Indeed, enslaved people at court described unions that were a far cry from the idealized marital customs and regulations that Africans unfolded for Oldendorp in the 1760s. Their trial depositions were filled with tense disagreements about the meaning of marriage in a world of slavery. For the men and women who came to court, sharing an ideological background did not mean agreeing; rather, sharing a tradition or a set of ideas meant that they contested and negotiated their relationships on common ground. Africans in the Danish West Indies came from societies wherein marriage and the rules regulating it changed in response to the growing intensity of the slave trade during the eighteenth century. The trade in people stimulated the conjoined practices of slavery, marriage, and polygyny and thereby it strengthened patriarchal structures and deepened social divisions in large swaths of West Africa.[400] In the Danish West Indies, African and Afro-Caribbean men and women were engulfed in these broad Atlantic processes. They agreed that marriage entailed a set of mutual obligations and entertained the idea that spouses should be faithful toward one another. However, they had conflicting expectations of marital life, they disagreed about the distribution of authority between the spouses, and they debated the role that external authorities

— such as masters and drivers — should play in their intimate lives. For them, their ties to African-Atlantic traditions were central to the common ground upon which they sought, as best they could, to find their way through tense conflicts about marriage and authority in the Danish West Indies.

CHAPTER 5

Repressing Slave Stories: Guilt and Punishment

During proceedings in Christiansted Lower Court and Christiansted Police Court, enslaved people had few and severely restricted possibilities for developing their defense. As the chorus of enslaved voices in the previous pages evince, some slaves seized this opportunity, establishing themselves as modest Christians, caring parents, loving partners, and people who firmly believed that African-Atlantic traditions were useful and meaningful in the Danish West Indies. Enslaved men and women, in other words, provided descriptions of who they might be, of themselves, as it were. When, however, the proceedings finished, when the court scribe put down his quill and testified that his trial transcription was correct, these restricted windows for self-representation evaporated. At this stage of the judicial process, enslaved men and women were imprisoned at Fort Christiansværn, while the lower court judge retired to adjudicate and pass verdict in isolation.[401] It was at this specific point of the legal process that the actual decisions about guilt and punishment were made. Whatever influence enslaved men and women had on the court's decisions, therefore, depended on the interpretative practices developed by judges to master the abundance of slave testimony recorded during interrogations.

Evidence in Slave Trials

Sentencing a slave was not a simple matter in the Danish West Indies. Christiansted's judges moved in an unsettled legislative landscape. Even though the 1733 slave code, as mentioned, stipulated that the sworn deposition of one person, "white or Christian," would be sufficient evidence for the conviction of a slave, Danish West Indian judges followed Danish procedural tradition and gathered as many forms of evidence as possible. Sworn depositions by free Danish West Indians, testimonies and confessions from enslaved people, and various significant

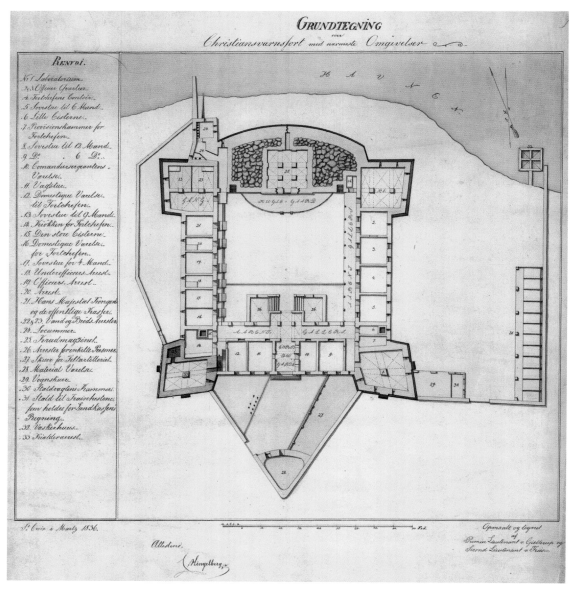

Ground plan of Fort Christiansværn, 1836. The fort was used as a prison for enslaved defendants as they awaited trial and punishment and, more rarely, served as a place of custody for enslaved people mistreated by their owners. The plan presents an ideal picture of Danish colonial occupation and administration; its straight lines and empty spaces create the impression of a colonial state able to impose order on society. However, fort life was not entirely regulated and enslaved prisoners did not live in complete isolation from the outside world. A few even managed to escape imprisonment in the 1780s (courtesy of *Rigsarkivet*, the Danish National Archives).

circumstances were regularly mobilized and weighed against one another by Christiansted's judges in order to decide whether an enslaved defendant was guilty. Hence, Judge Brown's verdict against the enslaved man John Danneson, who was convicted of attempted murder in 1783, was by no means unique. In his verdict Judge Brown drew on depositions by Danneson's alleged victim, his master, and two enslaved witnesses, as well as on Danneson's own statement and the "circumstances" of the attack in order to establish his guilt.[402]

Indeed, judges appear to have been wary of using only one sworn deposition to convict slaves, despite the fact that the slave code of 1733 provided the legal basis for such a procedure. In 1764, Judge Juul, for instance, argued that the sworn deposition of a certain Smith, who had been robbed, was not enough to turn a presumption against the enslaved woman Catharina into a full proof against her. Therefore, he settled for a lower, arbitrary sentence rather than the one stipulated in slave legislation.[403] Likewise, the court denied Cornelius Stallard's request, based on the 1733 slave code, that he be allowed to swear against the slave Gibraltar in 1769. Judge Juul found the request "rather" dubious since proceedings had shown Stallard to harbor an "implacable hatred" of Gibraltar.[404] Indeed, during the everyday, run-of-the-mill, proceedings in Christiansted Lower Court, a single sworn deposition was rarely considered sufficient proof against a slave.[405]

Instead of relying on the 1733 slave code, Christiansted's judges accumulated as much evidence as they could possibly collect from the trial transcripts. This practice was supported both by royal slave legislation and by metropolitan law. As mentioned, the 1755 slave code stipulated that enslaved defendants were to be tried following the same procedural rules as those pertaining to the king's free subjects.[406] These rules were spelled out in *The Danish Law*. The *Law* operated under the notion of full proof, based on Deuteronomy (17:6), which emerged when two witnesses had given corresponding sworn testimony.[407] In addition, however, Danish jurisprudence also operated with so-called presumptive sentences. These sentences were handed down when rumors, material evidence, significant circumstances and confessions in various combinations resulted in strong and well-founded presumptions against defendants.[408] Although the 1755 slave code explicitly prohibited that slave testimony be used to form "presumptions or corroborate evidence," this was exactly what Danish West Indian judges did. Moreover, they operated with both presumptions, strong presumptions, and full proof. As they juggled with evidence, judges diverged from metropolitan practice. In Denmark, verdicts based on presumptions were no longer fashionable in the eighteenth century and were generally reversed by the Supreme Court in the many criminal cases it heard, but Christiansted's judges argued that the tense nature of Danish West Indian society made presumptive sentencing necessary.[409]

The notion of the strong presumption enabled judges to broaden the evidential basis of their verdicts because presumptions could be obtained from a wide variety of information and facts, not only from the sworn statement.[410] Importantly, presumptions allowed judges to include slave testimony in their adjudicative deliberations. This was vital, Judge Winding noted in 1795, because only a minority of slaves could be proven guilty and punished if slave testimony was rejected.[411] Judge Winding was not alone in this concern. Christiansted's judges developed tortuous arguments in order to bypass the problems associated with slave testimony. In 1778, for instance, when acting Judge Rogiers convicted the enslaved man Bob for the murder of the enslaved man Hannibal, the only two witnesses were the slave women Bogatte and Ebbo Betti, both of whom emphatically testified against Bob. Rogiers argued that he had refrained from asking the women to swear on their statements because they were not Christians. By emphasizing their lack of faith rather than their enslavement, Rogiers closely followed the phrasing of the 1733 slave code's article concerning the evidential requirements needed to convict an enslaved person (i.e., an oath from a "white or a Christian").[412] Therefore there was no proof against Bob. However, Rogiers argued, when the women's statements were combined with the fact that Bob had been found with a knife beside Hannibal's dead body, there was a "strong presumption" against him. Judge Rogiers could not sentence Bob to death, but he could, he believed, sentence him to flogging, branding, and transportation.[413] Likewise, Paris was sentenced to transportation in 1779 because there was "a certain presumption" that he had tricked a fellow slave into poisoning their master.[414]

The confessions of enslaved defendants were the only statements that bondsmen and -women could make that were accepted as legally valid evidence.[415] Slaves were banned from oath taking, but since defendants were not required to swear on their depositions, this ban did not diminish the evidential status of their confessions. The confession was an important step toward establishing guilt, and judges referred to the alleged confessions of enslaved defendants in approximately half of their verdicts.[416] In 1786, Judge Brown argued that, since the intention of the enslaved man Jack was "an inner act, about which he himself must be the more conscious," it was safest to assume that Jack's statement was correct, and likewise, in 1795, the testimony of the enslaved man Juba was considered to be the "surest thing against him."[417] Indeed, judges went to great lengths to obtain confessions and believed they were the best proof to be had of the motives and intentions that guided the behavior and actions of enslaved people.

However, in the proficient and ingeniously manipulative hands of Christiansted's judges, the confession became a term applicable to a wide range of court statements. Naturally, statements in which enslaved defendants declared their guilt and responsibility were considered confessions. So too, however, were statements of defendants who had not accepted their guilt. In 1775, Judge Hellvad convicted the enslaved woman Raina, whom we met earlier, of poisoning her master Mr. Osborn. During long interrogations, facing threats of torture, Raina maintained that she had not known that the powder she added to her master's wine whey was poisonous. Nevertheless, Judge Hellvad described her statement as a confession in his verdict. Likewise, the enslaved man Acra, who, as we have seen, was sentenced for the murder of his wife in 1783, explained that she ran into a knife he was carrying. He did not admit that he had stabbed her. Nevertheless, his court statement was characterized by Judge Brown as a confession and used by Brown to conclude that Acra had committed premeditated murder.[418]

Expert Readings of Slave Testimony

In Christiansted Lower Court slave testimony was important. Indeed, of the enslaved defendants tried in Christiansted Lower Court one-sixth was convicted on the basis of slave testimony alone.[419] Formally, Christiansted's judges solved the problem of slaves' unsworn depositions by introducing the idea of the presumption. This idea in turn required judges to portray themselves as adept readers of slaves' statements. In verdict after verdict, Christiansted's judges pursued the argument, more or less openly, that it was legal expertise rather than mechanical rules that secured the fair working of justice. In 1802, Lower Court Judge Winding explained that a fair-minded judge would have to pay more than ordinary attention to slave testimonies. Judges had to look for "signs of partiality, contradictions, and even of ignorance and the lack of a clear mind;" in the latter case, a statement was probably useless, if not false. Alternatively, however, if a statement bore the "signs of a clear mind," was "coherent and correspond[ed ...] to the facts," it was to have the "effect" of evidence.[420] Only the expert judge could decide on — or, indeed, effectuate — the elevation of enslaved testimony to evidence.

When judges evaluated slave testimony, they used a series of critical techniques sanctioned by *The Danish Law*, thereby linking their own practice to the authority of metropolitan law. The internal coherence of a statement and its degree of correspondence to other statements were understood as a sign of its reliability.[421] Statements given under particular pressure, such as torture, face-to-face confrontations, or facing imminent death, were considered particularly trustworthy.[422] When, for instance, the enslaved Lembrecht maintained his accusation against a fellow slave, despite threats of torture, the court found that this constituted a "presumption" against said slave.[423] Confrontations were also viewed as producing truth. Judge Brown, for instance, believed that the enslaved couple, Rachel and Tony, had "looked at each other with such amazement [during a confrontation] that one could read the guilt in their face [sic]."[424] Likewise, it was the "contradictory explanation" of the enslaved woman Catharina that gave Judge Juul reason to convict her of handling stolen goods.[425] Christiansted Lower Court judges did not use their exegetical tools mechanically; they mobilized them in order to corroborate their broader conception of the events tried in court. Thus, when Judge Mouritzen believed that other evidence proved the guilt of Phillis and Oxford, he convicted them of attempted poisoning despite their steadfast denials during confrontations with witnesses.[426]

Particularly in the eighteenth century, judges, as described above, believed that enslaved peoples' familiarity with or conversion to Christianity enhanced their credibility. Christianity brought slaves into the realm of government, providing a form of control that was, judges opined, not grounded in fear. In contrast, it was "only fear of punishment" that could "prevent the wild and ignorant negro" from committing crimes.[427] Christiansted's judges primarily linked Christianity and credibility in order to exclude depositions by non-Christian witnesses, but the association also made judges attentive to a few defendants and witnesses whom they believed spoke with true Christian conviction.[428] When, for instance, in 1795, Juba was convicted of the murder of a fellow slave and attempted suicide, Judge Winding was clearly influenced by Juba's use of Christian rhetoric, noting that Juba had "ask[ed] God for mercy" during interrogations.[429] Juba's testimony, Winding believed, made it clear that he had no intention of committing murder. Juba, Winding stated, "repented the wretched incident, he […] invoked his God to forgive him, [… and he] confessed against himself."[430] With this reading of Juba's character, Winding decided that a death sentence was improper. Instead, he sentenced Juba to 150 lashes and transportation; a sentence which Governor General Lindemann confirmed.[431]

Yet as more and more enslaved men and women adopted Christianity in the nineteenth century and began to rely on Christian traditions to formulate their courtroom narratives, their faith, as such, ceased to serve judges as a means of distinguishing between supposedly more or less trustworthy slaves. In 1802 Judge Winding clarified how this change in the depositional weight of Christianity had come about. He believed that it would be unfair to make Christian faith a precondition for accepting slave testimony. In his opinion, the "idolater […] would often have more culture and morality" than the Christian.[432] In fact, Winding was arguing against the use of any set criteria in the validation of slave testimony. Instead, he suggested that such validation should be left to individual judges; it was their interpretative expertise that should determine whether slave testimony could operate as legal evidence. As noted, it was only in October 1830 and by royal decree that enslaved people of so-called good Christian character were allowed to give sworn evidence. This came at a point in time when most procedures against enslaved people had been removed from the formal setting of the Danish West Indian courts. Increasingly, enslaved people confronted the less formal and discretionary powers of the chief of police and the Danish West Indian Government (see Figure D, Chapter 2).

Appropriating Slave Voices

Christiansted Lower Court judges had to make sense of the many testimonies taken down during interrogations. To do so, they crafted case stories that they referred to as the "history of the case," the "circumstances of the case," or "the nature of the case."[433] In these case stories, judges postulated a sequence of events, a number of characters, and a set of motives.[434] Subsequently, they could explain how events were connected and specify the crimes committed. Motives were accepted or rejected, facts were included or excluded, and circumstances were highlighted or ignored. It was through this creative act of forging a coherent account out of many, sometimes irreconcilable, statements that the judges of Christiansted Lower Court exercised their legal power. In standard, dry legalese, they concluded their verdicts with the phrase: "According to the nature of the case, the court finds […]." Accordingly, it was not only what enslaved people said that determined the outcome of a trial. Rather, expressions like the "nature of the case" underlined the interpretative labor judges performed in order to uncover what they saw as the deeper truth of what was said during proceedings. Hence, the overall narrative frame into which judges placed excerpts of slave statements critically shaped legal decisions about guilt and innocence.

When judges refined their case stories, they relied on the transcripts generated during the trials. They drew on the records of preliminary investigations, police court examinations, and lower court sessions, and they inserted references to specific court documents into their written decisions. As Judge Hellvad set out to determine the sentences of nine enslaved people accused, collectively, of arson in 1774-75, he began by clarifying the documentary trail of the case. First, one Christian Friedrich Kipnasse had petitioned the Danish West Indian Government for a trial, then *Advocatus Regius* Buus had been instructed by government order of June 24, 1774, to arrange an interrogation of the slaves. The interrogation was conducted during the period from July 6 to August 16, 1774. Referring to the interrogation protocol, Judge Hellvad noted what the slave defendant Jacob had said on "pag. 100 [...] 101 [...] 198-200 [... and] 206," and he continued to do the same for each of the defendants, spinning a fine web of references that tied the nine slaves to the deed.[435] In this way, Christiansted Lower Court judges ensured and demonstrated that their interpretation of a case was crafted with a tangible relationship to what defendants, plaintiffs, and witnesses said during the proceedings.[436] However, judges' written decisions also demonstrated their ability to select between the many statements available to them in the court books.

When judges construed their case stories, they drew on a strong Atlantic judicial ideology that justified the exclusion of enslaved Africans and Afro-Caribbeans from ordinary legal practice by stressing, repeatedly, the evil nature of black bondsmen and -women. In 1781, Chubs was described as a man with a "wicked and mean heart" and an "evil obstinacy;" in 1800, Coachy was characterized as a "dangerous person for the state and his fellow brothers," and, in 1840, George supposedly had a "bold and dangerous mindset" and was described as a person "inclined to crime."[437] Many other slaves were characterized in similar terms, particularly during the eighteenth century while the 1733 slave code was in use. In the nineteenth century, judges became more subdued and settled on the expression "bad subject" to describe enslaved people whom they found suspicious and criminal.[438]

Nevertheless, and although the terrifying legislative portrait of the criminal slave dominated judges' interpretation of slave testimony, it did not determine it altogether. The idea that enslaved Africans and their descendants, like Europeans, could be categorized as men and women and that their sex shaped their behavior gave Christiansted's judges one more interpretive framework against which they could evaluate slave depositions. So, when enslaved Africans and Afro-Caribbeans described behavior that resembled judges' own gender norms, judges accepted motives that differed from those outlined in slave legislation. Lower court judges for instance believed that enslaved women were driven to crime by their desire for fancy clothes and jewelry and not, as stipulated in the slave code of 1733, by their evil nature. For these judges, slaves could act out of passion and jealousy rather than out of excess and stupidity. Similarly, Christiansted's judges saw behavior that they interpreted as the natural result of affection between husband and wife rather than as disloyalty and impertinence against a master.

Indeed, Christiansted's judges at times imagined that there was a sort of congruence between their own gendered constitution and that of the enslaved defendants and witnesses they met in court. This stands out with particular clarity in Judge Juul's verdict against the enslaved man Jaque in 1768. Juul stated that the accusations against Jaque were true. It was obvious that Jaque had attacked his wife Hannah with a *kapmesser* (i.e., a cane knife) in the backyard of one Mr. David Porth. In the commotion that followed, Jaque had used "indecent" words and thrown stones at the white people in the yard. Juul believed he understood Jaque's motives. During the examination in Christiansted Lower Court, Jaque had explained that he beat his wife because she "did not care for him." This was sufficient for Judge Juul. To Juul it was clear that Jaque was "jealous" and had acted in passionate "desperation." Jealousy, Juul reflected, was an emotion that "people," and he meant white people, who had learned better to control their "passions only mastered and suppressed with difficulty." No wonder then, that the "negro" Jaque had been unable to control his feelings. For Juul, Jaque was somewhat similar to other men, although his skin color made him less able to control his feelings. Juul believed that these considerations "appeared" to call for a milder punishment, yet he maintained that they did not exempt Jaque from capital punishment. In this way, Judge Juul's attempt at understanding Jaque's emotional life by establishing it as an analogue to that of white men could be seamlessly combined with a death sentence.[439]

Danish West Indian judges' recognition that gender shaped slaves' behavior rarely influenced the sentences enslaved people received, but there were notable exceptions. When Judge Rogiers acquitted the enslaved woman Felicite in 1778, he referred to the statement she had given in court. Felicite had argued that she and an enslaved woman friend often went to parties in Christiansted town. Her friend had given her a skirt and a waistcoat to wear for these festive events; what she had not known was that the clothes were stolen. Felicite's desire for fine dress, Rogiers believed, removed the suspicion against her of knowingly handling stolen goods, although she was still thought to deserve a flogging at the public whipping post.[440] In 1784, the enslaved man Tuseing, charged with murderous assault, was acquitted for similar reasons. Judge Brown believed Tuseing's Christian wife, the slave woman Jenny, who explained that he had been in a white man's backyard because the couple wanted to spend the night together.[441]

Familiar Behavior: Slave Couples

Christiansted's judges acknowledged that the affectionate relationships between enslaved men and women, particularly their marital unions, shaped their behavior. In a number of trials, mostly against enslaved men charged with theft and burglary, judges argued that the disputed incidents were most credibly understood as the result of the relationships between the defendants and their wives in "natural marriage." Thus, in 1765, Isaak, accused of theft in the yard of one Mr. Thomas Stretz, received a milder punishment because Judge Juul accepted Isaak's deposition. Juul believed Isaak when he explained that he had a *"rendezvous"* with a "negress" living in the yard.[442]

Likewise, Judge Rogiers accepted that the enslaved man Dick, charged with trespassing and burglary in 1778, had been visiting his former wife. During proceedings, the prosecution argued that the crime of trespassing had been aggravated by the fact that Dick had brandished an unsheathed knife. In contrast, the legal guardian of Dick's mistress argued that Dick had not entered the yard to murder or steal, "but only in order to visit his former wife." Therefore, some lashes at the public whipping post would be sufficient punishment.[443] Judge Rogiers agreed. Since Dick "previously had Sylvia as his wife" it was "credible," Rogiers argued, that there was "some *conexion* between them." Therefore he would not consider Dick's behavior as a "criminal offense."[444] Despite this conclusion, Judge Rogiers convicted Dick, as well as two other slave defendants whom he had found guilty, to a harsh flogging of 200 lashes under the gallows. In St. Croix Upper Court, Dick's sentence was later commuted to 150 lashes at the public whipping post.[445]

Judge Winding, in 1802, also operated under the idea — absent from slave legislation — that the domestic life of enslaved couples explained their behavior. Winding argued that the enslaved man Jack, charged with burglary, had been involved in a domestic dispute. In his verdict Winding quoted Jack's explanation from the police court, where Jack had explained that he

> entered the yard […] he had lodged there with a negress […] who was his wife /natural marriage/ […] he found the house or room, where she usually lives locked – took a *kapmesser* and broke up the door.[446]

The relationship between Jack and his wife comprised an alternative context against which Winding could explain Jack's behavior. Instead of figuring Jack as an ill-natured slave, Winding described him as a husband who had misbehaved. Consequently, he sentenced Jack to fifty lashes at the public whipping post for breaking into his former wife's room but acquitted him of the charge of burglary.[447] Drawing on slave depositions that described the relationships between enslaved couples, Christiansted's judges explained the nightly presence of enslaved men in the backyards of the white inhabitants of Christiansted town as the natural consequence of those relationships.

Although Christiansted's judges accepted that enslaved partners sought each other's company, they did not always agree on the interpretations such behavior should occasion. Some believed that intimacy would or should generate knowledge; others, it appears, believed it generated trust or ignorance. So, in 1772, when Botsvain was tried for theft, his defense attorney argued that Botsvain did not know that the money he took from his wife belonged to her owner and therefore the act could not be categorized as theft. Judge Gluckstadt disagreed. In his opinion, Botsvain, "as her husband," should have known that the money she kept was not her own.[448] When Aletta and Hans Jørgen were charged with theft and the handling of stolen goods in 1806, the question of what kind of knowledge their relationship generated was similarly central to the case. The defense attorney argued that there was no reason to believe that Hans Jørgen would know "what clothes Aletta, as his wife, brought to his house."[449] Mouritzen, however, stated that, since it had been proven that Aletta was not Hans Jørgen's wife but only his "*maitresse*," he ought to have known what she brought into his house.[450] Likewise, in 1811, Mouritzen argued that an enslaved husband could not be expected to know that his wife had stolen jewelry and therefore he should be acquitted.[451] In a peculiar twist of logic, the trust between partners and the free access they enjoyed to each other's dwellings became an extenuating, rather than incriminating, circumstance in these interpretations.

Familiar Speech: Christian Models of Gender

Christiansted's judges developed particular interpretations of the ways in which enslaved men behaved by arguing that such behavior was grounded in the slaves' emotional, often marital, lives. In addition to explicating enslaved behavior by grounding in it ideas about enslaved peoples' gendered nature, however, the particular words and phrases enslaved people used in their testimonies also influenced Christiansted's judges and the case stories they construed. When judges thought they recognized familiar Christian speech and models of gender in slaves' depositions, they often incorporated such gendered elements into their verdicts. These acts of appropriation allowed judges to further pursue their legal reasoning.

Judge Wiel, from a Norwegian merchant family, appears to have exempted the slave woman Ancilla from the death penalty because he heard a description of feminine dependence in her speech that he recognized from his own background as a Lutheran protestant and as part of an educated elite of legal experts.[452] After hearing the testimonies of Ancilla and her husband Louis in 1773, Judge Wiel was convinced that Louis had "persuaded" his wife, Ancilla, to escape the island by canoe. Therefore "one could say something in her favor," and while he sentenced her husband to hanging, Ancilla was to receive 150 lashes at the public whipping post.[453]

Yet the adoption of a Christian vocabulary could also be used against enslaved people. In 1779, the enslaved man Cudjoe had a conflict at his wife's estate with Peru, another enslaved man. Cudjoe claimed that the dispute arose because Peru owed him money for his services as a "doctor" — a term that could refer both to the (male) nurses appointed by white plantation staff and to African-Atlantic healers and spiritual experts.[454] Cudjoe maintained that his marital arrangement was in perfect agreement with his wife's parents. Yet Peru, a member of the Moravian Church, claimed that Cudjoe quarreled because "he cared for a negro girl" but had been rejected by the girl's parents. This was why he had exclaimed, "God dam'd the Estate, Negroes & All. I will burne it." Cudjoe's alleged swearing made such an impression on Judge Cooper that he put Cudjoe's blasphemous words first on a long list of reasons that there was great presumption against him. Indeed, Cooper was convinced that Cudjoe was a "chain of pure evil […] a dangerous creature […] an evil and depraved negro […] who […] can commit the greatest acts of ungodliness at night."[455] In both cases, therefore, Christiansted's judges deemed trustworthy those enslaved who spoke in familiar Christian modes.

The ruling against Eva, Dublin, and Hannibal who were charged with theft in 1784, underlines just how effective slave speech could be in influencing the wording of verdicts. In 1784, Judge Brown felt "justified" in quoting Eva's "comprehensive and coherent statement with the same words as it has been given by Eva."[456] The statement that sounded "coherent" and "comprehensive" to Brown contained Eva's description of a theft she had committed with Dublin and another committed with Hannibal. Although they denied Eva's accusations — Hannibal despite being tortured and Dublin in the face of "serious admonitions" — Judge Brown sentenced both to transportation.[457]

The reason for the convictions of Dublin and Hannibal can be found first and foremost in Judge Brown's appropriation of Eva's court statement. Eva delivered her deposition in Dutch-Creole, a language that, as mentioned above, had a rich Christian vocabulary. While not a member, she explained that she attended the

Church of the Moravian Brethren.[458] She appeared, in Brown's view, to be well informed about the truths of Christianity and, in court, she had declared that a minister, who had visited her in Fort Christiansværn, had "admonished her to say the right and pure truth."[459] According to Brown, Eva explained that

> she had as her husband a negro called Dublin […] some time ago she came to town and he asked her to stay with him. She did so and did it willingly since it was evening at that time, but I [sic] complained to him that she [sic] was very hungry. He answered her that she should wait for a while, then she would get money […] Shortly afterwards she again said to Dublin: I am pregnant and very hungry. Dublin answered her: Wait until my master returns home. Then you shall get money.[460]

Judge Brown was convinced. In his verdict, he referred to this conversation between a pregnant wife and her husband in which she requested support and he provided it. This was a distribution of tasks that must have squared nicely with his own gendered ideals. He was the son of a Danish church dean, had gone through grammar school and university, and ended his career at a higher rank than his father as a Supreme Court judge; a career that suggests that Brown was a man of his time and, presumably, conversant with the emerging middling gender norms shaping life among the urban elite in Copenhagen.[461]

Word-for-word, Brown incorporated Eva's deposition into his verdict.[462] Yet he had to turn a blind eye to several disturbing facts. The relationships between Eva, Hannibal, and Dublin were complicated. Dublin was probably not Eva's only partner. She had stayed with Hannibal as a runaway. According to the testimony of Eva's mother, Hannibal was actually the father of Eva's unborn child. Although Brown noticed these contradictions, he refrained from clarifying them. When summarizing the case, he insisted on an explanation that figured Eva in relation to each man in isolation. While Eva's behavior could be understood as promiscuous, Brown chose to emphasize those elements of her deposition that allowed him to figure her as an honest Christian woman. This choice allowed him to exploit Eva's testimony to convict Dublin and Hannibal.

In his verdict Brown departed from the idea, widespread among Danish colonial staff, that Africans and Afro-Caribbeans had only fleeting and informal relationships. Instead, he argued that enslaved men and women, particularly Christians, were caring toward and appreciative of each other — a vision that had been developed, as we have seen, by the Moravian missionaries since the early eighteenth century. In Eva's description of her theft, her pregnancy played a significant role. Hannibal and Eva stole together because her condition made her "incapable" of stealing alone. Dublin stole money because Eva was pregnant and hungry.[463] Eva was not, in other words, one of those strong, entirely fictional, African women who reproduced without any difficulties or, for that matter, induced abortions merely to seek further pleasure. In Brown's rendering of the "nature" of the "case," Eva was part of a community of marital love. Brown "could not imagine" that a wife, like Eva, would bring harm to her husband, whom she owed "gratitude and love," and therefore Eva's court statement was, in his opinion, trustworthy.[464]

Judge Brown's framing of the case — his case story — was not allowed to stand, however, and the tangible effect that Eva's deposition made on him was only provisional. Brown sentenced Eva to death and Dublin and Hannibal to transportation, but his verdict was altered after the trial. Eva's sentence was commuted, presumably to flogging, branding and banishment. For unknown reasons, perhaps she needed to get away from her owners, Eva turned up at Judge Brown's house two months after her verdict to complain that she had not yet been sent off the island. She had no wish to stay in St. Croix.[465] What happened to Dublin remains unclear, but Hannibal was released and returned to his owner, Sir Robert Tuite, who, as owner of Sion Farm Estate and more than 200 slaves, was one of St. Croix' most significant planters.[466] Unsatisfied with Brown's ruling, Tuite had appealed the case to St. Croix Upper Court, and, after two years of waiting, he petitioned Governor General Schimmelmann who invited the opinion of Government Member, Legal Councilor Edvard Colbjørnsen. Colbjørnsen deemed Eva's deposition inadmissible not because she was a slave but because she was a felon. Therefore there was absolutely no evidence against Hannibal and he was released after more than two years in Fort Christiansværn.[467]

As Eva's trial illustrates, Christiansted's judges were strangely persuaded by enslaved peoples' testimonies, yet they also interpreted them in such a way that they effectively supported their repressive sentencing practices. The importance of enslaved testimony also stands out in the extraordinary trial against Luke Codwise who was charged with maltreatment of Peggy in 1803. As mentioned, the case was tried at every tier of the Danish Atlantic legal system: Christiansted Lower Court, St. Croix Upper Court, and finally the Supreme Court in Copenhagen, Denmark. Christiansted Lower Court fined Codwise and ordered him to cover the trial costs, St. Croix Upper Court acquitted Codwise of all charges, and the Supreme Court reversed this decision, sentencing Codwise to free Peggy.

The deliberations of the Danish West Indian judges in the Lower Court of Christiansted and the West Indian Upper Court demonstrate how the processes of inclusion and exclusion of slave testimony shaped legal decision-making.[468]

To fashion his argument, Judge Winding of Christiansted Lower Court relied heavily on the statement Peggy made in Christiansted Police Court.[469] He noted that Peggy had "from childhood been raised as a house negress" and that she had asked for "forgiveness but was not granted any."[470] Both these expressions came from Peggy's statement in Christiansted Police Court. Judge Winding appropriated them in order to fashion his argument against Codwise.[471] Winding found that Codwise had been harder on Peggy than "required by circumstances and allowed by law."[472] Although Peggy's crimes could not be "legally excused," Judge Winding believed that when the case was considered from the point of view of "morality" it was in Peggy's favor.[473]

According to Winding, Peggy's moral advantage was related to the fact that Codwise had broken unspoken rules concerning female domestics and shown himself insensitive to Peggy's womanly lot. In his verdict, Winding momentarily imagined that he could put himself in the place of enslaved women, and noted

> the difference between the tasks [of house and field negroes], between the situations in daily life where house negroes are exempted from the heat and cold of the climate, from the rain and sunshine to which field negroes are exposed. Imagine a house negress who is suddenly taken away from the life she has been living and exposed to fieldwork. I am convinced that such negress will find it a double burden, and a negress such as Peggy who has a slender build will find it even more oppressing.[474]

In Peggy's case, Lower Court Judge Winding argued that both custom and nature established Peggy as a gendered subject who should be mastered according to her particular constitution. The decision to move Peggy was wrong because it was improper to move female domestic workers to the cane fields. Trained for domestic service these women would find fieldwork a "double burden." The move was also wrong, however, because it did not take into account the difficulties that female domestic slaves of a "slender build" would have in performing fieldwork. The delicate enslaved women that Judge Winding imagined were indeed a far cry from the tropes of strong African women workers propagated by earlier observers of Danish West Indian slavery.[475]

Peggy's well-phrased deposition had an extraordinary power to shape, indeed to change, legal decisions. This becomes clear when the verdicts of Christiansted Lower Court and St. Croix Upper Court are compared. The Upper Court did not reflect on Peggy's court statement. Instead, the court gave a purely statutory reading of the case. Pointing to the 1755 slave code, the Upper Court concluded that the floggings Peggy had received were not particularly harsh. Whereas Lower Court Judge Winding had incorporated central elements of Peggy's deposition into his verdict, the Upper Court verdict contained only faint traces of the statement Peggy had given in Christiansted Police Court.[476] Whereas Winding painted a sentimental picture of a vulnerable woman slave and convicted Codwise, the St. Croix Upper Court excluded Peggy's statement and moved for his acquittal.

Indeed, judges paid acute attention, often appropriating their words and phrases, when enslaved men and women established themselves as subjects who acted according to the sorts of gender conventions Christiansted's judges recognized. It was a process of appropriation that aimed at securing procedural legitimacy; only seldom (as in Peggy's case) did it result in sentences that recognized the narratives crafted by enslaved men and women in court. Two almost identical trials concerning the collective walkout of the enslaved from Hermon Hill Estate and Mount Welcome Estate, respectively, underscore this point. In 1804, all of the enslaved fieldworkers — perhaps as many as seventy people — ran away from Hermon Hill Estate.[477] At court they explained that they had acted without prior planning. Judge Winding did not believe them. To him, it was "clear that there was a conspiracy."[478] Their act could have the most "dangerous consequences" and cause "rebellion."[479] In contrast, when the slaves of Mount Welcome Estate ran away in 1816, they convinced Judge Mouritzen that their action resulted from "affection and kindness" for the estate where they were "born or had lived since their childhood or for very long."[480] Citing the statements of Mount Welcome's slaves, Mouritzen related that they had sworn that "they would not be sold […] so help them God and his Holy word." They had pledged that if sold "the women would not breed children" and the men "would not serve any other owner." These testimonies, in which enslaved people spoke with Christian words about their gendered responses to a sale, allowed Judge Mouritzen to conclude that Mount Welcome's slaves were misguided rather than rebellious.[481] Indeed, the slaves of Mount Welcome and Hermon Hill provided their judges with very different narrative feedstock; in turn they emerged with different subjective characteristics in the verdicts penned by their judges. Notwithstanding these verbal ripples, however, the alleged leaders of the collective walkout at Hermon Hill were flogged and exiled and those of Mount Welcome were flogged and sentenced to work for life.[482]

In strange and distorted ways, slaves' statements had a rhetorical effect on the manner in which Christiansted's judges formulated their verdicts. When judges could recognize, rightly or wrongly, descriptions of a gender order that echoed their own, they would often incorporate these descriptions into their written verdicts. This meant that slaves' stories and fragments of slave voices were present in the verdicts. It did not mean, however, that lower court judges were particularly good listeners. Judges were interested in establishing a formal relationship between their verdicts and what enslaved people said during legal proceedings. Their exegetical work was geared at turning a polyphonic transcript of interrogations into a coherent case story. It was this move, rather than the oaths of one or more white West Indians, that ensured legal legitimacy in the eyes of the Danish West Indian judges.

Distorting Slave Stories

To ensure the inclusion of slave voices, lower court judges twisted and turned depositions, highlighting one element and ignoring another. They came up with peculiar palimpsests that contained much, but far from all, of what slaves said during proceedings. Indeed, judges were powerful and cunning editors of slave testimony. Their ability to pick and choose among depositions, to tear individual depositions apart, to ignore the wider context of what enslaved men and women said, and to focus on those elements which they found meaningful was an indispensable part of their expertise. It was this peculiar, distorted inclusion of slave testimony that allowed judges to declare most enslaved defendants guilty.

By selectively accentuating some elements of slaves' statements while giving others less explanatory weight or excluding them altogether, Christiansted Lower Court judges de-contextualized the statements slaves gave during proceedings. This editorial practice served to legitimize legal decisions about guilt and innocence, but it also further effaced the ideational outlooks — already marginalized by slave legislation and interrogative procedures — that enslaved men and women relied on to explain their behavior. Christiansted Lower Court judges consistently ignored descriptions of African-Atlantic practices and ideas. The trial against five enslaved Africans charged and convicted for disobedience, arson, and mutiny in Christiansted Lower Court in 1802 is an incisive example of this willful ignorance. The trial record included no references to the defendants' African background.[483] Yet colonial administrators were aware that they were not generic Africans. Government Councilor Bentzon related that the group had all been of "one nation," and he connected the assault to a "kind" of "agreement" that existed among the "Gold Coast negroes." Bentzon feared that the Danish West Indies were witnessing the fomenting of a rebellion such as the one organized among Akan-speaking slaves and led by the enslaved man Tacky in Jamaica in 1760.[484] This was a piece of information that Judge Winding supposedly could have used to further incriminate the five defendants, yet he did not reference it in his verdict. Apparently, such detailed knowledge of African bonds and loyalties was unnecessary for the legal process to proceed.

Indeed, the erasure of information about enslaved Africans' backgrounds was due more to the efficiency of the Danish West Indian courts, wherein such information was unnecessary for the enactment of repressive sentences, and less to judges' lack of knowledge. Many judges had lived for many years in the Danish West Indies. Although they did not possess detailed knowledge of West Africa's many languages and peoples, these men were familiar with the lifestyles of enslaved Africans and Afro-Caribbeans. From the uprising in St. John in 1733, organized by Akan speakers, colonial officials learned that African ethnic bonds still mattered in the Americas.[485] By the late eighteenth century, some would have read the work of Christian Oldendorp, edited into an abridged version in 1777 by Johann Jakob Bossart, and would have been able to further familiarize themselves with the various African nations present in St. Croix.[486] It is not, therefore, surprising that Judge Winding easily located an enslaved boy who could translate the slave woman Carolina's statement from Mandingo to English in 1805.[487]

Judges also systematically overlooked slaves' descriptions of African-Atlantic cosmologies even when such descriptions could have strengthened their convictions. In 1794, the enslaved couple Bucan and Anna Maria were charged with theft. The interrogation records at Judge Winding's disposal contained explicit references to African-Atlantic practices and cosmologies. One slave witness related that Anna Maria had claimed that ghosts were involved in the affair, but Judge Winding believed this claim had merely been Anna Maria's way of scaring off witnesses. Perhaps he was correct, but Anna Maria may also have referred to ghosts because she believed spiritual beings were involved in the event.[488] Another witness explained that Anna Maria and Bucan had taken an oath of silence in "the manner of the Coast," an indication that Anna Maria and Bucan may have oriented themselves toward African-Atlantic legal practices.[489] Winding, however, chose to ignore this information even though he could have referred to the alleged oath to undermine the couple's declarations of innocence. Instead, Winding preferred to rely on a familiar narrative frame. In the verdict against Bucan and Anna Maria, their marital relationship carried sufficient explanatory power to legitimize a reading in which they had assisted each other in committing a crime. Judge Winding acknowledged that there was no evidence against Anna Maria and Bucan, wherefore they cannot be sentenced as thieves, but as they have made themselves guilty of strong suspicion and thus justly can be considered harmful for the country if they are returned to their masters, [and] as they would provide a wicked example for other negroes, who would likely imagine that they can escape punishment for a secret misdeed, if they could only endure interrogation with firmness, the court finds it appropriate to impose an arbitrary sentence on Anna Maria and Bucan.

Basing his judgment on this argument, Winding sentenced them to fifty lashes each and transportation.[490]

By distorting slaves' courtroom stories, judges managed to portray slaves as guilty while maintaining that their verdicts were based on the inclusion of slave testimony. This was exactly what happened to Sally in 1799. When she was sentenced to death, Judge Winding ignored the main thrust of her court statement, namely that her acts had been provoked by her husband's adultery. Instead, Winding emphasized that Sally had set fire to a cane field because she hated her overseer. In his verdict, Winding examined this act on the basis of Sally's court statement. Likewise, he adopted Sally's explanation of why she had not confessed to her crime immediately, namely that she would not give the overseer such "satisfaction."[491] Winding quoted selected terms from Sally's statement from the interrogation protocol, "hatred" and "satisfaction," in the register of verdicts.[492] Thus, Winding's peculiar inclusion of Sally's court statement allowed him to represent Sally's behavior as the result of a conflict between a slave and her manager. In fact, however, Sally had stressed that her behavior had more to do with her troubled marital situation than with her enslaved condition.

A shrewd and calculating reading of slave testimony was also at play when the enslaved man Daniel was convicted in 1804. Daniel was charged with disobedience, theft, and threats of arson.[493] In his decision, Judge Mouritzen provided a reading of the interrogation transcripts that rendered Daniel's wider story irrelevant to his actions. In court, Daniel focused on the difficulties he and his wife had faced. He related how, despite his pleadings, the overseer had flogged his wife so hard that she was incapable of working for seven weeks. Additionally, the overseer had forbidden him from staying on his wife's estate. Nevertheless, he returned to his wife and the house he had built for her. On his return he was assaulted and this, Daniel argued, was the only reason he had voiced threats of arson.[494]

At first, Daniel's statement convinced Governor General Mühlenfels. He warned the overseer against such "hard and gruesome behavior" and instructed him to make an agreement with Daniel so that the couple could live together.[495]

The owners of Daniel and Felicity, however, agreed to press criminal charges against Daniel. The case went from Christiansted Police Court to Christiansted Lower Court and a verdict was handed down. In the verdict, Judge Mouritzen failed to mention the heavy beatings Felicity received or the "good-natured" relationship between Daniel and Felicity.[496] Although Mouritzen acknowledged that Daniel might have acted out of "jealousy and anger because he had been forbidden to stay with his wife," such feelings were "weak grounds for his defense." Daniel was guilty. This conclusion was obtained by disregarding the main thrust of Daniel's defense, namely that his wife had been maltreated and his attempts to care for her had been impeded. When Governor General Mühlenfels read about Daniel for the second time, he supported Judge Mouritzen's sentence, albeit with some modifications. Daniel was flogged one hundred, not 150 times, and, while he was spared branding, he was sold off the island.[497]

Judicial practice in the trials of Sally and Daniel, and in many more, was characterized by the subtle exclusion of particular pieces of information and narrative sequences. This elective exclusion allowed judges to construe a new and incriminating context against which to evaluate slave behavior. Exclusion became more thorough, however, when enslaved Africans and Afro-Caribbeans spoke of sexual intimidation, abuse, and rape by white West Indians. The tense narrative developments of enslaved men and women regarding their superiors' sexual misbehavior, as they emerged in the nineteenth century, were deftly excluded from Christiansted Lower Court and, instead, dealt with through the discretionary powers of the police judge and the governor general. Francky, charged with theft in 1788, who argued that she had been the victim of a rape attempt, was not convicted, but neither was the man she accused of attempted rape.[498] Cecilie's case against her overseer, Davis, in 1830, was also displaced from the ordinary courts. While Police Judge Frederiksen believed that Cecilie's charge, among others, was true because of the cruel punishment meted out by Cecilie's mistress, he informed acting Governor General Johan Frederik Bardenfleth that he did not have any legal evidence. Both Cecilie's master and her mistress denied the charge. Accordingly, Cecilie's case never made it out of the police court and into the lower court. Instead, Governor General Bardenfleth ordered Judge Frederiksen to fine Davis 10 rix-dollars and instruct the couple that Cecilie was no longer to serve in the house.[499]

Likewise, Margrethe, who accused her manager Lier of rape in 1840, that is, after enslaved people were allowed to provide sworn evidence, never had her claim tested in Christiansted Lower Court. Police Judge Frederiksen was not convinced by her story. A doctor had declared that Margrethe's bruises were not necessarily the outcome of a rape attempt. Margrethe's main witness, a young boy, had provided what Frederiksen believed to be inconsistent statements, and two white men, who alleged that they had stayed overnight at Lier's on the relevant dates, denied hearing or seeing anything. Indeed, Frederiksen found it "incredible" that Lier would commit rape with strangers in the house. Therefore he chose to believe the white witnesses and suggested to Governor General Peter von Scholten that Margrethe's mother was given a few weeks to find out what had really happened. Scholten agreed and ordered mother and daughter to be released from the prison. The case, Scholten noted, was not "solved, but only on hold for the time being." This decision, however, appears to have dissolved Margrethe's charge and removed it permanently from the court. Lier was neither convicted nor acquitted in the courts of Christiansted.[500]

Slave depositions about sexual violence disappeared, almost unnoticed, from the annals of the Danish Atlantic legal regime. Even the backing of one of the most important Cruzian planters Sir Robert Tuite was not enough to catapult claims about sexual coercion into Christiansted Lower Court. In June 1799, Robert Tuite notified Judge Mouritzen that

> A Negro Girl called Grace […] was stopped near La Rein Estate, by Mr. Ferral Manager on […] Lime Tree Estate, who applied to her to permit him to be connected with her; on her refusal he threw her down and attempted to rape her, not being able to succeed in that attempt he tor[e] open that part in a most cruel Manner with his Fingers. This is what the Negro Girl has declared to me, she knows of no Person being present except a Negro Man called Joe.[501]

Mouritzen questioned Ferral, but did not summon Grace and Joe to court.

Indeed, the fact that the witness to the rape of Grace was a slave in combination with the "peculiar circumstances" of the case prompted Judge Mouritzen to turn to Governor General Lindemann for advice.[502] Together Mouritzen and Governor Lindemann found a neat way by which to avoid a courtroom confrontation. Lindemann informed Mouritzen that he should not take the statements of Grace and Joe because of the "caution" needed when slaves were to testify against whites. Yet the "peculiar circumstances" of the case had generated so much suspicion against Ferral that he should be warned against such behavior.[503] Thus, Judge Mouritzen resolved the matter out of court. He spoke with Sir Tuite once again to ensure that there were no legal witnesses and spoke to Grace and Joe who repeated their statements. According to Mouritzen, Grace explained that she met Ferral who dismounted his horse and grabbed her, and when she would not amicably allow him to have sexual intercourse with her, he put her on the ground […] and with his fingers he cleaved open her secret part, but as the negro Joe came at that moment, he rose and rode away.[504]

Here the case ended. Grace's words never entered into the paper trail of the Danish Atlantic legal archive, and, therefore, her experiences did not become part of the written record upon which justice was grounded in the Danish legal system.

Like those of Grace, Anna Catherina's accusations against her owner, Count de Bretton, were never heard in court. Anna Catherina made her claim in June 1807. Thereafter she was kept in a sort of protective custody in Fort Christiansværn for the next year. Judge Mouritzen and British Governor Hartcourt, who presided under the British occupation of the Danish West Indies from 1807 to 1815, were unwilling to release her because they feared that Count de Bretton would sue for damages if she ran away.[505] After one year in prison, Anna Catherina was sold at auction for 525 rix-dollars in July 1808 to John Heyliger Abrahamson, a member of the influential Heyliger family and owner of Work and Rest Estate with approximately 180 slaves. From the point of view of Danish West Indian authorities, a thorny case had finally been solved. Yet Count de Bretton was not convicted of attempted rape.[506] Indeed, Anna Catherina's, like Grace's, rape accusation never rose beyond the lowest, most informal end of the representational economy of the Danish Atlantic regime.

Christiansted judges established control of the depositions enslaved men and women made in court in a variety of ways. Tales of sexual coercion and abuse were quickly censored away while slaves' descriptions of their domestic troubles were distorted beyond recognition. Judges picked apart the statements of enslaved men and women and came up with interpretations that proved, for their purposes, the existence of criminal activity and justified harsh punishments. This was a sophisticated process of refinement during which Christiansted's judges removed those semantic impurities that, in their opinion, would otherwise have polluted white justice in the Danish West Indies.

Changing Punitive Practices

Christiansted Lower Court judges needed enslaved peoples' courtroom stories to appear within their verdicts, but when judges decided the punishment of enslaved defendants, such stories no longer served a purpose. Christiansted Lower

Court judges moved smoothly from a case story, which established proof or presumption against a defendant, to a brutal sentence. When full proof existed, conviction was simple. However, it was only slightly more complicated for lower court judges to convict slaves when full proof did not exist. The idea of the strong presumption, which enabled judges to rely on slave testimony, allowed judges to convict enslaved Africans and Afro-Caribbeans when they lacked sufficient evidence.[507] Often judges acknowledged that full proof did not exist, "but," as they wrote, there were strong presumptions and therefore an arbitrary sentence was in place. The presumptive sentences, especially, were used in the eighteenth century. This was a period during which the judges' control of the judicial process was comparatively weak as witnessed by the number of slaves acquitted (see Figure E). Judges, therefore, needed the presumptions in order to uphold the security of the white population. Or, as Judge Hesselberg wrote in 1760 in response to a group of enslaved people suspected of participation in the alleged conspiracy of 1759, "even though the Court finds relatively large presumptions [...] it has not been fully proven [that they are guilty ...] nevertheless, as the *securitas* of the island is challenged, the Court finds that such suspicious negroes should not remain on the island."[508]

Rhetorically, the move from the construction of a case story that had not conclusively settled the question of guilt and conviction to sentencing was simple. Words such as *although, nevertheless, still, however*, and *but* frequently appeared as judges moved from considerations of guilt to specifying exactly what punishments they thought fitting.[509] These tiny words made the existence of many versions of justice possible within a single verdict.[510] In so far as words could prove dangerous in the Danish West Indian judicial system, these small modifiers were dangerous, even deadly, for enslaved Africans and their descendants. They introduced a shift of focus from evidential proof to politics that allowed judges to evaluate bondspeoples' actions against what they believed to be the security needs of Danish West Indian society.

Christiansted Lower Court judges achieved impressive and terrifying conviction rates because they compiled evidence, operated with an all-encompassing notion of proof, and shifted smoothly between legal and political arguments when justifying their decisions. Altogether, 493 enslaved men and women were tried in Christiansted Lower Court from 1756 to 1848 in 339 trials. Eighty-five percent of these defendants were convicted, not including the fate of those seventy-one defendants tried for conspiracy to rebel in 1759 and 1760. During the winter of 1759-1760, planters panicked and brought slaves to court whom even Christiansted Lower Court judges, with their sophisticated readings of slave testimony, could not find evidence against. Out of the seventy-one defendants, fifty were acquitted; resulting in a conviction rate of 30 percent for this particular group of defendants. In general, however, everyday convictions rates were much higher and increased toward the turn of the century. So, even though slaves did their best to exploit and even expand the narrow formal possibilities of self-representation provided by Danish West Indian legal procedure — as witnessed by their skillfully developed accounts of sexual misconduct and rape in the nineteenth century — such representation seldom resulted in convictions of their white adversaries or their own escape from the violent punitive practices of the Danish Atlantic legal regime.

Figure E: Verdicts in Slave Trials, Christiansted Lower Court, 1756-1848

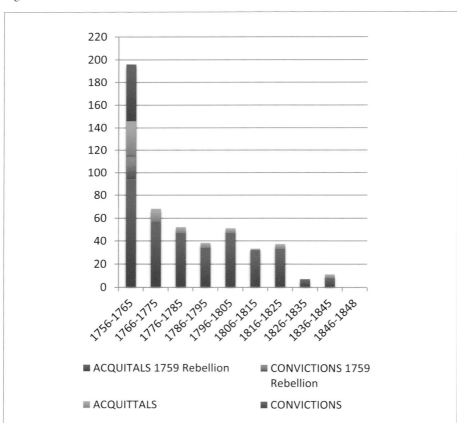

38.6.1-32. Christiansted Byfoged, Domprotokoller, 1756-1848 and 38.18.4-5. Christiansted By-foged, Pådømte sager, 1756-1848.

During the late eighteenth and the nineteenth centuries, Christiansted Lower Court judges expanded their control of the judicial process. Judges ensured that only the most serious cases were tried in court and they became better at detecting what they believed to be the guilt of enslaved defendants. In the mid-eighteenth century, a quarter of the defendants were acquitted — more if the 1759-conspiracy trials are included. By the late eighteenth and into the nineteenth centuries, the acquittal rate had fallen to around 10 percent.[511] The correspondingly higher conviction rate emerged because more incidents were solved out of court (see Chapter 2, Figure D) and because Christiansted Lower Court judges' became better at crafting incriminating case stories. Judges in the mid-eighteenth century regularly settled for short verdicts wherein they laconically stated that a slave was guilty and had to be punished. Later, more sonorous case stories that paid greater attention to slave testimonies became the norm. These longer, incriminating verdicts allowed judges to reach an even higher conviction rate in the nineteenth century.

Figure F: Punishments in Slave Trials, Christiansted Lower Court, 1756-1848

38.6.1-32. Christiansted Byfoged, Domprotokoller, 1756-1848 and 38.18.4-5. Christiansted Byfoged, Pådømte sager, 1756-1848.

Furthermore, the hierarchical structure of the Danish Atlantic legal system, which necessitated scribes, often made enslaved peoples' legal representation indirect and opaque. The chain of appeal and mitigation that went from Christiansted Lower Court to the West Indian Upper Court and the Supreme Court with detours to the West Indian governors and the Chancellery in Copenhagen and the Danish-Norwegian kings ensured that enslaved people in the Danish West Indies had a wide set of readers. Some were members of the Danish West Indian white elite, others were high ranking nobles, jurists, or successful merchants who served in the royal administration in Copenhagen. Indeed, enslaved men and women were not merely communicating with the police court and lower court judges of Christiansted, they also spoke to distant institutions and legal personae, whom they rarely, if ever met. With such a complex audience, enslaved peoples' chances of developing effective rhetorical strategies were very slim.

However, during the period from the 1750s to emancipation in 1848, the most important external reader of slave testimony was the governor general. He represented the absolutist monarchy in the islands and, as the king's representative, he held the power to confirm, mitigate or appeal verdicts. In some ways, however, he held powers greater than those of the Danish-Norwegian king. In Denmark, capital sentences were automatically appealed to higher tiers of the legal system during the eighteenth century, meaning that at least two courts were involved when capital punishments were meted out. Moreover, by 1758 capital sentences were to be submitted to royal confirmation before execution could take place. However, such checks were not available to enslaved men and women. In the Danish West Indies, the governor general resolved on lower court verdicts against slaves.[512]

The governor's power to make the final decision in all verdicts against slaves passed by the Danish West Indian courts endowed the judiciary with a high degree of flexibility. Christiansted Lower Court judges counted on this. If they believed that a sentence stipulated by legislation was improper, they would hint at this to the governor general, particularly during the eighteenth century when they still followed slave legislation to the letter. In 1761, Judge Juul submitted to Governor General Christian Lebrecht von Pröck that he should decide if the enslaved man Bristol could be returned to his owner after he had suffered his punishment. Bristol's owner, Judge Juul noted, would incur a substantial loss if Bristol were to be banished from the island. Juul offered as "*ratio mitigandi*" that Bristol was a first time offender.[513] Likewise, in 1764, Juul noted that the enslaved man Andre had been provoked to attack a white man and this fact could "serve to his mercy" if Governor General von Pröck was so inclined.[514] Like Christiansted's judges, slave

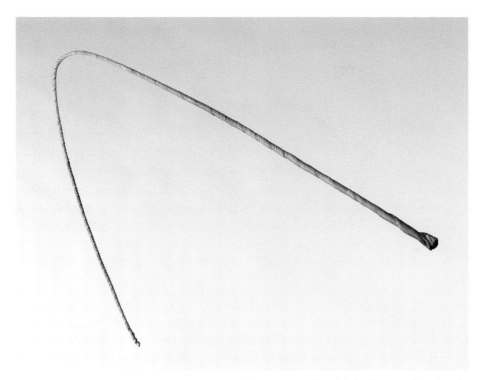

Slave whip, undated. Most of the instruments used to torture enslaved defendants, such as thumb-screws and the so-called Barbadian gloves, have not survived. However, the photograph shows one of the most common tools — the whip — used to scare, hurt, and punish enslaved people in the Danish West Indies (courtesy of *Nationalmuseet*, National Museum of Denmark, photo by John Lee).

owners also swayed the governors with well-turned petitions. In 1766, Governor Clausen, for instance, commuted the enslaved man Telemark's death sentence to 150 cart-whip lashes under the gallows, because of his "good character and the several received petitions interceding for his life."[515]

For most enslaved Africans and Afro-Caribbeans, however, the governor general's power over the legal system did not significantly alter its thoroughly violent nature. Mitigation, as specious as it may sound, was a far cry from acquittal. In the period from 1776 to 1823, 41 percent of the enslaved people convicted by Christiansted Lower Court had their verdict confirmed, 34 percent received a milder punishment, and 22 percent had their verdict appealed following gubernatorial decision (see Figure G). Forty percent of the slaves convicted by Christiansted Lower Court received one of the many ingenious capital punishments contained

Figure G: Distribution of Gubernatorial Decisions in Slave Trials, Christiansted Lower Court, 1776-1823[516]

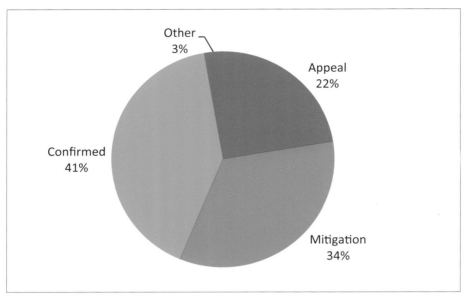

in slave legislation and *The Danish Law* — spanning from simple hanging, post-mortem mutilation and burning to pre-mortem mutilation on the wheel and live burning. Of those receiving a death penalty, half had their sentence commuted to heavy flogging, branding, and transportation or work for life. For the few enslaved people sentenced to dismemberment, mitigation meant that this part of their sentence was commuted to flogging. Others received a smaller number of lashes or had branding removed from their sentences. Indeed, for the vast majority of enslaved Africans and Afro-Caribbeans, their encounter with the Danish West Indian courts resulted in death or violent punishments that had far reaching consequences. Their health would suffer and their bodies would be scarred beyond recognition, leaving them with marks that probably influenced their relationships with owners and managers as well as with fellow slaves for the rest of their lives.

During the nineteenth century, with the abolition of the transatlantic slave trade taking effect in 1803, colonial officers were searching for ways of securing enslaved peoples' reproduction; they hoped to achieve this by altering the relationship between the colonial state, slave masters, and slaves. In line with this concern, Christiansted Lower Court judges gave up some of the brutal punishments found in the slave codes of 1733 and 1755 (see Figure F). While Christiansted Lower Court judges sentenced one-third of all defendants to death in the eighteenth century, they handed down a death penalty against approximately one-sixth of the enslaved defendants in the nineteenth century. Similarly, dismemberment fell out of use. In 1774, Governor General Peter Clausen asserted that such mutilation was "horrible."[517] Five years later, in 1779, the last enslaved person — Plymouth — was sentenced to amputation of the leg, and Governor Clausen mitigated this sentence to 200 lashes and transportation.[518] Floggings of 200 lashes soon fell out of favor as well and, instead, sentences of one hundred or fifty lashes became more frequent.

The concern with the reproductive lives of the enslaved, particularly the belief among government officials that widespread promiscuity worked against natural reproduction, may also have informed what appears to have been a new gender distinction in punishment that had not hitherto been part of legal practice. The majority of defendants appearing before Christiansted Lower Court were enslaved men, but slightly less than 20 percent were women. When, in the nineteenth century, Christiansted Lower Court judges substituted work sentences for death sentences, they reserved these for men. For enslaved women, judges used transportation. This practice emerged because Danish West Indian officers were wary of the results of imprisoning men and women together in Fort Christiansværn. Already in the late eighteenth century, Governor General Peter Clausen and Commander of St. Thomas, Thomas Malleville, believed that women in the fort would encourage promiscuous behavior; indeed, not even separate cells, they ventured, would prevent enslaved men and women from "sexual intercourse." Thus, in the nineteenth century and with a colonial government that increasingly positioned itself as the caretaker of its enslaved subjects' sexual morality, convicted women slaves had to be banished from the islands to avoid promiscuity among enslaved inmates.[519]

Judge Winding described this repositioning of the colonial government vis-à-vis masters and slaves when he argued that the main responsibility of the Danish West Indian state was to "safeguard the rights of the negroes" who, in consequence, had "duties." Winding believed that "[t]he free citizen is obliged to work — and the laborer to submit to his master's castigation."[520] After 1800 the corps of Danish West Indian royal officials, including Christiansted's judges, began to argue that their main function was to ensure the stability of a society ridden by tensions between masters and slaves.

To transform their practice from one concerned with the safety of white West Indians, especially slave owners, to one concerned with reproducing labor in the long run, Christiansted Lower Court judges needed another legal framework; they could not continue to sentence slaves to death at the same rate as they had so far. The reform of punishments that Christiansted's judges carried through in the nineteenth century came about by questioning the validity of slave legislation and by appropriating new Danish legislation. Judges engaged in an intense dialogue with statute law, both metropolitan and colonial, and teased out the finest legal details by referring to high principles of law to support those decisions that departed from slave legislation.

As part of their attempts at reform, judges began to operate under idea that it was possible for slaves to be simultaneously innocent and guilty. When, in 1816, Judith Lydia complained that she had too many children and was too frail to perform fieldwork, Judge Rosenørn admonished her owner to treat her with moderation and warned her family not to encourage her to quarrel with her master.[521] In 1818, Judge Mouritzen likewise directed himself to both slave and owner. The enslaved man Titus, charged with self-mutilation, had been "treated in an incorrect and irresponsible way," but "still" Titus had no excuse for cutting his left arm. Judge Mouritzen found that Titus had offended his owner and the state by robbing the colony of an able-bodied slave.[522] Slowly, enslaved people and their masters, or rather the relationship between them, became the object of legal regulation.

Reforming judges also turned to metropolitan legislation. In 1789, Crown Prince Frederik issued an ordinance that abolished capital punishment for theft in Denmark-Norway. The ordinance did not have any immediate impact in the West Indies, but in the early nineteenth century Danish West Indian judges realized that they could use it to reason against the death sentences stipulated in slave legislation.[523] In 1814, Judge Mouritzen thus stated that, in so far as Danish legislation was applicable in the West Indies, the ordinance on theft of 1789 meant that the death sentence for theft was no longer to be used.[524] Likewise, in 1817, Mouritzen explained that the correct sentence of a thief was to be found by combining the milder metropolitan legislation with the demands set by the special "colonial constitution" of the islands.[525] Indeed, Mouritzen found that the courts in the West Indies had departed from the "old, hard punishments" and had turned to the "mitigating legislation in Denmark." The result was a "middle way" between the old slave codes and new Danish law.[526]

In the nineteenth century, slave legislation was no longer taken for granted by Christiansted's judges. In 1804, Judge Winding stated that slave legislation stipulated too harsh a punishment for Daniel who was charged with arson, theft, and disobedience (see above). The 1733 slave code could "rightly be called cruel" and it had not received royal confirmation.[527] With this conclusion in mind, Judge Winding applied, what he believed to be, "milder measures" and sentenced Daniel to flogging, branding, and transportation.[528] In 1805, Judge Mouritzen likewise made clear that older legislation was inadequate for the "mild government" he represented and regretted that he had to punish according to the slave codes.[529] In Daniel's case, and in a slew of other cases, then, the legislation that had so far been accepted was cast into doubt, thereby allowing Christiansted's judges to choose an alternative, arbitrary punishment.[530]

Christiansted Lower Court judges were, step by step, invalidating older slave codes when they moved to decide the exact punishments fitting for slaves found guilty of specific crimes. The result was a legal terrain wherein judges, in the absence of suitable legislation, could pronounce arbitrary sentences. The most important result of their punitive reform was the significant decline in death penalties. Christiansted Lower Court judges never said so, but their position as the bearers of legal expertise allowed them to support the vision of a reformed slave society promoted among Danish West Indian colonial officers and supported by state departments such as the Chamber of Customs and the Danish Chancellery, in the metropolitan part of the Danish Atlantic empire. Indeed, it made sense to refrain from killing off members of the enslaved population at the very moment when demographic decline threatened Danish West Indian sugar production. Yet there was one conspicuous absence in the many pages judges wrote regarding the sentences they handed down. Slave voices played no part in arguments for or against specific punishments.

The enslaved Africans and Afro-Caribbeans who attempted to forge a persuasive account of their behavior faced a series of dislocations in the Danish Atlantic legal system. When judges set out to determine justice, they did not simply dismiss slave testimonies. Slaves' interpretations of events, their self-portraits, and their suggestions of interpretative frameworks often entered the verdicts of Christiansted's judges. Judges inserted direct quotes and, occasionally, more substantive extracts from police court and lower court interrogations in their written decisions. Yet inclusion went hand in hand with sly distortion. Terms such as fragmentation, deformation, and de-contextualization come to mind as adequate descriptions of the interpretive practices developed by judges in Christiansted Lower Court. Misrepresentation and erasure were used more frequently when enslaved men and women attempted to broaden the scope of the judicial inquiry; for example, when enslaved men and women referred to African-Atlantic spiritual authority to craft their statements or when they drew attention to white West Indians' sexual misconduct, abuse, and rape of enslaved girls and women.

In the eyes of Christiansted Lower Court judges, just verdicts were not obtained by simple reference to slaves' inherent guilt, the tidy exclusion of slave testimony, or by mobilizing the sworn testimony of a free Danish West Indian inhabitant. The just sentence, these judges believed, was established by forwarding a set of arguments about credibility and trustworthiness that were critically dependent on the use of slave testimony. For Christiansted Lower Court judges, justice emerged when they could show that they had based their verdicts on a formal multiplicity of voices. Consequently, they had to be deeply attentive to what enslaved Africans and Afro-Caribbeans said.

Slave testimony was fundamental to justice in the Danish West Indies and since gender was a powerful organizing principle in both the European and African societies from which judges and slaves came, it became central to the skewed conversation between judges and slaves. Christiansted Lower Court judges looked for the familiar, or, at least, the recognizable, when they sought to interpret slave depositions. The idea that a fundamental difference existed between men and women constituted such a recognizable arena. Christian gender norms were familiar ground for judges and many enslaved Africans and Afro-Caribbeans and when judges heard slave testimonies that they could place within their own gendered worldview, they latched on to them. This did not mean the Christiansted Lower Court judges and enslaved witnesses and defendants understood each other well. Rather, it meant that Christiansted Lower Court judges and enslaved men and women shared a limited common ground through which judges could misrepresent what enslaved people said.

Christiansted Lower Court judges balanced between the inclusion and exclusion of slave testimony in order to establish coherent case stories and guilt. If this balancing act was not successful, the strong presumption ensured that even weak case stories could result in convictions. Outright dismissal of slave depositions, their complete exclusion from the representative processes of litigation, mostly occurred in the final conclusive paragraphs of a verdict. It was at this point — and seldom earlier — in the judicial process that the slave voice was finally silenced. Indeed, when it came to determining punishment, the statements enslaved men and women made in Christiansted Police Court and Lower Court were dismissed as irrelevant.

This meant that the influence enslaved Africans and Afro-Caribbeans had on their fate within the Danish Atlantic legal system was above all rhetorical; slaves sometimes succeeded in shaping the wording of verdicts. For Christiansted's judges, their twisted inclusion of slave testimony allowed them to maintain the claim that they were dealing in truth and justice rather than in control and repression. For enslaved men and women distortion meant that they had little influence on the punishments they received. With few exceptions, enslaved peoples' words did not seriously shape the outcome of trials. Indeed the distance between slave testimony and final punishment was as great as the distance between raw cane and fine sugar. Speech and penalty were obviously related, but to get from one to the other involved, if we remain in the mechanical language of sugar production, harvesting and crushing slave depositions and then cleaning and condensing them until, finally, Christiansted's judges could crystalize white verdicts that had little resemblance to the original stories crafted by enslaved men and women.

EPILOGUE

Words with Little Power

Words can lose their power. They can be ignored, distorted, and fragmented beyond recognition. They can be appropriated for purposes entirely different from those of their initial speakers. In a sense this is what happened to most of the stories narrated by enslaved men and women in the Danish West Indian courtrooms. But words can also be enduring, establishing a haunting significance — only partly understood by those who recorded them — that allow us a closer, albeit still incomplete, understanding of those who spoke them. This is also what happened to many of the stories crafted by enslaved men and women in the Danish West Indies. Consider, for example, the trajectory of Sally who argued that her violent actions were grounded in love for her husband and her refusal to accept his polygyny. Consider also the testimony of Ancilla who apologized to her husband for having stayed in the room of the estate overseer — an apology that possibly drew on a Moravian narrative of enslaved female sacrifice. Together the stories of Sally and Ancilla exemplify the three intersecting questions about law, representation, and gender that inform this study. Both women were included in processes of litigation, but both were also excluded and repressed by these same processes. Sally received a death sentence and Judge Brown paid scant attention to her explication of her actions and motives during proceedings in Christiansted Lower Court. Ancilla crafted a courtroom story that established her actions as an individual choice for which she ventured an apology. In her testimony, legal distortions worked by establishing individual agency in a violent environment where such a notion had little bearing.

The reconstructions in *Slave Stories* of the narratives crafted by enslaved people — who testified as defendants, witnesses, and, more rarely, as informal plaintiffs in Christiansted's courts — elucidate how these statements were shaped by processes of inclusion and exclusion as they unfolded in Danish Atlantic legal institutions. As such, *Slave Stories* can be understood as a contribution to a more nuanced history of how enslaved Africans and their descendants were inserted into the representational practices of various colonial regimes, particularly those modeled on the legal traditions of continental Europe. If nothing else, the history of how enslaved men and women expressed themselves, remained silent, or were made silent, in Christiansted's courts in St. Croix shows that the voices of enslaved men and women were not absent in this particular legal regime.

In *Slave Stories* I present the argument that a remarkably inclusive legal power was also dangerously repressive. Legal formality opened up a constrained space in which enslaved men and women could explain themselves. The narratives they crafted were shaped by law and procedure, but also, importantly, by what may be described as a slim ideological overlap between Africans — from many parts of West Africa — and Europeans, specifically Danes, many of whom had stakes in emergent ideas about middling gender roles that circulated in Copenhagen, the metropolitan capital. Enslaved men and women and their judges accepted, for different reasons and with different implications, gender as a category that organized society and divided its members into men and women. The importance of this gender division in framing how judges encountered enslaved Africans is visible, at its most basic level, in the terms adopted by legal scribes to characterize enslaved people. In the courts of Christiansted, enslaved Africans and their descendants were described as *'negere'* and *'negerinder'* (i.e., 'negroes' and 'negresses'). These terms blended race, status and gender into a classifying label that provided the matrix through which enslaved men and women emerged in the courtrooms of Christiansted and in the legal records of the Danish Atlantic regime. They underline that the "racialist discourse" that undergirded slavery in the Americas, as Jennifer Morgan has noted, "was deeply implicated by gendered notions of difference and human hierarchy."[531]

Historians of Caribbean slavery have established that plantation slavery involved what Hilary Beckles has called a "revolutionary restructuring" of traditional gender orders that shaped experiences of enslavement for men and women in different ways.[532] Indeed, the groundbreaking social histories of enslaved women by Marietta Morrissey and Lucille Mathurin Mair, among others, have documented enslaved women's particular and vulnerable structural position within the productive and reproductive processes that constituted racial slavery in the Caribbean.[533] Likewise, newer cultural histories of gender, sexuality, and women have highlighted the fact that the intersection of race and gender lay at the very core of the ideological establishment of Atlantic slavery and undergirded everyday practices of domination.[534]

Historians have pointed to processes of degendering and hypersexualization to approach and explain the restructuring of gender regimes that enslaved men and women, as well as their masters and mistresses, experienced in the Caribbean.

These same processes were in play in the Danish West Indies. While the idea of degendering stresses that gender divisions were often suspended during the daily toil in the fields of sugar estates,[535] the idea of hypersexualization illuminates the myriad ways in which Europeans attributed abnormal sexuality to African men and women in order to legitimize their enslavement.[536] These two analytical metaphors highlight, each in their own way, how the categories of enslaved men and women were made and remade — manipulated, violated, and illuminated — by Europeans in their efforts to establish and maintain slavery. Restructuring revolutions, however, can extend through long periods of time. Europeans and Africans in the Danish West Indies came to the islands equipped with gender ideologies from their home communities and these were continually crossing paths in the Danish West Indies. This meant that many intersecting narratives about the kind of subjects enslaved men and women could be and how they ought to behave informed the encounters between enslaved Africans and Afro-Caribbeans and Danish legal staff up until emancipation in 1848.

Enslaved African men and women responded with adaptation, accommodation, and resistance to the changing configurations of race, gender, and status that marked the slave societies of the Caribbean. An important way of getting closer to such responses has been through the study of behavioral patterns, either as these emerge in aggregate figures —such as demographic trends, fertility levels, and marriage patterns — or as they appear in the lives of particular groups and individuals. Considering the low number of Christian marriages in the British and the French Caribbean, historian Barbara Bush, for instance, argues that this figure can be understood as a sign of women's refusal of "a dual patriarchy" of both African and European origin. Likewise, Bernard Moitt, considering the low number of marriages in the French Caribbean, draws attention to enslaved peoples' limited choice of marriage partners.[537] Another approach has been to zoom in on the trajectories of individual slaves. Historian Trevor Burnard has highlighted the range of responses — from rebelliousness to demoralization to accommodation — exhibited by the enslaved women owned by the small-scale planter Thomas Thistlewood in eighteenth-century Jamaica. Similarly, Hilary Beckles' study of a family of five enslaved women in Barbados has established their relative success at obtaining authority among their fellow slaves while securing themselves from fieldwork.[538] In such studies, enslaved men and women are often and of necessity depicted through a focus on their responses to a strenuous working regime, degrading treatment, extremely brutal punishments, and sexual intimidation, assault and rape.

In *Slave Stories* I have sought to contribute to these Caribbean gender histories by etching out in detail — in time, space, and substance — the changing contours of how enslaved men and women negotiated their encounters with slave-owners, plantation managers, colonial officials, and fellow slaves in the Danish West Indies through words, rather than actions. These reconstructions are obviously not a full exposure of enslaved men and women's inner selves and how gendered notions informed their subjectivity (which would have been a futile exercise in any case). Nonetheless, the reconstruction of the gendered voices of enslaved people as they emerge in court testimonies provides a glimpse of the ideational repertoire that undergirded enslaved people's experiences and concerns. In Christiansted's courts, enslaved men and women crafted stories with spatial horizons that went far beyond the shores of the island of St. Croix. These stories encompassed African-Atlantic cosmologies, notions of power, and contestations about patriarchy, as well as intimate knowledge of emergent ideas about Christian respectability with roots in Northwestern Europe, pietism, and, eventually, abolitionism.

The content of enslaved peoples' narratives about sexual violence and rape, as they unfolded in the courts of Christiansted, changed from the eighteenth to the nineteenth century. Indeed, it was only in the nineteenth century that rape became a legal fact, rather than simply a common experience for enslaved women in the Danish West Indies. The emergence and development of enslaved peoples' stories allow us to follow an increasingly explicit Christian-based narrative and critique, emerging from estates and towns, of the sexual violence and power exercised by white West Indians. These stories show us that enslaved Africans and Afro-Caribbeans creatively used their knowledge of Christian gender conventions to position themselves as subjects that were defined, not by enslavement, but by their respectable behavior. Thus, in Christiansted's courts enslaved women and their families countered sexual violence with a strong ideological opposition to Atlantic tropes of African men and women as promiscuous and sexually aggressive.

In contrast, the unnerving stories about domestic conflict, violence and murder that emerged when enslaved men were accused of murder or of murderous assault on their common law wives, show little change in content and form. These stories also illustrate that legal representation was severely constrained in the nineteenth century, leaving highly fragmented accounts of how enslaved men and women imagined their intimate relationships. Nevertheless, enslaved peoples' testimonies about their domestic troubles offer glimpses of the ideas on which they drew in their struggle to bring some measure of order to their intimate affairs. The stories crafted by men and women suggest that they were engaged in fierce debates about what to make of African-Atlantic and Christian gender conventions, particularly in regards to the question of how to distribute authority between men and women. As Sally and her husband's statements indicate, these traditions were a resource but a contested resource among men and women in St. Croix. Clearly, bonds of material dependence tied enslaved men and women together, perhaps more than they did other couples in the early modern world, but these men and women were also employing a significant emotional language of love and care that gave deeper meaning to the practical necessity of cooperation. In doing so, they argued that they were capable of a wide repertoire of fine sentiment that could not be subsumed under — or understood through — the notions of African insolence and conjugal informality that characterized slave law and Atlantic racial discourses.

Slave Stories establishes many different enslaved voices that were not fully determined by the oppressive structures that shaped the lives of enslaved men and women. However, these voices were not unrestrained and freely expressed in the courtrooms of Christiansted, St. Croix. The testimonies of Sally and Ancilla were different because Sally spoke as a defendant facing a life sentence whereas Ancilla spoke as a witness, possibly in defense of her common law husband. Their stories also differ because Sally narrated a domestic conflict whereas Ancilla described a case of enforced intimacy, possibly rape. Yet there was also an ideational difference between the two women. Sally desired monogamous love and hinted at African-Atlantic supernatural support. Ancilla accepted, in her testimony, her husband's duty to instruct her in the norms of proper marital conduct. She framed herself as a young Christian woman who repented her choice of accompanying her overseer to his room, although it was a decision that obviously cannot be fully understood as an act of will. In highlighting these different ideational positions, and those of many other enslaved men and women, *Slave Stories,* I hope, can be read as a chapter in the history of ideas, or better, the intellectual history of people in the African diaspora. It is a preliminary answer to the question of how "enslaved people theorized their own actions" posed by the historian Walter Johnson in his call to historians to pay attention to the ideational elements of enslaved peoples' daily lives and struggles.[539]

By offering reconstructions of the narrative practices employed by enslaved men and women in St. Croix, the preceding chapters participate in a long-standing debate over how scholars should approach the worldviews of subjugated people, women particularly. More than twenty years ago, the literary critic Gayatri Spivak argued that the subaltern voice or subject, especially the female subject, was impossible to retrieve from the colonial archive.[540] What could be found in texts produced by European colonial agents was a phantom subject, a textual effect that served to legitimize colonial domination. Actual people — whoever they were — appeared as gaps in colonial texts.[541] Moving on from this conclusion, the reconstructions of enslaved men and women's experiences with slavery in the Danish West Indies, as they were mediated by Christiansted's courts, highlight how those gaps and silences work as concrete instances of censorship rather than as abstract qualities of colonial archives. Studies of colonialism and gender in the Atlantic world (and beyond) have generated an awareness of the deep constraints that past power structures impose on the formation of historical knowledge by silencing the perspectives and worldviews of enslaved men and women (as well as other colonial subjects).[542] To this awareness, *Slave Stories* adds the perspective that representation, misrepresentation, and erasure are contextual and concrete. Consider again the trial of Sally whose testimony did not explicate the meaning of the marl and water she prepared for herself and her husband beyond the claiming that it had the power to "terrify." The silencing process that marked the trial against Sally probably erased a particular reference to and use of African-Atlantic spiritual power in the handling of marriage and affection in the Danish West Indies of the late eighteenth century; it did not erase an abstract female subject.

In his work on the silencing processes at work in the making of Caribbean history, Michel-Rolph Trouillot argued that these were multilayered — shaping the generation of facts, sources, archives, and narratives — and he suggested that we "deconstruct these silences" as the *particular* "bundle" of censorship that they are.[543] This means that we should be wary of filling archival silence with abstraction and, further, it suggests a different conclusion than the one advocated by Spivak when she argued that subaltern women are caught in a position wherein "the free will and agency of the sexed subject as female […] is successfully effaced."[544] Indeed, the study of slave resistance and, more recently, agency in the Americas constitutes a telling example of how contemporary historians have filled archival silence with abstract notions of the will to freedom. As a result, enslaved peoples' multifaceted behavior and complex ideological horizons have often been reduced to signs of (often rationalist) resistance.[545] However, analyzing the concrete practices of inclusion, distortion and erasure enacted by Danish West Indian judges suggests a way of working with silencing processes that does not presume that we can know what is being silenced at particular times and places. Returning to Sally's trial, Judge Brown understood Sally's behavior as a response to her troubled relationship to her overseer, whereas Sally was preoccupied with her relationship to her husband. Likewise, George, who attempted suicide, gave a number of overlapping reasons, spanning from vexation with fellow slaves to hatred of the driver, that cannot all be subsumed under the category of resistance or opposition, to slavery. Testimonies like these suggest that conflicts about marriage, love, and authority were shaped by struggles between enslaved people and their superiors, but also, and significantly, by ideological differences among the enslaved in St. Croix about how regimes of affection should be organized.

The history of law, representation, and gender in the Danish West Indies suggests that it may be useful to think about the links between legal agency and testimonial subjectivity as less direct, instrumental, and strategic than we have been used to. In *Slave Stories* I have tried to disentangle the notion of agency (understood as a capacity to act or exert power) from ideas about enslaved peoples' volition and subjectivity. In a broad sense, the history of enslaved testimony in the Danish West Indies emphasizes that there were many enslaved subjects and very few enslaved agents in Christiansted's courts — subjects in the sense that enslaved people were requested to and also attempted to explain their version of events in dispute and thereby emerge as literal subjects in court prose. Understood as a process, extended in time, divided into various phases, civil and criminal proceedings were geared toward the restrictive inclusion of enslaved peoples' testimony; on such testimony decisions about guilt or innocence were later based. Enslaved men and women could occasionally persuade Danish West Indian judges to turn away from a life sentence. However, the high rates of conviction and the use of extremely brutal punishments is evidence that the opportunity enslaved people had to give testimony in the Danish West Indies did not significantly alter the repressive power of the islands' courts.

Such a conclusion can be used to think about the nature of legal power in the Danish West Indies and in the slave societies of the Americas more broadly. Historian of the Danish West Indies, Neville Hall, has noted that law in the Danish West Indies was primarily directed toward the control of a resistant enslaved population, concluding that slaves were "not conceived as having rights" in the Danish West Indian legal system.[546] It is a conclusion that is also borne out in *Slave Stories* and follows legal scholarship about Atlantic slave societies more broadly. Historians of slave law have pointed to the restrictions on slave testimony in order to document that slaves had no say in Atlantic courts.[547] They have stressed that "a major function of slave laws and the slave courts was to enforce the subordination and deference of slaves to white people," as historian Diana Paton concluded regarding eighteenth-century Jamaica.[548]

Nevertheless, in studies of the encounter between enslaved Africans and specific Atlantic courts, historians have also documented how enslaved people used the courts to negotiate status and resist various forms of misuse and abuse. Summarizing the situation in the Spanish colonies, Alejandro de la Fuente notes that enslaved people had some possibility of making legal claims, not least because the authority owners held over their slaves was shared with crown and church.[549] Although enslaved men and women's ability to access the law was greater in colonial regimes that drew on elements of Roman law and were ruled by a strongly centralizing state, it was not altogether absent from the English-speaking Caribbean. In the nineteenth century, the British occupation of Dutch, French and Spanish colonies and ameliorative legal reforms meant that enslaved people in the British Caribbean, particularly in Crown colonies, had some, albeit severely circumscribed, access to redress.[550]

Such access to colonial courts was also a feature of legal culture in the Danish West Indies. Neville Hall has noted that enslaved people in the Danish West Indies were becoming increasingly aware that "their masters had other masters who represented a higher jurisdiction that could be invoked to their advantage" in the nineteenth century.[551] Clearly, complaining to colonial authorities, such as Christiansted's chief of police or the governor general, emerged as an important element in everyday conflicts on estates in St. Croix in the nineteenth century. Yet few slaves received vindication. The trajectory of enslaved people and their testimonies in the Danish Atlantic legal system reveal that agency was only part of the story of how enslaved people met the law in the islands.

Historians have provided a number of different answers to the question of what such legal openings meant for enslaved peoples' uses of the law and the function of law in Caribbean slave societies. In her study of the uprising in Demerara in 1823, Emilia Viotti da Costa argued that enslaved peoples' hundreds of complaints testify to the "importance, they attributed to a grievance procedure, that whatever its limitations, at least allowed them occasionally to be dealt with as people rather than as things."[552] Mindie Lazarus-Black has gone a step further by suggesting that the access enslaved people had to courts made these institutions "agents of a system of hegemony that united master and slave."[553] However, considering the high rates of conviction confronting enslaved defendants in Danish West Indian courts, the concept of hegemony does not seem to adequately explain how enslaved people engaged with the law. Rather, the Danish West Indian courts appear to parallel the Jamaican slave courts that historian Diana Paton has shown were consistently ruling against enslaved defendants, at least before ameliorative reforms refigured the legal landscape of the island.[554] Noting that enslaved people in the Danish West Indies seldom achieved legal redress and were often dismissed and punished for their complaints in the nineteenth century as well only further emphasizes Paton's point.

The many slave testimonies produced in the Danish West Indian courts, and in other courts in the Caribbean, nevertheless, suggest that repression is only part of the story of how legal power worked in the Atlantic world. By reconstructing the everyday proceedings against enslaved men and women in the Danish West Indies, *Slave Stories* shows that repression can go hand in hand with a certain degree of legal integration of enslaved people and their testimony. Indeed, legal power can be vitally dependent on such integration. In the Danish West Indies, the notion of justice held by colonial Danish jurists relied on the distortion of slave testimony rather than its formal exclusion from the legal process. To understand this phenomenon, I suggest that we approach Danish West Indian legal culture as a highly sophisticated phenomenon. Indeed, the Danish West Indian courts can be viewed as sites that were equal in refinement to the long, intricate, and destructive process of turning cane juice into sugar; these courts were sites in which production and destruction went hand in hand. With such an image in mind, the court statements of enslaved men and women can be recognized as part of, rather than exceptions to, a remarkably brutal legal regime. We can recognize Danish West Indian legal power as devious, twisted, and cunning as well as brutal and repressive.

MANUSCRIPT SOURCES

To write *Slave Stories* I worked in the collections of the *Rigsarkiv*, the National Archives, in Copenhagen, Denmark. The Danish National Archives hold most of the documents produced by the central absolutist administration of the Danish-Norwegian state, including the colonial administration and the so-called *Vestindiske lokalarkiver*, the Danish West Indian Local Archives. This collection of material, produced by authorities in the Danish West Indies, lies at the core of my work. It was brought to Denmark in the years immediately after 1917, when the Danish West Indies were sold to the United States.[555]

Some institutions and record types (legal proceedings, verdicts and the like) appear again and again in the notes of *Slave Stories* and therefore I have chosen to abbreviate references to some of these sources. When I refer to court proceedings, I either provide the number of the case or the date when the case began. When I refer to verdicts, I refer to the date when the verdict was pronounced or the number of the verdict.

Abbreviations

CB	Christiansted Byfoged	Office of Christiansted's Judge
DP	Domprotokoller	Register of Verdicts
ERP	Ekstraretsprotokoller	Proceedings of the Extra Court
GG	Generalguvernementet	Office of the Governor General
GRP	Gæsteretsprotokoller	Proceedings of the Guest Court
KP	Kriminalprotokoller	Proceedings of Criminal Trials
PB	Plakatbøger	Books of Placards
PJ	Politijournaler	Police Journals
PRP	Politiretsprotokoller	Proceedings of the Police Court
RP	Referatprotokoller	Registers (journals) of Letters Received

De vestindiske lokalarkiver
(The Danish West Indian Local Archives)

Generalguvernementet

2.1.1-8	Plakatbøger, 1733-1821
2.2.3	Korrespondance- og ordreprotokoller (kopibøger), 1818
2.5.1-3	Kopibøger til lokale myndigheder og personer, 1773-1807
2.6.4-6	Koncepter til skrivelser overvejende til lokale myndigheder og personer, 1799-1801
2.10.1	Kopibøger, 1820-1822
2.16.1-13	Referatprotokoller (journaler) for indkomne skrivelser fra myndigheder m.m. i Dansk Vestindien, 1790-1825
2.17.1, 17-19 & 23	Journaliserede og ikke-journaliserede skrivelser fra myndigheder m.m. i Dansk Vestindien, 1760-1776, 1799-1800, 1802
2.26.3 & 6	Kopibøger B, 1831-1833, 1837-1839
2.27.1-18	Referatprotokoller B (journaler), 1820-1846
2.28.1-7	Sager til referatprotokoller B, 1821-1822
2.49	Rapporter fra Christiansteds politikammer, 1777-1787

Den Vestindiske Regering

3.1.2	Forhandlingsprotokoller, 1771-1825
3.31.2	Kopibog for skrivelser til lokaladministrationen m.fl., 1768-1776
3.33.4-6	Kopibrevprotokoller for skrivelser til lokaladministrationen m.fl., 1779-1783
3.40	Instruktionsprotokol, 1723-1784
3.41.6, 32 & 34	Referatprotokoller (journaler) for breve fra lokaladministrationen, 1780, 1800, 1801-1807
3.56.2.	Indgåede breve til den engelske guvernør, 1809-1810

3.59.3, 5, 8-12, 20, 36-38 & 42	Referatprotokoller A, 1817, 1819, 1820-1824, 1828, 1838-1840, 1843
3.81.73	Gruppeordnede sager 2. Lokale myndigheder: Breve vedr. justits- og politivæsenet, 1782-1790
3.81.175	Gruppeordnede sager 3. Retsvæsen: Retsdokumenter fundet i generalguvernør P. Clausens bo, 1774-1804
3.81.219	Gruppeordnede sager 3. Retsvæsen: Mord på plantageforvalter P. Machin, 1832

Landsoverretten for De Vestindiske Øer

5.2.3	Justitsprotokoller, V 1815-X 1819
5.5.3-4	Domprotokoller, Litra Q-R, 1814-1820 to Litra S, 1820-1822
5.7	Alfabetisk navneregister til pådømte sager. 1806-1906

Landstinget på St. Croix

37.7.7 & 10	Domprotokoller, Litra H, 1780-1784 & Litra L, 1798-1804

Christiansted Byfoged

38.2.8	Ekstraretsprotokoller, 1820-1824
38.5.2, 8, 10, 16, 18-19, 23-24 & 30	Gæsteretsprotokoller, 1759-1761, 1765-1766, 1767-1768, 1773-1776, 1778-1783, 1792-1800, 1805-1806
38.6.1-32	Domprotokoller, 1756-1857
38.9.1-24	Politiretsprotokoller, 1756-1841
38.11.2, 4 & 6	Kriminalprotokoller, 1817-1821, 1824-1839, 1845-1851
38.18.1-9	Pådømte sager, 1746-1849
38.22.27, 40 & 43	Fogedprotokoller, 1803-1805, 1817-1820, 1822-1824
38.31.1-6	Politijournaler, 1798-1822

Centraladministrationens arkiver
(Central Government Archives)

Danske Kancelli

F26	Vestindiske Sager, 1773-1786

Generalkirkeinspektionskollegiet

F4-3-2	Kopibøger for forestillinger og breve, 1763-1791
F4-8-20-21	Indkomne sager, 1784-91
F4-8-18-19	Indkomne sager, 1779-1783

Generaltoldkammerets vestindiske og guineiske sager

390	Visdomsbog, 1733-1783
420	Genpart af adskillige anmærkninger og plakater ang. slaver samt udkast til slavelov, 1672-1787
421	Anmærkninger ved forslaget til negerloven. Tillige med supplement, grunde og analogi for samme, 1783-1787
424	Dokumenter vedr. Kommissionen for Negerhandelens bedre indretning II, 1783-1806

Kommercekollegiet, Dansk-norske Sekretariat

17	Forordninger, 1735-1770

Reviderede Regnskaber, Vestindiske Regnskaber

86.4-8, 36, 64-65	Matrikler for St. Croix, 1758-1768, 1803-1804, 1837-1838

Håndskriftssamlingen
(The Manuscript Collection)

18. VII, D, 2	Species facti over den paa Eilandet St. Croix i Aaret 1759 intenderede Neger Rebellion, forfattet efter Ordre af Byfoged Engelbret Hesselberg

Privatarkiverne
(The Archives of Private Persons)

6285	Heinrich Ernst Schimmelmann (1747-1831), ny aflevering, pk. 32, Breve fra administratorerne på plantagen "La Princesse," St. Croix, Charles Vanderbourg og La Porte

NOTES

1   38.5.24, CB, GRP, case 1799-10-04, and 38.9.10, CB, PRP, case 1799-08-29.

2   38.6.21, CB, DP, verdict 1799-11-01.

3   A fine introduction to Danish West Indian history and detailed catalogues of the Danish West Indian holdings in the Danish National Archives is provided at www.virgin-islands-history.dk. The number of volumes concerning law in Christiansted is calculated on the basis of information provided on this site. At the time of writing, information at this site is being moved to www.virgin-islands-history. org which also include the digitized versions of the great majority of material related to the Danish possessions in the Caribbean (accessed 2017-05-01). For an overview of Scandinavian involvement in the Atlantic, see G. Simonsen, "Northern Europe and the Atlantic World," ed. Trevor Burnard, *Oxford Online Encyclopaedia of the Atlantic World* (Oxford University Press, 2011).

4   For an excellent analysis of how gender provides a basic grammar for cross-cultural encounters, see J. Barr, *Peace Came in the Form of a Woman. Indians and Spaniards in the Texas Borderlands* (Chapel Hill: University of North Carolina Press, 2007).

5   See for instance E.V.d. Costa, *Crowns of Glory, Tears of Blood: The Demerara Slave Rebellion of 1823* (New York and Oxford: Oxford University Press, 1994); J. De Barros, "'Setting Things Right': Medicine and Magic in British Guiana, 1803-38," *Slavery & Abolitim* 25, no. 1 (2004); J.H. Sweet, *Recreating Africa: Culture, Kinship, and Religion in the African-Portuguese World, 1441-1770* (Chapel Hill: University of North Carolina Press, 2003); M.W. Ghachem, *The Old Regime and the Haitian Revolution* (Cambridge: Cambridge University Press, 2012).

6   D. Paton, "Punishment, Crime, and the Bodies of Slaves in Eighteenth-Century Jamaica," *Journal of Social History* 34, no. 4 (2001), 923.

7   J.H. Lean, The Secret Lives of Slaves: Berbice 1819 to 1827 (Ph.D.-thesis, University of Canterbury, 2002); Costa, *Crowns of Glory*; R.M. Browne, "The 'Bad Business' of Obeah: Power, Authority, and the Politics of Slave Culture in the British Caribbean," *William and Mary Quarterly* 68, no. 3 (2011); J.K. Schafer, *Slavery, the Civil Law, and the Supreme Court of Louisiana* (Baton Rouge: Louisiana State University Press, 1994).

8   D.B. Gaspar, *Bondmen and Rebels: A Study of Master-Slave Relations in Antigua* (Durham: Duke University Press, 1985), 12; quote from Costa, *Crowns of Glory*, 238.

9   See the debate about the so-called Vesey conspiracy, begun by M.P. Johnson, "Denmark Vesey and His Co-Conspirators," *William and Mary Quarterly* 58, no. 4 (2001). See also E.A. Pearson, "Trials and Errors: Denmark Vesey and His Historians," *William and Mary Quarterly* 59, no. 1 (2002); D.R. Egerton, "Forgetting Denmark Vesey; Or, Oliver Stone Meets Richard Wade," *William and Mary Quarterly* 59, no. 1 (2002); D. Robertson, "Inconsistent Contextualism: The Hermeneutics of Michael Johnson," *William and Mary Quarterly* 59, no. 1 (2002); P.D. Morgan, "Conspiracy Scares," *William and Mary Quarterly* 59, no. 1 (2002); J. Sidbury, "Plausible Stories and Varnished Truths," *William and Mary Quarterly* 59, no. 1 (2002); T.J. Davis, "Conspiracy and Credibility: Look Who's Talking, about What — Law Talk and Loose Talk," *William and Mary Quarterly* 59, no. 1 (2002); R.L. Paquette, "Jacobins of the Lowcountry: The Vesey Plot on Trial," *William and Mary Quarterly* 59, no. 1 (2002); W.D. Jordan, "The Charleston Hurricane of 1822; Or, the Law's Rampage," *William and Mary Quarterly* 59, no. 1 (2002); M.P. Johnson, "Reading Evidence," *William and Mary Quarterly* 59, no. 1 (2002).

10   H. Beckles, *Centering Woman: Gender Discourses in Caribbean Slave Society* (Kingston: Ian Randle Publishers, 1999); V. Shepherd, B. Brereton, and B. Bailey, eds., *Engendering History: Caribbean*

Women in Historical Perspective (New York: St. Martin's Press, 1995); J.L. Morgan, *Laboring Women: Reproduction and Gender in New World Slavery* (Philadelphia: University of Pennsylvania Press, 2004); B. Bush, *Slave Women in Caribbean Society 1650-1838* (Kingston: Ian Randle, 1990).

11 Morgan, *Laboring Women*, 198-99. Scholars noting the absence, repression or rarity of the enslaved voice include T. Burnard and G. Heuman, "Introduction," in *The Routledge History of Slavery*, ed. Trevor Burnard and Gad Heuman (London and New York: Routledge, 2011), 9; P. Scully and D. Paton, "Introduction: Gender and Slave Emancipation in Comparative Perspective," in *Gender and Slave Emancipation in the Atlantic World*, ed. Pamela Scully and Diana Paton (Durham and London: Duke University Press, 2005), 20; B. Brereton, "Text, Testimony and Gender: An Examination of some Texts by Women in the English-speaking Caribbean from the 1770s to the 1920s," in *Engendering History: Caribbean Women in Historical Perspective*, ed. Verene Shepherd, Bridget Brereton, and Barbara Bailey (New York: St. Martin's Press, 1995). In a wider colonial context, Laura A. L. Stoler has explored how postcolonial subjects can be "'speaking back to the archives'," Stoler, *Carnal Knowledge and Imperial Power: Race and the Intimate in Colonial Rule* (Berkeley: University of California Press, 2002), 162-65.

12 See for instance Burnard and Heuman, "Introduction," 9; Scully and Paton, "Introduction: Gender and Slave Emancipation in Comparative Perspective," 20. D. Paton, *No Bond but the Law: Punishment, Race, and Gender in Jamaican State Formation, 1780-1870* (Durham: Duke University Press, 2004), 17; Brereton, "Text, Testimony and Gender: An Examination of some Texts by Women in the English-speaking Caribbean from the 1770s to the 1920s; M.J. Fuentes, *Dispossessed Lives, Enslaved Women, Violence, and the Archive* (Philadelphia: University of Pennsylvania Press, 2016).

13 T. Burnard and J. Lean, "Hearing Slave Voices: The Fiscal's Reports of Berbice and Demarara-Esseqeubo," *Archives [Britain]* 27, no. 107 (2002), 133. See also K. Hilliard, "Finding Slave Voices," in *The Oxford Handbook of Slavery in the Americas*, ed. Robert L. Paquette and Mark M. Smith (Oxford: Oxford University Press, 2010). The engagement with the question of what historical texts represent has been a primary focus of the microhistorial tradition attributed to, among others, Carlo Ginzburg. Ginzburg argues that certain types of historical texts can be shown to contain polyphonic and dialogic elements, and that these texts enable us to explore the worlds of groups and individuals who never wrote themselves, C. Ginzburg, *History, Rhetoric, and Proof* (Hanover and London: The University Press of New England, 1999), 71-91; C. Ginzburg, *Clues, Myths, and the Historical Method* (Baltimore: Johns Hopkins University Press, 1989), 156-164. Also see the debate of Ginzburg's ideas in P. Chatterjee, *A Princely Imposter? The Strange and Universal History of the Kumar of Bhawal* (Princeton: Princeton University Press, 2002), 356-357.

14 The notion of 'voice' could have been substituted by other, more precise, notions such as echoes, resonance, and ventriloquisms. Holding on to voice, however, signals the persistent attempt of historians to locate those instances where enslaved men and women were able to participate in processes of representation. See for example M. Hodes, *White Women, Black Men: Illicit Sex in the Nineteenth-Century South* (New Haven and London: Yale University Press, 1997), 86-95; J.E. Mason, *Social Death and Resurrection: Slavery and Emancipation in South Africa* (Charlottesville and London: University of Virginia Press, 2003), 5; J. Smolenski, "Hearing Voices: Microhistory, Dialogicality and the Recovery of Popular Culture on an Eighteenth-Century Virginia Plantation," *Slavery & Abolition* 24, no. 1 (2003); N. Zacek, "Voices and Silences: The Problem of Slave Testimony in the English West Indian Law Court," *Slavery & Abolition* 24, no. 3 (December 2003); Hilliard, "Finding Slave Voices."

15 C. Steedman, "Enforced Narratives. Stories of Another Self," in *Feminism and Autobiography*, ed. Tess Cosslett, Celia Lury, and Penny Summerfield (London: Routledge, 2000).

16 M.-R. Trouillot, *Silencing the Past: Power and the Production of History* (Boston: Beacon Press, 1995), 23.

17 M. Foucault, "The Subject and Power," *Critical Inquiry* 8 (1982), 781. Subjectivity — as I use the concept — is not merely a better word for individuality. As I use the term, it denotes the meanings people attribute to themselves, but it does not indicate that a person understands him- or herself as

wholly self-determined; see N.Z. Davis, "Boundaries and the Sense of Self in Sixteenth-Century France," in *Reconstructing Individualism: Autonomy, Individuality, and the Sense of Self in Western Thought*, ed. Thomas C. Heller, Morton Sosna, and David E. Wellbery (Palo Alto, CA: Stanford University Press, 1986), 58.

18   V. Carretta, *Unchained Voices: An Anthology of Black Authors in the English Speaking World of the Eighteenth Century* (Lexington: University Press of Kentucky, 1996); A. Costanzo, *Surprising Narrative: Olaudah Equiano and the Beginnings of Black Autobiography* (New York: Greenwood Press, 1987); J. Olney, "'I Was Born': Slave Narratives, Their Status as Autobiography and as Literature," *Callaloo*, no. 20 (1984); P. Gilroy, *The Black Atlantic: Modernity and Double Consciousness* (Cambridge, MA: Harvard University Press, 1993).

19   D.A. McBride, *Impossible Witnesses: Truth, Abolitionism, and Slave Testimony* (New York: New York University Press, 2001), 3.

20   The ideological shaping of colonial discourses are powerfully explored in the, by now, classic works of scholars, such as E.W. Said, *Orientalism: Western Conceptions of the Orient* (London: Penguin Books, 1995); S.J. Greenblatt, *Marvelous Possessions: The Wonder of the New World* (New York: Clarendon Press, 1991); G.C. Spivak, *A Critique of Postcolonial Reason: Toward a History of the Vanishing Present* (Cambridge, MA: Harvard University Press, 1999); G.C. Spivak, "Can the Subaltern Speak?," in *Marxism and the Interpretation of Culture*, ed. Cary Nelson and Lawrence Grossberg (Macmillan Education Ltd, 1988).

21   V. Brown, *The Reaper's Garden, Death and Power in the World of Atlantic Slavery* (Cambridge, MA: Harvard University Press, 2008), 145; G. Simonsen, "Magic, Obeah and Law in the Danish West Indies, 1750s-1840s," in *Ports of Globalisation, Places of Creolisation: Nordic Possessions in the Atlantic World during the Era of the Slave Trade*, ed. Holger Weiss (Leiden: Brill, 2015). In the records of the Danish West Indian colonial administration, obeah was spelled variously as *obia*, *obiah*, and *obeah*. I have chosen to use the English spelling *obeah*.

22   38.9.20. CB, PRP, case 1828-11-01.

23   F.G. Cassidy and R.B.L. Page, *Dictionary of Jamaican English* (Cambridge: Cambridge University Press, 1967); Paton, "Punishment," 942-943; V. Brown, "Spiritual Terror and Sacred Authority in Jamaican Slave Society," *Slavery & Abolition* 24, no. 1 (2003), 36.

24   For the way gender intersected with race, slavery and religion in other Atlantic areas see C. Hall, *Civilising Subjects: Metropole and Colony in the English Imagination 1830-1867* (Chicago and London: University of Chicago Press, 2002); D.B. Gaspar and D.C. Hine, eds., *More than Chattel: Black Women and Slavery in the Americas* (Bloomington: Indiana University Press, 1996); K.M. Brown, *Good Wives, Nasty Wenches, and Anxious Patriarchs: Gender, Race, and Power in Colonial Virginia* (Chapel Hill: University of North Carolina Press, 1996); M. Hodes, ed. *Sex, Love, Race: Crossing Boundaries in North American History* (New York: New York University Press, 1999).

25   N.T. Jensen, *For the Health of the Enslaved: Slaves, Medicine and Power in the Danish West Indies, 1803-1848* (København: Museum Tusculanum Press, 2012), 57-58.

26   N. A. T. Hall, *Slave Society in the Danish West Indies. St. Thomas, St. John and St. Croix* (Mona, Jamaica: University of the West Indies Press, 1992), 1-33. For other introductions to Danish West Indian history, see L. Müller, G. Rydén, and H. Weiss, eds., *Global historia från periferin. Norden 1600-1850* (Lund: Studentlitteratur, 2010); J. Brøndsted, ed. *Vore Gamle Tropekolonier*, vol. 1-4 (Denmark: Fremad, 1966); G. Simonsen, "Nye og gamle perspektiver på dansk kolonihistorie," *1066 – Tidsskrift for Historie* 2 (2003).

27   J. B. Christensen, "Jord, slaver og plantere. Kolonisamfundet på St. Croix 1742-1804," in *Dansk kolonihistorie. Indføring og studier*, ed. Peter Hoxcer Jensen, et al. (Århus: Historia, 1981), 147. See also Hall, *Slave Society*, 10, table 1.2. Studies that similarly emphasize the processes of cultural blending marking the Americas, see K. F. Olwig, "African Culture in the Danish West Indies. The Slave Trade and its Aftermath," in *The Danish West Indian Slave Trade*, ed. Arnold R. Highfield and George F. Tyson

(St. Croix: Virgin Islands Humanities Council, 1994); K. F. Olwig, "African Cultural Principles in the Caribbean Slave Societies," in *Slave Cultures and the Cultures of Slavery*, ed. Stephan Palmié (Knoxville: University of Tennessee Press, 1995); P. D. Morgan, "The Cultural Implications of the Atlantic Slave Trade: African Regional Origins, American Destinations and New World Developments," *Slavery & Abolition* 18, no. 1 (1997).

28   D. Hopkins, "Jens Michelsen Beck's Map of a Danish West Indian Sugar-Plantation Island: Eighteenth-Century Colonial Cartography, Land Administration, Speculation and Fraud," *Terrae Incognitae* 25 (1993).

29   G. F. Tyson, "On the Periphery of the Peripheries: The Cotton Plantations of St. Croix, Danish West Indies, 1735-1815," *The Journal of Caribbean History* 26, no. 1 (1992).

30   O. Hornby, *Kolonierne i Vestindien* (København: Politikens Forlag, 1980), 130.

31   S.E. Holsoe, "The Origin, Transport, Introduction and Distribution of Africans on St. Croix: An Overview," in *The Danish West Indian Slave Trade*, ed. Arnold R. Highfiled and George F. Tyson (St. Croix: Virgin Islands Humanities Council, 1994), 33.

32   J. Vibæk, *Dansk Vestindien 1755-1848: Vestindiens Storhedstid*, ed. Johannes Brøndsted, vol. 2, *Vore Gamle Tropekolonier* (Denmark: Fremad, 1966), 319-323.

33   Jensen, *For the Health*, 135.

34   I use the term African-Atlantic to capture those elements of enslaved people's lives that developed in dialogue with African social and cultural practices, yet were shaped by the integration of West Africans and West Central Africans into the Atlantic slave trading system. Two interpretations have dominated the understanding of the cultural transformations Africans experienced in the Americas. In 1976 Richard Price and Sidney Mintz hypothesized that enslaved Africans underwent a relatively fast process of creolization in which slaves' African pasts were retained through "unconscious 'grammatical' principles" uniting otherwise diverse West and West Central African people, see S. W. Mintz and R. Price, *The Birth of African American Culture: An Anthropological Perspective* (Boston: Beacon Press, 1992), 9. Historians such as John Thornton, Michael A. Gomez, Gwendolyn Hall and James Sweet have revised this interpretation. Creolization was, they argue, a slow and extended process involving people from regionally defined African cultures and involving neo-African inventions in the Americas (J. Thornton, *Africa and Africans in the Making of the Atlantic World, 1400-1800*, 2nd ed. (Cambridge: Cambridge University Press, 1998); P. E. Lovejoy, ed. *Identity in the Shadow of Slavery* (London: Continuum, 2000); G. M. Hall, *Africans in Colonial Louisiana: The Development of Afro-Creole Culture in the Eighteenth Century* (Baton Rouge: Louisiana State University Press, 1992); M. A. Gomez, *Exchanging our Country Marks: The Transformation of African Identities in the Colonial and Antebellum South* (Chapel Hill: University of North Carolina Press, 1998); J. H. Sweet, *Domingos Álvares, African Healing, and the Intellectual History of the Atlantic World* (Chapel Hill: University of North Carolina Press, 2011). These two ways of understanding the early African diaspora are sometimes presented as contradictory, but they can be understood as mutually beneficial analytical strategies, and this is the approach I follow here. See also G. Simonsen, "Moving in Circles: African and Black History in the Atlantic World," *Nuevo Mundo Mundos Nuevos* (2008).

35   In each decade from 1760 to 1800 the Moravians baptized from 8 to 16 percent of the enslaved African population in St. Croix. Over time they may have baptized as much as one-third of the enslaved Africans in St. Croix. The figures are calculated on the basis of P. H. Pope, Cruzan Slavery: An Ethnohistorical Study of Differential Responses to Slavery in the Danish West Indies (Ph.D.-thesis, University of California, 1969), 59-69, table 1; S. E. Green-Pedersen, "Slave Demography in the Danish West Indies and the Abolition of the Danish Slave Trade," in *The Abolition of the Atlantic Slave Trade: Origins and Effects in Europe, Africa and the Americas*, ed. David Eltis and James Walvin (Madison: University of Wisconsin Press, 1981), 247-248, table 13.1. There is a relatively fine accordance between Oldendorp's impression of the ethnic composition of the African population in the late 1760s, the ethnic designations used by planters and overseers in runaway-slave notices in the 1770s, and the

Moravian registers of baptism. This indicates that the registers represent the nations of Africans present in St. Croix fairly well, see C. G. A. Oldendorp, *Historie der caribischen Inseln Sanct Thomas, Sanct Crux und Sanct Jan. Kommentierte Edition des Originalmanskriptes*, ed. Gudrun Meir, et al., vol. I (Dresden: Verlag für Wissenschaft und Bildung, 2000), 449; Holsoe, "The Origin, Transport, Introduction and Distribution of Africans on St. Croix: An Overview," 36.

36   The history of the Amina nation is not entirely clear. Here I follow Oldendorp's classification and the editorial annotations in the 2000-version of his manuscript. For a different interpretation see G. M. Hall, "African Ethnicities and the Meanings of 'Mina'," in *Identity in the Shadow of Slavery*, ed. Paul E. Lovejoy (London: Continuum, 2000), 63-81; G.M. Hall, *Slavery and African Ethnicities in the Americas: Restoring the Links* (Chapel Hill: University of North Carolina Press, 2005), 111-125; for a critique of Hall see R. Law, "Ethnicities of Enslaved Africans in the Diaspora: On the Meaning of Mina (Again)," *History in Africa* 32 (2005).

37   The two men Sylvester and David, born in Africa, explained that they were brothers, see 38.9.11. CB, PRP, case no. 1802-10.

38   Hall, *Slave Society*, 73, table 4.1; P. E. Olsen, "Godserne på St. Croix 1733-1800," *Bol og by* 2 (1996), 87, table 1.

39   L. Sebro, *Mellem afrikaner og kreol: Etnisk identitet og social navigation i Dansk Vestindien 1730-1770* (Lund: Historiska Institutionen ved Lunds Universitet, 2010), 105-118.

40   For a detailed analysis of Moravian recording practices and the meaning of national labels that concentrates on St. Thomas see ibid., 51-103.

41   38.9.3. CB, PRP, case 1774-09-10 and 1777-01-08 and 38.9.10. CB, PRP, case 1798-01-18. It has not been possible to identify the location of this fort, see A. W. Lawrence, *Trade Castles & Forts of West Africa* (London: The Trinity Press, 1963).

42   38.9.15. CB, PRP, case no. 1813-2. See also CB, DP, verdict 1804-04-23 where two enslaved men carry names pointing to a Congo-identity, namely Congo Peter and Congo George, both of the Belvedere Estate; and 38.9.4. CB, PRP, case 1781-03-22, in which the "under-Bomba," or assistant driver, is called Congo Jack. For the importance of references to Africa in African American names, see J. Thornton, "Central African Names and African-American Naming Patterns," *William and Mary Quarterly* 50, no. 4 (1993).

43   38.9.2. CB, PRP, case 1773-12-20; and 38.9.17. CB, PRP, case no. 1815-34.

44   38.31.5. CB, PJ, entry 1815-08-02; and 38.9.1. CB, PRP, case 1758-10-05.

45   CB, PRP, case 1778-03-20.

46   A *skelm*, or in Dutch a *schelm*, has at least two competing meanings. It can denote a rogue, but it can also refer to a person who is making fun, is playful, flirtatious and often liminal. The compound with the word *treck*, possibly trick, or perhaps the Dutch *trek* (i.e., appetite or desire), indicates that *skelmtrek* may have meant something like "flirtatious tricks." See Oldendorp, *Historie*, I, 642; P. Stein and H. v. d. Voort, eds., *Christian Georg Andreas Oldendorp: Criolisches Wörterbuch sowie das anonyme, J. C. Kingo zugeschriebene Vestindisk Glossarium*, Lexicographica (Tübingen: Max Niemeyer Verlag, 1996), 61, 104.

47   Oldendorp, *Historie*, I, 724-725.

48   Ibid., 377, 418, 440.

49   Each African nation described the legal measures used to combat adultery in their home region, see ibid., 394-395, 412, 418, 428, 431, 440-441, 446-447. This conclusion is supported by the sketch of pre-colonial West African legal systems provided by P. J. Schwarz, *Slave Laws in Virginia* (Athens and London: University of Georgia Press, 1996), 13-34.

50   C. Robertson, "Africa into the Americas? Slavery and Women, the Family, and the Gender Division of Labor," in *More than Chattel: Black Women and Slavery in the Americas*, ed. David Barry Gaspar and Darlene Clark Hine (Bloomington: Indiana University Press, 1996), 18-19; P. M. Martin, *The External Trade of the Loango Coast, 1576-1870: The Effects of Changing Commercial Relations on the Vili Kingdom of Loango* (Oxford: Oxford University Press, 1972), 24-25; S. E. Greene, *Gender, Ethnicity, and Social*

Change on the Upper Slave Coast: A History of the Anlo-Ewe (Portsmouth, NH: Heinemann, 1996), 90;
E. G. Bay, *Wives of the Leopard. Gender, Politics, and Culture in the Kingdom of Dahomey* (Charlottesville:
University of Virginia Press, 1998), 19, 144-145.

51 Oldendorp, *Historie*, I, 738-739. For the presence of similar practices in Denmark in the eighteenth
century see T. Krogh, *Det store natmandskomplot: En historie om 1700-tallets kriminelle underverden*
(København: Samleren, 2000), 72.

52 38.9.17. CB, PRP, case 1815-05-17. The identity of the *duddlido* leaves are established through H.
West, *Hans West's Accounts of St. Croix in the West Indies*, trans. Nina York and Arnold R. Highfield
(US Virgin Islands: The Virgin Islands Humanities Council, 2004), 246. This particular ordeal is also
known from Antigua and Trinidad. In Trinidad the test was described in the caption to sketch twenty-
one, "Negro Superstition. The Doo di Doo Bush — or which is the thief" in Richard Bridgen's *West
Indian Scenery […] from sketches taken during a voyage to and residence of seven years in* […] *Trinidad*
(London, 1836), image reference NW0171, as shown on www.slaveryimages.org compiled by Jerome
S. Handler and Michael Tuite (accessed 2015-01-01). For Antigua see M. Lazarus-Black, "Slaves,
Masters and Magistrates: Law and the Politics of Resistance in the British Caribbean, 1736-1834," in
Law, Hegemony and Resistance, ed. Mindie Lazarus-Black and Susan F. Hirsch (New York: Routledge,
1994), 261. The circulation of African-Caribbean spiritual expertise in the Caribbean archipelago in
the late nineteenth and twentieth centuries is analysed by L. Putman, "Rites of Power and Rumors of
Race: The Circulation of Supernatural Knowledge in the Greater Caribbean, 1890-1940," in *Obeah
and Other Powers: The Politics of Caribbean Religion and Healing*, ed. Diana Paton and Maarit Forde
(Durham: Duke University Press, 2012). Independent courts among slaves appear to have been a
wider Caribbean phenomenon. It has been described by, among others, R. Dirks, *The Black Saturnalia:
Conflict and its Ritual Expression on British West Indian Slave Plantations* (Gainesville: University of
Florida Press, 1987), 141-142; and N. Z. Davis, "Judges, Masters, Diviners: Slaves' Experience of
Criminal Justice in Colonial Suriname," *Law and History Review* 29, no. 4, special issue (2011).

53 38.9.20. CB, PRP, case 1825-04-07. Neville Hall argues that obeah disappeared in the nineteenth
century (Hall, *Slave Society*, 113.). However, the appearance of court cases involving obeah or other
spiritual practices continued long into the nineteenth century, see Simonsen, "Magic," 266.

54 H.C. Johansen, "The Reality behind the Demographic Argument to Abolish the Danish Slave Trade,"
in *The Abolition of the Atlantic Slave Trade: Origins and Effects in Europe, Africa and the Americas*, ed.
David Eltis and James Walvin (Madison: University of Wisconsin Press, 1981), 226, table 12.2; Green-
Pedersen, "Slave Demography," 247-249; Hall, *Slave Society*, 125, table 7.1. For the wider Caribbean
see R. S. Dunn, "Sugar Production and Slave Women in Jamaica," in *Culture and Cultivation: Labor and
the Shaping of Slave Life in the Americas*, ed. Ira Berlin and Philip D. Morgan (Chalottesville: University
Press of Virginia, 1993); B. Moitt, *Women and Slavery in the French Antilles, 1635-1848* (Bloomington:
Indiana University Press, 2001), 36-56.

55 Jensen, *For the Health*, 134.

56 The complementary economic roles played by men and woman in West Africa are described by Morgan,
Laboring Women, 50-58; G. E. Brooks, *Eurafricans in Western Africa: Commerce, Social Status, Gender and
Religious Observance from the Sixteenth to the Eighteenth Century* (Athens, Ohio: Ohio University Press,
2003), 28-32; K. Okonjo, "The Dual-Sex Political System in Operation: Igbo Women and Community
Politics in Midwestern Nigeria," in *Women in Africa: Studies in Social and Economic Change*, ed. Edna
G. Bay and Nancy J. Hafkin (Palo Alto, CA: Stanford University Press, 1976).

57 G. U. Nwokeji, "African Conceptions of Gender and the Slave Traffic," *William and Mary Quarterly*
58, no. 1 (2001); C. C. Robertson and M. A. Klein, "Women's Importance in African Slave Systems,"
in *Women and Slavery in Africa*, ed. Claire C. Robertson and Martin A. Klein (Madison: University
of Wisconsin Press, 1983); Robertson, "Africa into the Americas"; Beckles, *Centering Woman*, 7; H.
Beckles, "Black Masculinity in Caribbean Slavery," in *Interrogating Caribbean Masculinities: Theoretical*

and Empirical Analyses ed. Rhoda Rheddock (Kingston: University of the West Indies Press, 2004); Morgan, *Laboring Women*, 50-68.

58   For the complementary economic roles played by rural men and women in Denmark in the eighteenth century, see A.R. Thomsen, *Lykkens smedje? Social mobilitet og social stabilitet over fem generationer i tre sogne i Salling 1750-1850* (Viborg: Landbohistorisk Selskab, 2011), 249-297; S. Busck, *Et landbosamfund i opbrud. Tradition og modernisering i Sundby sogn på Mors i tiden 1660-1800*, vol. 1 (Århus: Klim, 2011), 425-433.

59   L. Bendtsen, Intern Slavehandel på St. Croix, 1750-1848 (MA-thesis, Københavns Universitet, 2010), 88-97. See also L. Bendtsen, "Domestic Slave Trading in St. Croix, 1764-1848," *Scandinavian Journal of History* 41, no. 4-5 (2016).

60   For an introduction to the idea of the neuter as a category outside the feminine and the masculine, see E. B. Higginbotham, "African-American Women's History and the Metalanguage of Race," in *Feminism and History*, ed. Joan Wallach Scott (Oxford: Oxford University Press, 1997).

61   The amount of West Indian account material in the Danish National Archives demonstrates the time colonial administrators spent thinking about slaves as labor and capital. Account material constitutes 150 shelf-meters, whereas all other material produced by the colonial administration and kept in the National Archives constitutes 800 shelf-meters. Another illustration of this way of thinking about slaves is the fact that, in cases where free Europeans or Afro-Caribbeans helped slaves to flee, they were prosecuted according to a metropolitan legal code on the grand theft of cattle, see P. E. Olsen, "Danske Lov på de vestindiske øer," in *Danske og Norske Lov i 300 år*, ed. Ditlev Tamm (København: Jurist- og Økonomforbundets Forlag, 1983), 307.

62   R. Haagensen, *Description of the Island of St. Croix in America in the West Indies*, trans. Arnold R. Highfield (St. Croix: The Virgin Islands Humanities Council, 1995), 22. See also P.L. Oxholm, *De Danske Vestindiske Öers Tilstand i Henseende til Population, Cultur og Finance-Forfatning, i anledning af nogle Breve fra St. Croix indrykkede i det Politiske og Physiske Magazin for Marts og April Maaneder 1797 hvortil er föiet Beskrivelse om Sukkerets Fabrikation, med 4 Planer* (København: Johan Frederik Schultz, 1797), 42.

63   *J.L. Carstens' St. Thomas in early Danish Times: A General Description of all the Danish, American or West Indian Islands*, trans. Arnold R. Highfield (St. Croix: Virgin Islands Humanities Council, 1997), 77-78; Oldendorp, *Historie*, I, 615, 623. For the idea that African women gave birth without pain, see *A General*, 77; Haagensen, *Description*, 55-56. See also *J. L. Carstens: En Almindelig Beskrivelse om alle de Danske, Americanske eller West-Jndiske Ey-Lande* (København: Dansk Vestindisk Forlag, 1981); R. Haagensen, *Beskrivelse over Eylandet St. Croix i America i Vest-Indien* (København: Lillies Enke, 1758).

64   Morgan, *Laboring Women*.

65   *A General*, 50; Oldendorp, *Historie*, I, 545, 560; West, *Accounts of St. Croix*, 38. For the wider Atlantic see for instance Moitt, *Women and Slavery*, 55; Morgan, *Laboring Women*, 62-63; R. Olwell, "'Loose, Idle and Disorderly': Slave Women in the Eighteenth-Century Charleston Marketplace," in *More than Chattel: Black Women and Slavery in the Americas*, ed. David Barry Gaspar and Darlene Clark Hine (Bloomington: Indiana University Press, 1996).

66   For court cases involving drivers, all men, see 38.5.19. CB, GRP, case 1781-03-08; 38.9.4. CB, PRP, case 1779-09-22, 1780-01-15, 1781-03-22; 38.9.5. CB, PRP, case 1781-09-06; 38.9.11. CB, PRP, case no. 1800-28, 1800-29, 1802-06, 1802-07, 1802-10, 1802-27, 1802-28, 1803-17; 38.9.18. CB, PRP, case no. 1820-36, 1820-39; and 38.9.19. CB, PRP, case no. 1821-48, 1821-49, 1821-53.

67   Johansen, "The Reality," 226, table 12.

68   Hall, *Slave Society*, 88-90.

69   For an overview of the development of racial thinking in the early modern period, see W.D. Jordan, *White over Black: American Attitudes Toward the Negro 1550-1812* (Chapel Hill: University of North Carolina Press, 1968); B. Braude, "The Sons of Noah and the Construction of Ethnic and Geographical Identities in the Medieval and Early Modern Periods," *William and Mary Quarterly* 54, no. 1 (1997); K.F.

Hall, *Things of Darkness. Economies of Race and Gender in Early Modern England* (Ithaca and London: Cornell University Press, 1995); see also P. Brantlinger, *Dark Vanishings. Discourse on the Extinction of Primitive Races, 1800-1930* (Ithaca, New York: Cornell University Press, 2003).

70 Cited from J.E. Loftin, The Abolition of the Danish Slave Trade (Ph.D.-thesis, Louisiana State University, 1977), 223.

71 38.9.2. CB, PRP, case 1774-07-02, the interrogation is continued in 38.9.3. CB, PRP, case 1774-07-05. See also 38.9.5. CB, PRP, case 1783-04-03.

72 Oldendorp, *Historie*, I, 641; *A General*, 65-66.

73 Generalkirkeinspektionskollegiet. F4-8-20-21, Indkomne sager 1784-1791, Torkild Lund to August Kreydal, entry 1788-12-13.

74 Oldendorp, *Historie*, I, 727-728.

75 Generalkirkeinspektionskollegiet. F4-8-20-21, Indkomne sager 1784-1791, Torkild Lund to August Kreydal, entry 1788-12-13.

76 *A General*, 65-66.

77 M.V. Olsen, Frie afrocaribiske kvinder i Christiansted, St. Croix, Dansk Vestindien ca. 1780-1820 (MA-thesis, Københavns Universitet, 2010), 32, 35-36. See also M.V. Olsen, "Sexual Relationships and Working Lives of Free Afro-Caribbean Women," *Scandinavian Journal of History* 41, no. 4-5 (2016).

78 E. Rezende, Cultural Identity of the Free Colored in Christiansted, St. Croix, Danish West Indies 1800-1848 (Ph.D.-thesis, The Union Institute, 1997), 411-420. See also https://www.virgin-islands-history.org/historien/skaebnehistorier/maria-elizabeth-yard-frifarvet-forretningskvinde/ (accessed 2016-11-14).

79 West, *Accounts of St. Croix*, 24. See also H. West, *Beretning om det danske Eiland St. Croix i Vestindien fra Junii Maaned 1789 til Junii Maaneds Udgang 1790* (København1790); H. West, *Bidrag til Beskrivelse over Ste Croix med en kort udsigt over St. Thomas, St. Jean, Tortola, Spanish Town and Crabeneiland* (København: Friderik Wilhelm Thiele, 1793).

80 Haagensen, *Description*, 55-56.

81 For the Moravian missionaries in the Danish West Indies, see H. Lawaetz, *Brødremenighedens Mission i Dansk-Vestindien, 1769-1848* (København: Otto B. Wroblewski, 1902); A.R. Highfield, "Patterns of Accommodation and Resistance: The Moravian Witness To Slavery in the Danish West Indies," *The Journal of Caribbean History* 28, no. 2 (1994); J.F. Sensbach, *Rebecca's Revival: Creating Black Christianity in the Atlantic World* (Cambridge, MA: Harvard University Press, 2005). The Moravians were also active in other parts of the Caribbean and in North America and appear to have modeled their engagements on their experiences in the Danish West Indies, see E.V. Goveia, *Slave Society in the British Leeward Islands at the End of the Eighteenth Century* (Westport, CT: Greenwood Publishers, 1980), 263-310; J.F. Sensbach, *A Separate Canaan: The Making of an Afro-Moravian World in North Carolina, 1763-1840* (Chapel Hill: University of North Carolina Press, 1998). According to Fogleman, the early Moravians experimented with a radical transformation of their gender order. His findings pertain to the first part of the eighteenth century after which the Church adopted more conventional ideas about the relationship between men and women, see A.S. Fogleman, *Jesus Is Female: Moravians and Radical Religion in Early America* (Philadelphia: University of Pennsylvania Press, 2007).

82 Oldendorp, *Historie*, I, 531, 566-567, quote from 567.

83 F. Lindvad, De afrikanske hjælpere i Brødremenigheden i Dansk Vestindien: En undersøgelse af menighedsfællesskabet og omvendelsen (MA-thesis, Københavns Universitet, 2014), 66.

84 Lawaetz states that the following governors supported the mission: Clausen, Roepstorff, Lindemann, Malleville, and von Scholten, see Lawaetz, *Brødremenighedens Mission i Dansk-Vestindien, 1769-1848*, 30, 34, 116-121, 133, 160-162.

85 Ibid., 134-139, 155. Oldendorp, *Historie*, I, 567, 646-647.

86 Sensbach, *Rebecca's*, 102-105.

87   C.G.A. Oldendorp, *History of the Mission of the Evangelical Brethern on the Caribbean Islands of St. Thomas, St. Croix and St. John*, trans. A.R. Highfield and Vladimir Barac (Ann Arbor: Karoma Publishers, Inc., 1987), 541-543. The African helpers in the Moravian mission are treated in Lawaetz, *Brødremenighedens Mission i Dansk-Vestindien, 1769-1848*, 87, 130 and 140; C. Degn, *Die Schimmelmanns im atlantischen Dreickshandel. Gewinn und Gewissen* (Neumünster: Karl Wachholtz Verlag, 1984), 338-339; Sensbach, *Rebecca's*.

88   Pope, "Cruzan Slavery," table 1, 59-69.

89   Generalkirkeinspektionskollegiet. F4-8-20-21. Indkomne sager 1784-1791. Torkild Lund to August Kreydal, entry 1788-12-13.

90   Pope, "Cruzan Slavery," 16, 56-69, table 1. The number of baptisms per year is calculated on the basis of figures in table 1. See also Lawaetz' description of the mission stations Friedensfeld and Friedensberg. The missionary efforts of the Moravians were, according to Lawaetz, successful until 1817. In 1817-1823 the mission suffered a crisis when older and experienced personnel passed away. The arriving staff showed more interest in craft and trade than in evangelizing; see Lawaetz, *Brødremenighedens Mission i Dansk-Vestindien, 1769-1848*, 52,111,139-160.

91   If all slaves who were baptized on the Friedensthal mission between 1760 and 1799 had survived until 1799, then they would have constituted around 18 percent of the enslaved population in St. Croix. With a mortality rate of 36 deaths per 1000 slaves, Moravian baptized slaves would constitute around 13 percent of all slaves in 1799 (the mortality rate is calculated on the basis of a census of plantation slaves made in 1804, see Johansen, "The Reality," 225-229; Green-Pedersen, "Slave Demography," 247-249, table 13.1.

92   Oldendorp, *Historie*, I, 533, 566-570, 643-649, 725-726.

93   K.H. Jansson, "Marriage, Family and Gender in Swedish Political Language, 1750-1820," in *Scandinavia in the Age of Revolution. Nordic Political Cultures, 1740-1820*, ed. Pasi Ihalainen, et al. (Surrey: Ashgate, 2011).

94   K. Lützen, *Byen Tæmmes. Kernefamilie, sociale reformer og velgørenhed i 1800-tallets København* (København: Hans Reitzels Forlag, 1998); B. Possing, *Viljens Styrke: Natalie Zahle – En biografi om dannelse, køn og magtfuldkommenhed* (København: Gyldendal, 1992); J. Engelhardt, *Borgerskab og fællesskab. De patriotiske selskaber i den danske helstat, 1769-1814* (København: Museum Tusculanums Forlag, 2010), 333-342; T. Bredsdorff, *Den brogede oplysning. Om følelsernes fornuft og fornuftens følelse i 1700-tallets nordiske litteratur* (København: Gyldendal, 2003); S.M.S. Pearsall, *Atlantic Families. Lives and Letters in the Later Eighteenth Century* (Oxford: Oxford University Press, 2008).

95   C. Gold, *Educating Middle Class Daughters: Private Girls Schools in Copenhagen 1790-1820* (Copenhagen: Museum Tusculanum Press, 1996), 19; Lützen, *Byen Tæmmes*, 72-74; C. Gold, *Danish Cookbooks: Domesticity and National Identity, 1616-1901* (Seattle: University of Washington Press and Museum Tusculanum Press, 2007), 61-75, 81-89; Engelhardt, *Borgerskab og fællesskab*, 83-87, 195-199, 221-234, 333-344.

96   H.H. Knap, "Danskerne og slaveriet: Negerslavedebatten i Danmark indtil 1792," in *Dansk kolonihistorie. Indføring og studier*, ed. Peter Hoxcer Jensen, et al. (Århus: Historia, 1981), 153-174.

97   N.J. Koefoed, *Besovede kvindfolk og ukærlige barnefædre. Køn, ret og sædelighed i 1700-tallets Danmark* (København: Museum Tusculanums Forlag, 2008), 77-221.

98   Ibid., 223-307.

99   A. Clark, *Desire: A History of European Sexuality* (New York and London: Routledge, 2008), 139-140; Gold, *Educating Middle Class*, 17-52. For the gendering of whiteness, see C. Jones, *Engendering Whiteness: White Women and Colonialism in Barbados and North Carolina, 1627-1865* (Manchester: Manchester University Press, 2007).

100   Hall, *Slave Society*, 111 and 200, table 11.1.

101   Johansen, "The Reality," 226, table 12.2; Hall, *Slave Society*, 200, table 11.1.

102   Johansen, "The Reality," 226, table 12.2; Hall, *Slave Society*, 83-84.

103 The focus on the family lives of slaves and ex-slaves was by no means particular to the Danish West Indies, see for instance P. Scully, *Liberating the Family? Gender and British Slave Emancipation in the Rural Western Cape, South Africa, 1823-1853* (Portsmouth, NH: Heinemann, 1997); J. De Barros, *Reproducing the British Caribbean, Sex, Gender, and Population Politics after Slavery* (Chapel Hill: University of North Carolina Press, 2014); P. Scully and D. Paton, eds., *Gender and Slave Emancipation in the Atlantic World* (Durham: Duke University Press, 2005).

104 E. Gøbel, *Det danske slavehandelsforbud 1792, studier og kilder til forhistorien, forordningen og følgerne* (Odense: Syddansk Universitetsforlag, 2008), 69-73, 86-88; Loftin, "The Abolition of the Danish Slave Trade," 77. See also E. Gøbel, *The Danish Slave Trade and its Abolition* (Leiden and Boston: Brill, 2016); P. Røge, "Why the Danes Got There First: A Trans-Imperial Study of the Abolition of the Danish Slave Trade in 1792," *Slavery & Abolition* 35, no. 4 (2014); C.A. Trier, "Det dansk-vestindiske Negerindførselsforbud af 1792," *Historisk Tidsskrift* 5 (1904).

105 Privatarkiv nr. 6285, Heinrich Ernst Schimmelmann (1747-1831), ny aflevering, pk. 32, Breve fra administratorerne på plantagen "La Princesse," St. Croix, Charles Vanderbourg og La Porte, 1796-1798, Letter from Vanderbourg and La Porte to H.E. Schimmelmann, date 1796-02-18. See also U. Langen, *Revolutionens skygger. Franske emigranter og andre folk i København 1789-1814* (Denmark: Lindhardt og Ringhof, 2005), 298-299.

106 Loftin, "The Abolition of the Danish Slave Trade," 166.

107 Ibid., 193-198.

108 Ibid., 192, 240, 270.

109 K.F. Olwig, *Cultural Adaptation and Resistance on St. John: Three Centuries of Afro-Caribbean Life* (Gainesville: University of Florida Press, 1985), 42-85; Johansen, "The Reality," 225-227.

110 Gøbel, *Det danske slavehandelsforbud*, 124-131.

111 Loftin, "The Abolition of the Danish Slave Trade," 221-225, quotation from 224.

112 The increasing role played by the metropolitan states in the Caribbean in the late eighteenth and nineteenth centuries was a development that the Danish West Indies shared with the British, French and Spanish Caribbean colonies, see D.P. Geggus, "Slavery, War, and Revolution in the Greater Caribbean, 1789-1815," in *A Turbulent Time: The French Revolution and the Greater Caribbean*, ed. David Barry Gaspar and David Patrick Geggus (Bloomington: Indiana University Press, 1997), 2-3, 30; E. Brathwaite, *The Development of Creole Society in Jamaica 1770-1820* (Oxford: Clarendon Press, 1971). For Danish West Indian state formation see Jensen, *For the Health*, 151-244; J.F. Johansen, "Landskolerne — Skoler for slavebørn på landet," in *Skoler i palmernes skygge*, ed. Julie Fryd Johansen, Jesper Eckhardt Larsen, and Vagn Skovgaard-Petersen (Odense: Syddansk Universitetsforlag, 2008); R.B. Sielemann, Natures of Conduct: Governmentality and the Danish West Indies (Ph.D.-thesis, Købenavns Universitet, 2015).

113 38.5.28. CB, GRP, case 1804-07-27.

114 For works on the narrative elements of legal processes, see N.Z. Davis, *Fiction in the Archives: Pardon Tales and Their Tellers in Sixteenth-Century France* (Palo Alto, CA: Stanford University Press, 1987); L.W. Bennett and M.S. Feldman, *Reconstructing Reality in the Courtroom* (London: Tavistock Publications, 1981); P. Brooks and P. Gewirtz, eds., *Law's Stories* (London: Yale University Press, 1996); N. Mezey, "Law as Culture," in *Cultural Analysis, Cultural Studies, and the Law*, ed. Austin Sarat and Jonathan Simon (Durham and London: Duke University Press, 2003).

115 See n. 9 in the introduction.

116 1755-03-31, "Anordning om Justitiens og Politiets Administration paa St. Croix, St. Thomas og St. Jan" in *Chronologisk Register over de Kongelige Forordninger og Aabne Breve, som fra Aar 1670 af ere udkomne* (København: 1777-1850).

117 This practice received legal confirmation in a local ordinance of 1760, which underlined that the "*forum delicti*" for slaves were the ordinary Danish West Indian courts, see 2.1.1. GG, PB, ordinance

of 1760-11-01; and 421. Generaltoldkammerets vestindiske og guineiske sager, Anmærkninger ved forslaget til negerloven. Tillige med supplement, grunde og analogi for samme, 169.

118 1755-03-31, "Anordning om Justitiens og Politiets Administration paa St. Croix, St. Thomas og St. Jan" in *Chronologisk Register*. An early overview of the so-called 'police-law' is provided in J.L.U.K. Rosenvinge, *Grundrids af den danske politiret: Til brug ved Forelæsninger* (København: Den Gyldendalske Boghandels Forlag, 1825). Danish legal institutions and practices in the eighteenth and nineteenth centuries have not received comprehensive analysis. However, a good overview can be obtained through the following works: P. Bagge, J.L. Frost, and B. Hjejle, eds., *Højesteret, 1661-1961*, 2 vol. (København: GEC Gads Forlag, 1961); D. Tamm, *Retshistorie – Danmark – Europa – globale perspektiver* (København: Jurist- og Økonomforbundets Forlag, 2005); T. Krogh, *Oplysningstiden og det magisk: Henrettelser og korporlige straffe i 1700-tallets første halvdel* (København: Samleren, 2000); E. Österberg and S. Sogner, eds., *People Meet the Law: Control and Conflict Handling in the Courts, Nordic Countries in the Post-Reformation and Pre-Industrial Period* (Olso: Universitetsforlaget, 2000); P.U. Knudsen, *Lovkyndighed og vederhæftighed: Sjællandske byfogeder 1682-1801* (København: Jurist- og økonomforbundets Forlag, 2001); T. Munch, "Keeping the Peace. 'Good Police' and Civic Order in 18th-Century Copenhagen," *Scandinavian Journal of History* 32, no. 1 (2007); J. Mührmann-Lund, Borgerligt Regimente. Politiforvaltningen i købstæderne og på landet under den danske enevælde (Ph.D.-thesis, Aalborg University, 2011); I. Dübeck, "'alt hvis Politien egentlig vedkommer …' Forholdet mellem Danske Lov og den såkaldte politianordning," in *Danske og Norske Lov i 300 år*, ed. Ditlev Tamm (København: Jurist- og Økonomforbundets Forlag, 1983).

119 1755-03-31, "Anordning om Justitiens og Politiets Administration paa St. Croix, St. Thomas og St. Jan" in *Chronologisk Register*; Vibæk, *Dansk Vestindien 1755-1848*, 2, 16-18; Olsen, "Danske Lov," 291-299.

120 38.9.2. CB, PRP, case 1772-07-14.

121 In the years 1780-1782, 1800-1803 and 1820-1822 transcripts of interrogations in slave trials made in Christiansted Police Court were sent to the governor general in 40 percent of the trials whereas the overall percentage of such dispatches was around 20 percent. For cases with slave defendants, 37 out of 84 cases were sent on to other legal institutions (mainly the governor general). For all defendants, 132 out of a total of 616 cases were forwarded to other legal institutions (the estimates are based on 38.9.4, 38.9.5, 38.9.11, 38.9.18 and 38.9.19 CB, PRP).

122 Knudsen, *Lovkyndighed*, 203-212, 285-290, 324-348.

123 Olsen, "Danske Lov; P.E. Olsen, "De dansk-vestindiske øer og junigrundloven," *Historie* 18, ny række, no. 1 (1989); *Le Code Noir au le calvaire de Canaan*, ed. Louis Sala-Molins (Paris: Presses Universitaires de France, 1987); a study of the legal reverberations of the Code Noir is provided by Ghachem, *The Old Regime and the Haitian Revolution*. For legal borrowings in the Caribbean see also D.B. Gaspar, "With a Rod of Iron: Barbados Slave Laws as a Model for Jamaica, South Carolina, and Antigua, 1661-1697," in *Crossing Boundaries. Comparative History of Black People in Diaspora*, ed. Darlene Clark Hine and Jacqueline McLeod (Bloomington: Indiana University Press, 1999); D.B. Gaspar, "'Rigid and Inclement': Origins of the Jamaica Slave Laws of the Seventeenth Century," in *The Many Legalities of Early America*, ed. Bruce H. Mann and Christopher L. Tomlins (Chapel Hill: University of North Carolina Press, 2001); E.B. Rugemer, "The Development of Mastery and Race in the Comprehensive Slave Codes of the Greater Caribbean during the Seventeenth Century," *William and Mary Quarterly* 70, no. 3 (2013).

124 Verdicts containing references to the slave code of 1755, see 38.6.21. CB, DP, verdict 1801-02-14; 38.6.23. CB, DP, verdict 1805-10-24 and 1805-02-04; 38.6.24. CB, DP, verdict 1807-01-20 and 1809-02-06; 38.6.25. CB, DP, verdict 1811-12-06 and 1811-06-27; 38.6.26. CB, DP, verdict 1813-09-18, 1814-01-28 and 1814-03-09; 38.6.27. CB, DP, verdict 1816-11-16; and 38.6.29. CB, DP, verdict 1823-09-27; 38.6.30. CB, DP, verdict 1824-01-27; 38.6.31. CB, DP, verdict 1833-07-09 and 1838-04-09.

125 Kommercekollegiet, Dansk-norske sekretariat, nr. 17, forordninger, 1735-1770, 126-148.

126 Governor Gardelin's slave regulations from 1733 can be found in a Dutch-Creole version in 2.1.1. GG, PB, 1733-1782. For a Danish version of the code see 390. Generaltoldkammerets vestindiske og guineiske sager, Visdomsbog, 1733-1783, 359-363.

127 1830-10-22, "Rskr. (til den vestindiske Regjering) ang. Negerslavers Antagelse til edeligt Vidnesbyrd," in *Kongelige Rescripter, Resolutioner og Collegialbreve for Danmark, Norge, udtogsviis udgivne* (København: 1786-1871).

128 P.E. Olsen, "Fra ejendomsret til menneskeret," in *Fra slaveri til frihed. Det dansk-vestindiske slavesamfund 1672-1848*, ed. Per Nielsen (København: Nationalmuseet, 2001), 47-51; Hall, *Slave Society*, 69.

129 3.40. Den Vestindiske Regering, Guvernementet på St. Croix. Instruktionsprotokol, Instruktion for generalguvernøren, regeringen såvel som de secrete råd på de kongelige danske ejlande i Amerika i henseende til justitsvæsenet sammesteds, entry 1771-10-12, article 4.

130 *Kong Christian den Femtis Danske Lov*, ed. V.A. Secher (København: Schultz, 1891), 857.

131 Generaltoldkammeret, Vestindiske-guineiske Sager, Diverse, Visdomsbog, 1733-1783, 359-363.

132 38.9.11. CB, PRP, case 1802-09-25.

133 Whereas the Danish West Indian administration excluded references to the national affiliation of Africans, this was not the case in the British colony, Berbice, in the 1820s. Here the term "countryman" was regularly used in the records of the Protector of the Slaves, see Lean, "The Secret Lives," 235, 245-250.

134 2.1.1, 2.1.2, 2.1.4, 2.1.5, 2.1.7, 2.1.8, GG, PB, from 1755 to 1803; the two placards were 2.1.1. GG, PB, ordinance of 1759-12-23, and 2.1.7. GG, PB, ordinance of 1786-05-13.

135 2.1.7. GG, PB, ordinance of 1786-05-13, see also 2.1.1. GG, PB, ordinance of 1774-10-05. For other ordinances that described free Africans and Afro-Caribbeans as men and women, see 2.1.1. GG, PB, ordinance of 1774-01-20, 1775-09-27 and 1775-10-12. The same differentiation of punishment according to gender was present in *The Danish Law*, see Bagge, Frost, and Hjejle, *Højesteret, 1661-1961*, 79.

136 A thorough analysis of legal aspects of illegitimacy in Denmark can be found in Koefoed, *Besovede kvindfolk*.

137 Olsen, "Frie afrocaribiske kvinder," 43-45. I have only identified four trials concerning illegitimate children in the courts of Christiansted; none of them involved slave women, see 38.6.24. CB, DP, verdict 1807-12-15, 38.6.28. CB, DP, verdict 1819-09-11, 38.9.22. CB, PRP, case 1836-06-15, and 8.9.21. CB, PRP, case 1829-11-28.

138 Danske Kancelli, F26, Vestindiske Sager 1773-1786, royal ordinance 1784-12-24, 578-579. For a study of the conditions enabling sexual abuse of enslaved women see also E. Donoghue, *Black Women/White Men: The Sexual Exploitation of Female Slaves in the Danish West Indies* (Trenton: Africa World Press, Inc., 2002).

139 38.9.2. CB, PRP, case 1773-03-06.

140 For the presence of defense attorneys, see 38.6.13. CB, DP, verdict 1779-04-23; 38.6.14. CB, DP, verdict 1781-01-03; 2.5.1. GG, Kopibøger til lokale myndigheder og personer, entry 1796-08-06; and 2.27.1. GG, RP B, entry 1820-10-12. The first case in which slaves were sentenced with the participation of lay jurymen emerged in 1799. In this case an enslaved man was sentenced to work in the fortress for life, see 38.6.21. CB, DP, verdict 1799-05-01. In the period from 1803-1808 there are no references to these jurymen, but from 1809 onward they appear again in capital cases against slaves in Christiansted Lower Court. For verdicts prescribing death penalties and confirmed by lay jurymen, see 38.6.21. CB, DP, verdict 1801-07-03 and 1801-10-21; 38.6.22. CB, DP, verdict 1802-06-23 and 1802-10-20; 38.6.24. CB, DP, verdict 1809-02-06; 38.6.25. CB, DP, verdict 1812-07-07; 38.6.26. CB, DP, verdict 1813-05-07; 38.6.28. CB, DP, verdict, 1818-11-10; 38.6.29. CB, DP, verdict 1820-12-14; and 38.6.29. CB, DP, verdict 1823-09-27. For verdicts containing death penalties of slaves with no recorded confirmation of lay jurymen, see 38.6.21. CB, DP, verdict 1801-09-14; 38.6.22. CB, DP, verdict 1804-01-16; 38.6.23.

CB, DP, verdict 1805-02-04, 1804-11-02, 1804-11-05, 1805-12-04, 1806-05-05 and 1806-02-04; and 38.6.24. CB, DP, verdict 1807-01-20.) See also Olsen, in Tamm, ed., 1983, 313.

141 38.9.4. CB, PRP, case 1780-10-20; CB, PRP, case 1781-11-28; 38.9.11. CB, PRP, case 1802-08-14 and 1803-08-02.

142 For the various ways of translating the title *byfoged* into English, see E. Gøbel, *A Guide to Sources for the History of the Danish West Indies (U.S. Virgin Islands), 1671-1917* (Odense: University Press of Southern Denmark, 2002), 343; Hall, *Slave Society*, v.

143 Reviderede Regnskaber, Vestindiske Regnskaber, Matrikler for St. Croix, 86.4-86.8, 1761, 6; 1762, 12; 1763, 25; 1764, 9 and 29; 1765, 109; 1766, 153.

144 A. Falk-Jensen and H. Hjorth-Nielsen, *Candidati og examinati juris 1736-1939* (København: G.E.C. Gad, 1954), 294.

145 Vibæk, *Dansk Vestindien 1755-1848*, 2, 94-95.

146 In the period 1756-1848, there were, at least, thirteen officers holding the position as judge in Christiansted Lower Court, some with an interim appointment, and most also holding the corresponding office as chief of police, see *Hof- og Statskalenderen* (published by various publishers and with various titles since 1734). Short biographical data on most of these are provided in Falk-Jensen and Hjorth-Nielsen, *Candidati*.

147 K.A. Schmidt, Det kongelige civile vestindiske embedskorps 1800 til 1848 med særligt henblik på sammensætning og karriereforhold (MA-thesis, Københavns Universitet, 1980), 1-38; E. Gøbel, *De styrede rigerne: embedsmændene i den dansk-norske civile centraladministration 1660-1814* (Odense: Odense Universitets Forlag, 2000); L. Sebro, "Kreoliseringen af eurocaribierne i Dansk Vestindien – sociale relationer og selvopfattelse," *Fortid og nutid* 2 (2005). For Hesselberg, see *Dansk Biografisk Leksikon* online: http://denstoredanske.dk/Dansk_Biografisk_Leksikon (accessed 2016-04-08).

148 The family connection is documented in Falk-Jensen and Hjorth-Nielsen, *Candidati*, see under Edvard Røring Colbjørnsen. The careers of Jacob E. Colbjørnsen and Christian Colbjørnsen are described in *Dansk Biografisk Leksikon* online: http://denstoredanske.dk/Dansk_Biografisk_Leksikon (accessed 2016-04-08).

149 See for example 38.9.4. CB, PRP, case 1780-10-20; 38.5.19. CB, GRP, case 1783-06-28; and 38.6.25. CB, DP, verdict 1811-12-06.

150 38.6.6. CB, DP, verdict 1764-05-23.

151 The estimate is based on all cases appearing in Christiansted Police Court in the periods, 1780-82, 1800-03, 1820-22 (38.9.04, 38.9.05, 38.9.11, 38.9.18 and 38.9.19, CB, PRP). For examples of slaves testifying in slave trials, see 38.9.4. CB, PRP, case 1781-05-04; 38.9.5. CB, PRP, case 1781-07-27 and 1782-10-03; 38.9.11. CB, PRP, case 1800-08-26, 1801-01-03, 1802-03-07 and 1802-07-28; 38.9.18. CB, PRP, case 1820-07-20, 1821-06-15, 1822-02-28 and 1822-09-26. For examples of slaves testifying against free West Indians, see CB, PRP, case 1780-01-15, 1780-02-23; CB, PRP, case 1782-06-20 and 1782-10-05; CB, PRP, case 1800-08-14, 1800-12-03, 1802-05-22 and 1803-08-02; CB, PRP, case 1820-03-16 and 1820-10-26; 38.9.19. CB, PRP, case 1821-03-05 and 1822-02-06.

152 See, for example, T.D. Morris, "Slaves and the Rules of Evidence in Criminal Trials," *Chicago-Kent Law Review* 68 (1993); T.D. Morris, *Southern Slavery and the Law, 1619-1860* (Chapel Hill: University of North Carolina Press, 1996).

153 In the early 1780s there were no such recorded complaints, but from 1798 to 1816 as many as 122 complaints were made by slaves, individually and collectively to Christiansted's chief of police, see 38.31.1-38.31.5. CB, PJ, 1798-1816. For complaints reaching Christiansted Police Court and Lower Court see 38.6.1-32. CB, DP, 1756-1848 & 38.18.1-9, CB, Pådømte sager, 1756-1848, and 39.9.1-24. CB, PRP, 1756-1841.

154 See for example: 38.6.1-2. CB, DP, verdict 1756-08-02; 38.6.3. CB, DP, verdict 1760-12-08; 38.6.7. CB, DP, verdict no. 1765-315; 38.6.8-9. CB, DP, verdict 1769-06-14; 38.6.11. CB, DP, verdict 1772-11-21; 38.9.5. CB, PRP, case 1782-10-19 and 1781-10-15; 38.9.11. CB, PRP, case 1800-08-14, 1801-12-11

and 1803-07-13, 1803-03-21 and 1803-09-30; 38.9.18. CB, PRP, case 1820-09-13 and 1820-11-15; 38.9.19. CB, PRP, case 1821-01-24, 1821-04-17, 1821-07-12, 1821-10-16; 38.6.32. CB, DP, verdict 1845-07-01.

155   For the role of rumors, see 3.81.73. Den Vestindiske Regering, Guvernementet på St. Croix, Gruppeordnede sager 2, Lokale myndigheder: Breve vedr. justits- og politivæsenet, letter from Chief of Police Lundbye (Frederiksted) to Governor General Schimmelmann, entry 1785-06-10; 38.9.4. CB, PRP, case 1780-01-15; and 3.33.4. Den Vestindiske Regering, Guvernementet på St. Croix, Kopibrevprotokoller for skrivelser til lokaladministrationen m.fl., entry 1779-01-04.

156   See, for instance, 38.6.13. CB, DP, verdict 1778-08-10; 8.6.16. CB, DP, verdict 1786-11-04; 38.6.18. CB, DP, verdict 1794-12-03; 38.6.21. CB, DP, verdict 1799-11-01; 38.6.24. CB, DP, verdict 1806-11-25; 38.6.26. CB, DP, verdict 1813-05-07; and 38.6.28. CB, DP, verdict 1818-11-10. For short discussions of metropolitan law concerning illicit sexuality, see M.B. Pedersen, "Usædelige ugerninger – Utugt og straf indtil 1800-tallet," in *Det bedste selskab. Festskrift til Jens Engberg i anledning af halvfjerdsårsdagen*, ed. Merete Bøge Pedersen and Anne Trine Larsen (København: Selskabet til Forskning i Arbejderbevægelsens Historie, 2006); and H. Stevnsborg, "'Samfundets' og 'statens' strafferetspleje. Lovgivning og praksis i københavnske prostitutionssager i slutningen af det 17. og begyndelsen af det 18. århundrede," *Historisk tidsskrift* 82, no. 14. rk. bd. III (1982).

157   For marooning, see, for example, 38.9.5. CB, PRP, case 1782-04-17. For theft, see 38.6.20. CB, DP, verdict 1798-06-21.

158   Trials and police examinations concerned with the maltreatment of enslaved people grew significantly from the mid-eighteenth century on. The cases are distributed as follows: 1756-1770: 1; 1770-1789: 12; 1790-1809: 51; 1810-1829: 57; 1830-1848: 17. The numbers are based on 38.6.1-32. CB, DP, 1756-1848 & 38.18.1-9, CB, Pådømte sager, 1756-1848, and 38.9.1-24. CB, PRP, 1756-1841.

159   38.6.21. CB. DP, verdict 1801-02-14, see also 38.6.26. CB, DP, verdict 1815-12-30.

160   38.6.25. CB, DP, verdict 1812-07-07.

161   The fact that enslaved people appeared in court, either in person or as subjects of legal dispute, with a range of social characteristics also stands out in other studies of local litigation, see for instance A.J. Gross, *Double Character. Slavery and Mastery in the Antebellum Courtroom* (Princeton: Princeton University Press, 2000).

162   See, for instance, 38.5.19. CB, GRP, case 1783-06-28; CB, PRP, case 1783-06-02; 38.9.11. CB, PRP, case 1800-12-11; 38.9.12. CB, PRP, case 1804-07-16; 38.11.2. CB, KP, case 1818-10-28 and 1819-12-08; 38.9.19. CB, PRP, case 1821-02-07.

163   38.5.24. CB, GRP, case 1799-10-04.

164   38.9.5. CB, PRP, case 1782-06-20.

165   38.9.9. CB, PRP, case 1791-12-03.

166   38.9.11. CB, PRP, case 1802-04-24.

167   38.9.11. CB, PRP, case 1802-07-28.

168   38.9.10. CB. PRP, case 1797-07-06. For other examples of how enslaved people declared their Christian faith see 38.9.2. CB, PRP, case 1764-10-02; 38.9.10. CB, PRP, case 1798-01-02; 38.9.11. CB, PRP, case 1800-12-03.

169   The shifting role of Christianity in Danish perceptions of Africans has been analyzed by S.E. Green-Pedersen, "Teologi og negerslaveri. Om Erik Pontoppidans fortale til L.F. Rømer: Tilforladelig Efterretning om Kysten Guinea, 1760," in *Festskrift til Povl Bagge. På havlfjerdårsdagen 30. november 1972*, ed. Johny Leisner, Lorenz Rerup, and Vagn Skovgaard-Petersen (København: Den Danske Historiske Forening, 1972); S.E. Green-Pedersen, "Negro Slavery and Christianity: On Erik Pontoppidan's preface to L. F. Roemer Tilforladelig Efterretning om Kysten Guinea (A true account of the Coast of Guinea), 1760," *Transactions of the Historical Society of Ghana* 15, no. 1 (1974).

170   38.9.4. CB, PRP, case 1781-03-22.

171   *Kong Christian den Femtis Danske Lov*, 1009.

172 See, for example, 38.9.4. CB, PRP, case 1780-06-30; 38.9.5. CB, PRP, case 1782-06-12; and 38.9.11. CB, PRP, case 1803-08-02, 1803-09-30 and 1804-11-04.

173 See 38.9.4. CB, PRP, case 1779-09-23 and 1780-01-15; 38.9.5. CB, PRP, case 1781-09-11 and 1782-06-20; 38.9.11. CB, PRP, case 1800-08-26, 1800-09-03, 1801-08-04, 1802-06-23, 1802-09-13 and 1803-02-04.

174 38.9.11. CB, PRP, case no. 1800-29.

175 See, for instance, 38.9.4. CB, PRP, case 1780-03-22; 38.9.5. CB, PRP, case 1782-01-14; 38.6.15. CB, DP, verdict 1784-12-15; 38.9.11. CB, PRP, case 1800-08-26; and 38.9.18. CB, PRP, case 1820-07-20.

176 For examples, see 38.11.2. CB, KP, case 1818-10-28 and 38.6.15. CB, DP, verdict 1784-11-29.

177 38.9.2. CB, PRP, case 1773-03-06.

178 38.9.4. CB, PRP, case 1780-03-22.

179 38.6.15. CB, DP, verdict 1784-11-29; see also 38.9.5. CB, PRP, case 1782-10-14 and 1782-08-07; 38.5.19. CB, GRP, case 1783-08-06; and 38.9.19. CB, PRP, case 1822-10-07.

180 Generaltoldkammeret, Vestindiske-guineiske Sager, Diverse, Visdomsbog, 1733-1783, 359-363.

181 See 38.5.2. CB, GRP, 1759-1761, 138, 151, 153 and 155.

182 In Denmark torture was not part of common procedural practices. There were a few exceptions to the restrictions on the use of torture. In military jurisdiction torture was allowed, but only after special permission from the king. The historian Tyge Krogh has only found five instances of torture, all from the 1730s, in his study of the large jurisdiction of Zealand in Denmark. Torture was also allowed in a special inquisitorial commission based in Copenhagen, see Krogh, *Oplysningstiden*, 244; Knudsen, *Lovkyndighed*, 244; J. Smith, "Inkvisitionskommission i København. Tortur i Danmark," *Politihistorisk Selskab. Årsskrift* (1997).

183 These numbers do not include the instances of torture used against several defendants in the trials after the alleged conspiracy in 1759 (38.5.2. CB, GRP, 1759-1761, 138, 151, 153 and 155). References to torture emerged in the following verdicts and interrogations:
Christiansted Lower Court: 38.6.4. CB, DP, verdict 1761-11-20; 38.6.12. CB, DP, verdict 1775-01-16; 38.6.13. CB, DP, verdicts 1778-05-29, 1778-10-20, 1779-06-23 & 1779-12-23; and 38.6.18. CB, DP, verdict 1795-03-21. Christiansted Police Court: 38.9.1. CB, PRP, case 1758-10-05; 38.9.2. CB, PRP, case 1773-03-06; 38.9.4. CB, PRP, case 1778-03-20, 1779-05-07 & 1780-03-22; and 38.9.20. CB, PRP, case 1828-11-01. As in Christiansted's courts, the chief of police rarely noted the use of flogging, when it was performed as torture (it happened twice in the early 1780s and once in the period from 1798 to 1816), see 2.49. GG, Rapporter fra Christiansteds Politikammer, entries 1782-01-14, -15, -16 and 1782-04-23 and 38.31.1. CB, PJ, entry 1800-05-28.

184 421. Generaltoldkammerets vestindiske og guineiske sager, Anmærkninger ved forslaget til negerloven. Tillige med supplement, grunde og analogi for samme, 169-170. The role of torture, extralegal as well as legal, is further analyzed, in a French Caribbean context, by M.W. Ghachem, "Prosecuting Torture: The Strategic Ethics of Slavery in Pre-Revolutionary Saint-Domingue (Haiti)," *Law and History Review* 29, no. 4, special issue (2011).

185 For an analysis of how torture can produce false testimonies, see R.P.-c. Hsia, *Trent 1475: Stories of a Ritual Murder Trial* (New Haven and London: Yale University Press, 1992).

186 38.6.13. CB, DP, verdict 1779-06-23.

187 The draft slave code, compiled by Anton Lindemann in the 1780s, supports the conclusion that torture, other than flogging, was on its way out of the Danish West Indian courtrooms in the late eighteenth century. The draft code suggested that courts could use twenty-seven lashes against uncooperative slaves. Any other form of torture needed the approval of the governor general or the West Indian Government. Most comments made by colonial officers emphasized that flogging was the predominate form of torture used in the courts and the Burgher Council, a government body representing the important planters and merchants in St. Croix, suggested that all other forms of torture should be prohibited as they had proven inefficient; see 420. Generaltoldkammerets vestindiske og guineiske

sager, Genpart af adskillige anmærkninger og plakater ang. slaver samt udkast til slavelov, part 4, article 8 & 9, 6; and 421. Generaltoldkammerets vestindiske og guineiske sager, Anmærkninger ved forslaget til negerloven. Tillige med supplement, grunde og analogi for samme, entry 1787-08-01, 79, entry 1787-12-10, 94, and without date, 171.

188   2.16.1. GG, RP, entry 1795-01-25, no. 51.

189   38.6.18. CB, DP, verdict 1795-03-21.

190   For verdicts in which the crime of marronage operated as a sort of fall-back solution for judges when evidence for more serious crimes could not be obtained, see 38.6.5. CB, DP, verdict 1763-06-24 and verdict 1764-04-03; 38.6.7. CB, DP, verdict 1766-01-08; 38.18.4. CB, Pådømte sager, verdict 1766-12-05; 38.6.8-9. CB, DP, verdict 1769-10-20; 38.9.4. CB, PRP, case 1780-03-22; 38.5.19. CB, GRP, case 1780-12-05-02 and case 1782-04-03; 38.5.19. CB, GRP, verdict 1783-08-06; 38.6.22, CB, DP 1803-11-12; and 38.6.25. CB, DP, verdict 1811-12-06.

191   See for instance 38.31.1. CB, PJ, entry 1799-08-22 and 1799-08-25; 38.9.10. CB, PRP, case 1799-08-29; and 38.6.21. CB, DP, verdict 1799-11-01.

192   For an example of such precise questioning in a trial involving intra-slave crime, see 38.9.11. CB, PRP, case no. 1801-03.

193   38.5.16. CB, GRP, case 1774-10-15; for other examples of intimidating interrogations see 38.9.4. CB, PRP, case 1780-03-22, and 38.9.11. CB, PRP, case 1802-07-31.

194   For the black hole see 38.9.19. CB, PRP, case 1822-02-06; 38.9.20. CB, PRP, case 1831-04-24. For long arrests see 38.6.13. CB, DP, verdict 1778-09-07; 38.6.13. CB, DP, verdict 1778-10-20; 38.6.14. CB, DP, verdict 1781-01-15

195   G. Simonsen, "Legality outside the Courtroom: Practices of Law and Law Enforcement in the Danish West Indies at the End of the Eighteenth Century," *Quaderni Fiorentini. Per La Storia del Pensiero Giuridico Moderno* 33-34 (2005).

196   Attempts at crafting persuasive stories are presented in the chapters that follow. For examples of slaves who appear to have crafted incriminating stories, see 38.6.11. CB, DP, verdict 1772-09-26; 38.5.19. CB, GRP, case 1781-02-24 and case 1783-06-02, no. 1; 38.9.5. CB, PRP, case 1782-04-17 For examples of slaves who appear to have been unaware of the need to or unable to craft persuasive testimonies, see 38.6.13. CB, DP, verdict 1778-09-07; 38.6.21. CB, DP, verdict 1799-04-25; 38.6.31. CB, DP, verdict 1837-06-03; 38.5.16. CB, GRP, case 1774-10-15; 38.5.19. CB, GRP, case 1783-07-02 and 1783-06-28. James C. Scott has made an important contribution to the understanding of how dominated people are represented in public discourses. He distinguishes between a hidden and a public transcript. The former is largely hidden from view because dominated people strategically choose to keep silent, see J.C. Scott, *Domination and the Arts of Resistance: Hidden Transcripts* (New Haven and London: Yale University Press, 1990).

197   38.9.20. CB, PRP, case 1824-03-29.

198   38.9.5. CB, PRP, case 1783-04-03.

199   38.9.11. CB, PRP, case 1800-09-03. See also 38.9.11. CB, PRP, case 1802-06-01. I have located one episode in which the judge actively censored a slave's statement, see 38.9.11. CB, PRP, case 1800-08-20.

200   For a similar conceptualization of legal encounters as conversational, see B.P. Owensby, *Empire of Law and Indian Justice in Colonial Mexico* (Palo Alto, CA: Stanford University Press, 2008).

201   Scribes always noted when sessions began, and sometimes, when proceedings were cut short, for instance by nightfall, they also noted when they finished. The estimate provided here is based on such cases, see 38.9.4. CB, PRP, case 1780-01-15, 1780-08-19 and 1781-03-22; 38.9.5. CB, PRP, case 1781-07-27, 1781-08-03, 1782-08-07, 1782-08-17, 1782-11-01, 1782-11-07, 1782-12-11; 38.5.19. CB, GRP, case 1781-02-24, 1783-07-02 and 1783-06-02; 38.9.11. CB, PRP, case no. 1800-28, 1802-13, 1802-17, 1802-32, 1802-19, 1803-28 and 1803-34.

202   See, for example, 38.5.19. CB, GRP, case 1781-03-08; and 38.9.11. CB, PRP, case 1802-01-06.

203   See, for example, 38.5.19. CB, GRP, case 1781-03-08; 38.9.5. CB, PRP, case 1781-06-07; 38.9.11. CB, PRP, case 1800-10-06, 1802-01-06 and 1802-06-01; 38.5.28. CB, GRP, case 1804-07-27; 38.9.17. CB, PRP, case 1815-05-27; 38.11.2. CB, KP, case 1819-12-08; and 38.9.19. CB, PRP, case 1822-10-07.

204   See, for example, 38.9.5. CB, PRP, case 1782-06-14.

205   38.5.19. CB, GRP, case 1783-06-28; see also 38.5.19. CB, GRP, case 1780-12-05 and 1783-07-02; 38.9.10. CB, PRP, case 1799-08-29; 38.9.11. CB, PRP, case 1801-10-14 and 1803-02-02; 38.5.28. CB, GRP, case 1804-07-27; 38.11.2. CB, KP, case 1819-12-08.

206   38.9.11. CB, PRP, case 1802-03-05.

207   38.9.5. CB, PRP, case 1782-06-14; 38.9.11. CB, PRP, case 1800-10-28 and 1800-11-19.

208   For evidence of the continuing use of African languages, see 38.6.8-08. CB, DP, verdict 1769-12-13; 38.9.11. CB, PRP, case 1800-10-28; 38.31.1 CB, PJ, entry 1799-08-22; and 38.5.24. CB, GRP, case 1799-10-04; 38.9.14. CB, PRP, case 1806-05-23; 38.9.24. CB, PRP, case 1840-12-07.

209   38.9.4. CB, PRP, case 1780-03-22.

210   38.6.18. CB, DP, verdict 1795-03-21.

211   2.16.1. GG, RP, entry 1795-01-25, no. 51.

212   38.6.18. CB, DP, verdict 1795-03-21; and 2.16.1. GG, RP, entry 1795-03-30, no. 81.

213   38.9.11. CB, PRP, case no. 1802-17.

214   2.16.2. GG, RP, entry no. 1802-763. For other cases in which enslaved defendants could not make themselves understood see 38.9.5. CB, PRP, entry 1783-03-03; 38.9.10. CB, PRP, case 1799-02-20.

215   Oldendorp, *Historie*, I, 671-672.

216   For a rare example, see 38.6.18. CB, DP, verdict 1795-03-21, here the judge noted that an enslaved man had "clap[ped] his hands" to underscore his point.

217   Sibyll's story went like this: "my Budder in Law come in, and take me up and say he going to carry me to see his udder wife, he take and carry, carry, carry, carry, carry me all night and day, all night and day 'way from my Country […] As my budder in law carry me 'long, me hear great noise, and me wonder but he tell me no frighten. And he carry me to a long house full of new negurs talking and making sing […] and my budder in law sell me to de Back-erah [white] people [and he …] took up de gun and de powder which he sell me for and wanted to get 'way from me, but me hold he and cry and he stop wid me till me hold tongue and den he run away from me," quoted from J.S. Handler, "Survivors of the Middle Passage: Life Histories of Enslaved Africans in British America," *Slavery & Abolition* 3, no. 1 (2002), 32-33. See also W.J. Ong, *Orality and Literacy: Technologizing of the Word* (London and New York: Methuen, 1985), 33-71; J. Vansina, *Oral Tradition as History* (Madison: University of Wisconsin Press, 1985).

218   See, for example, 38.9.4. CB, PRP, case 1781-04-18; 38.9.5. CB, PRP, case 1781-08-31, 1782-04-17; 38.9.11. CB, PRP, case 1800-10-06, 1802-04-24 and 1803-03-21; 38.9.18. CB, PRP, case 1820-07-20 and 1820-08-04; 38.9.19. CB, PRP, case 1822-02-06.

219   See, for example, 38.6.13. CB, DP, verdict 1779-05-01; 38.5.19. CB, GRP, case 1781-03-08 and 1783-06-28; 38.9.11. CB, PRP, case 1802-05-19 and 1803-03-20; 38.9.19. CB, PRP, case 1821-06-15 and 1821-06-15.

220   *Kong Christian den Femtis Danske Lov*, 1-8-3.

221   See, for example, 38.9.4. CB, PRP, case 1779-09-23; 38.9.19. CB, PRP, case 1821-10-10; 38.9.5. CB, PRP, case 1782-06-20 and 1782-12-11; 38.9.11. CB, PRP, case 1801-10-14 and 1802-06-01.

222   38.9.5. CB, PRP, case 1781-09-11; see also 38.9.4. CB, PRP, case 1779-09-23.

223   38.5.28. CB, GRP, case 1804-09-18.

224   38.9.19. CB, PRP, case 1822-10-07.

225   38.9.4. CB, PRP, case 1779-09-23.

226   One of the best examples of how enslaved women encountered the sexuality of white men is provided by the diary of Thomas Thistlewood who was overseer and later pen keeper in Jamaica from 1750 until his death in 1786, see T. Burnard, *Mastery, Tyranny, and Desire: Thomas Thistlewood and His Slaves in*

the Anglo-Jamaican World (Chapel Hill: University of North Carolina Press, 2004); D. Hall, *In Miserable Slavery. Thomas Thistlewood in Jamaica 1750-1786* (London: Macmillan, 1992). About illicit sex in the Caribbean see also M. Lazarus-Black, *Legitimate Acts and Illegal Encounters: Law and Society in Antigua and Barbuda* (Washington, D.C.: Smithsonian Institute Press, 1994), 73-101; K.F. Olwig, "Ret og lov, magt og afmagt, et eksempel fra Dansk Vestindien," *Historie. Jyske samlinger* Ny række, 17, no. 3 (1988), 390; B. Moitt, "Slave Women and Resistance in the French Caribbean," in *More than Chattel: Black Women and Slavery in the Americas*, ed. David Barry Gaspar and Darlene Clark Hine (Bloomington: Indiana University Press, 1996), 80-100; Moitt, *Women and Slavery*, 99-100. For other slave societies see S. Block, "Lines of Color, Sex, and Service: Comparative Sexual Coercion in Early America," in *Sex, Love, Race: Crossing Boundaries in North American History*, ed. Martha Hodes (New York: New York University Press, 1999); Mason, *Social Death and Resurrection: Slavery and Emancipation in South Africa*; P. Scully, "Rape, Race, and Colonial Culture: The Sexual Politics of Identity in the Nineteenth-Century Cape," *American Historical Review* 100, no. 2 (1995).

227   38.9.21. CB, PRP, case 1829-12-18.

228   J.R. Oldfield, *Popular Politics and British Anti-Slavery: The Mobilisation of Public Opinion against the Slave Trade, 1787-1807* (London: Frank Cass, 1998); L.C. Jennings, *French Anti-Slavery: The Movement for the Abolition of Slavery in France, 1802-1848* (Cambridge: Cambridge University Press, 2000); D.P. Resnick, "The Société des Amis des Noirs and the Abolition of Slavery," *French Historical Studies* VII, no. 4 (Fall 1972); C.L. Brown, *Moral Capital: Foundations of British Abolitionism* (Chapel Hill: University of North Carolina Press, 2006); Vibæk, *Dansk Vestindien 1755-1848*, 2, 162-189.

229   M. Craton, *Testing the Chains. Resistance to Slavery in the British West Indies* (Ithaca and London: Cornell University Press, 1982), 161-290; D.B. Gaspar and D.P. Geggus, eds., *A Turbulent Time: The French Revolution and the Greater Caribbean* (Bloomington: Indiana University Press, 1997); C.L.R. James, *The Black Jacobins: Toussaint L'Ouverture and the San Domingo Revolution*, 2nd ed. (New York: Vintage Books, 1963); Ghachem, *The Old Regime and the Haitian Revolution*.

230   38.9.20. CB, PRP, case 1830-07-05.

231   Hall, *Slave Society*, 124-138, 178-190; P.E. Olsen, "Disse vilde karle: Negre i Danmark indtil 1848," in *Fremmede i Danmark*, ed. Bent Blüdnikow (Odense: Odense Universitets Forlag, 1987), 111. Concerning slaves in Copenhagen, see also K. Waaben, "A.S. Ørsted og negerslaverne i København," *Juristen* 46 (1964).

232   For the notion of respectability in a small Caribbean island, see K.F. Olwig, *Global Culture, Island Identity: Continuity and Change in the Afro-Caribbean Community of Nevis* (Chur: Harwood Academic Publishers, 1993), 13, 67-113. For a similar notion in eighteenth-century Denmark, see P. Henningsen, "Rang og titler klingre skal omkring mit navn som bjælder: titulaturer, prædikater og patronymer i 1700-tallets Danmark," *1066. Tidsskrift for historie* 32, no. 2. For the importance of interracial sexuality in the development of Caribbean slave societies and racial ideology, see D. Garraway, *The Libertine Colony: Creolization in the Early French Caribbean* (Durham, London: Duke University Press, 2005).

233   38.9.4. CB, PRP, case 1780-06-30; and 38.6.22. CB, DP, verdict 1804-03-19.

234   38.9.2. CB, PRP, case 1772-07-14. If not otherwise indicated, this is the reference for the discussion and the quotations concerning the trial where Maria Johanne appeared.

235   38.9.9. CB, PRP, case 1792-08-11.

236   C.v. Rossem and H.v.d. Voort, eds., *Die Creol Taal. 250 years of Negerhollands texts* (Amsterdam: Amsterdam University Press, 1996), 89-90.

237   38.9.5. CB, PRP, case 1782-06-20. If not otherwise indicated, this is the reference for the discussion concerning the trial involving Petrus.

238   421. Generaltoldkammerets vestindiske og guineiske sager, Anmærkninger ved forslaget til negerloven. Tillige med supplement, grunde og analogi for samme, entry 1787-12-10, 93-94; see also 420. Generaltoldkammerets vestindiske og guineiske sager, Genpart af adskillige anmærkninger og plakater ang. slaver samt udkast til slavelov, part 4, article 7 of Lindemann's draft proposal.

239 For a similar example see Oldendorp, *Historie*, I, 567.

240 38.9.5. CB, PRP, case 1783-06-02; 38.5.19. CB, GRP, case 1783-07-02; and 38.6.14. CB, DP, verdict 1783-08-19-01.

241 38.9.15. CB, PRP, case 1810-09-12.

242 38.31.5. CB, PJ, entry 1815-08-08.

243 2.16.5. GG, RP, entry 1815-08-16.

244 38.5.16. CB, GRP, case 1774-10-15, and 38.9.5. CB, PRP, case 1783-04-03.

245 38.9.19. CB, PRP, case 1822-10-07.

246 38.9.4. CB, PRP, case 1780-03-22. If not otherwise indicated, this is the reference for the discussion and the quotations concerning the trial against Louisa.

247 The relevant protocols of the Christiansted Lower Court's verdicts do not refer to Louisa; see 38.6.13-16. CB, DP, 1776-1786.

248 Vibæk, *Dansk Vestindien 1755-1848*, 2, 350-351.

249 38.9.4. CB, PRP, case 1780-03-22. If not otherwise indicated, this is the reference for the discussion and the quotations concerning the trial against Nanny.

250 P. Ariés, *Western Attitudes toward DEATH: From the Middle Ages to the Present* (Baltimore: Johns Hopkins University Press, 1974). For a thorough analysis of how death shaped colonial life in the British Caribbean societies, see Brown, *The Reaper's Garden*.

251 38.5.19. CB, GRP, case 1781-12-05; 38.6.14. CB, DP, verdict 1781-01-15.

252 2.5.1. GG, Kopibøger til lokale myndigheder og personer, letter from Governor General Clausen to attorney Balling, entry 1780-11-11, and letter from Governor General Clausen to member of the West Indian Government Lindemann, entry 1781-01-31.

253 Some of the pro-natalist policies in the Danish West Indies are described by N.T. Jensen, "'For the Benefit of the Planters and the Benefit of Mankind': The Struggle to Control Midwives and Obstetrics on St. Croix, Danish West Indies, 1800-1848," in *Health and Medicine in the Circum-Caribbean, 1800-1968*, ed. Juanita de Barros, Steven Palmer, and David Wright, *Routledge Studies in the Social History of Medicine* (New York: Routledge, 2009).

254 38.6.7. CB, DP, verdict 1764-12-11.

255 38.9.24. CB, PRP, case 1840-05-22; the expression "to the Judge" was rendered in English in the court book. See also 38.9.24. CB, PRP, case 1840-03-03; 38.9.11. CB, PRP, case 1802-05-19 and 38.6.22. CB, DP, verdict 1802-06-23.

256 38.9.17. CB, PRP, case 1815-05-27. A similar association between skin color and failing managerial authority appears in 38.9.24. CB, PRP, case 1840-03-03.

257 38.9.19. CB, PRP, case 1821-02-07. If not otherwise indicated, this is the reference for the discussion and the quotations that concern the slaves from La Reine.

258 38.31.6. CB, PJ, entry 1821-01-02, 1821-01-03, 1821-01-05, 1821-01-04, 1821-01-16, 1821-02-06, 1821-02-14 and 1821-02-15.

259 38.9.19. CB, PRP, case 1823-08-02, 1824-07-30, 1824-08-13, and 1824-08-30; 38.9.20. CB, PRP, case 1823-11-26, 1824-05-29, 1824-06-10, 1824-07-07, 1824-11-09, 1824-11-30, and 1825-11-11; 38.6.21. CB, DP, case 1825-10-05, and 1827-07-06.

260 38.9.18. CB, PRP, case 1816-12-20.

261 38.9.11. CB, PRP, case 1803-06-14. If not otherwise indicated, this is the reference for the discussion and the quotations concerning the trial involving Peggy. See also K.L. Rahbek, "Negerinden Peggy: En sandfærdig begivenhed, uddraget af Sagens Documenter," *Minerva* (1804), 298-321.

262 38.9.11. CB, PRP, case 1803-06-14.

263 Rahbek, "Negerinden Peggy," 304-305; O. Feldbæk and O. Justesen, *Kolonierne i Asien og Afrika* (København: Politikens Forlag, 1980).

264 38.9.11. CB, PRP, case 1803-06-14.

265 Rahbek, "Negerinden Peggy," 298-321. For abolitionist and proslavery representations of enslaved women, see H. Altink, "'An Outrage on all Decency': Abolitionist Reactions to Flogging Jamaican Slave Women, 1780-1834," *Slavery & Abolition* 23, no. 2 (2002); H. Altink, "Deviant and Dangerous. Proslavery Representations of Jamaican Slave Women's Sexuality, ca. 1780-1834," in *Women and Slavery: The Modern Atlantic*, ed. Gwyn Campbell, Suzanne Miers, and Joseph C. Miller (Athens: Ohio University Press, 2008); K. Halttunen, "Humanitarianism and the Pornography of Pain in Anglo-American Culture," *American Historical Review* 100, no. 2 (1995).

266 38.9.11. CB, PRP, case 1802-07-31. If not otherwise indicated, this is the reference for the discussion and the quotations concerning Polly and Cork.

267 2.16.2. GG, RP, entry 1802-07-17 and 1802-08-07; and 38.31.1. CB, PJ, entry 1802-07-16, 1802-07-17, 1802-07-19, 1802-07-31, 1802-08-03 and 1802-08-13.

268 38.31.1. CB, PJ, entry 1805-05-31.

269 For a story similar to that of Cork and Polly's see 38.31.2. CB, PJ, entry 1805-10-03.

270 38.6.21. CB, DP, verdict 1799-06-22; see also 38.6.31. CB, DP, verdict 1839-03-06; for slaves' strategies in cases of infanticide, see M. Echeverri, "'Enraged to the limit of despair': Infanticide and Slave Judicial Strategies in Barbacoas, 1788-98," *Slavery & Abolition* 30, no. 3 (2009).

271 38.6.30. CB, DP, verdict 1824-10-06.

272 38.9.24. CB, PRP, case 1840-09-15.

273 2.27.16. GG, RP B, entry 1840-09-26 no. 484.

274 38.6.29. CB, DP, verdict 1821-12-21 and 38.9.15. CB, PRP, case 1812-02-21.
There is no systematic research on rape in eighteenth- and nineteenth-century Denmark. Historian Inger Dübeck's overview of rape trials suggests that they sometimes constituted as much as 6 to 7 percent of the cases about sexual illegitimacy (fornication, adultery, sodomy and the like). At other times the number was lower, see I. Dübeck, "Voldtægtsforbrydelsen i retshistorisk belysning," *Historisk tidsskrift* 103, no. 1 (2003). Tyge Krogh's research on legal practice in the first half of the eighteenth century, likewise, suggests that rape accusations were rare but possible during this period, see Krogh, *Oplysningstiden*, 418, 501, 519, 532. In so far as Denmark and Sweden were similar, the work of Karen Hassan Jansson on rape in Sweden suggests that courts regularly heard rape trials in the seventeenth and eighteenth centuries and that women and girls had a fair chance of obtaining vindication (see K.H. Jansson, *Kvinnofrid. Synen på våldtäkt och konstruktionen av kön i Sverige 1600-1800* (Uppsala: Uppsala University, 2002).

275 38.5.2. CB, GRP, 1759-1761, case 1759-12-11, 151. For a case that resembles, see 38.9.5. CB, PRP, case 1783-06-02.

276 For another example see 38.6.23. CB, DP, verdict 1805-02-01.

277 See also 38.31.2. CB, PJ, entry 1805-07-24 and 1805-07-30. One eighteenth-century Danish equivalent to the notion of the 'respectable' was *honnet*, meaning an honorable, decent and reasonable person, according to *Ordbog over det danske Sprog* at http://ordnet.dk/ods (accessed 2016-05-06).

278 38.6.23. CB, DP, verdict 1805-02-01 and 1805-12-12.

279 38.9.9. CB, PRP, case 1793-04-03.

280 38.5.23. CB, GRP, case 1793-05-23.

281 38.9.9. CB, PRP, case 1793-04-03 and 38.6.18. CB, DP, verdict 1793-08-12.

282 38.9.8. CB, PRP, case 1788-11-26.

283 38.9.8. CB, PRP, case 1788-11-26. See also 38.9.10. CB, PRP, case 1799-06-10.

284 Such descriptions also emerged in the three cases where rape charges were raised against free and enslaved Afro-Caribbean men in the period 1755-1848, see 38.9.15. CB, PRP, case 1812-02-21 & 38.6.25. CB, DP, verdict 1812-03-23; 38.9.22. CB, PRP, case 1837-10-04; 38.9.24. CB, PRP, case 1839-06-29.

285 38.9.14. CB, PRP, case 1807-06-12. Narratives centered on Christian respectability and the vulnerability of enslaved women also circulated among abolitionists, see for example D. Paton, "Decency, Dependence

and the Lash: Gender and the British Debate over Slave Emancipation, 1830-1834," *Slavery & Abolition* 17, no. 3 (1996).

286 38.9.21. CB, PRP, case 1829-12-18.

287 38.9.18. CB, PRP, case 1820-04-22. If not otherwise indicated, this is the reference for the discussion and the quotations concerning the trial against Cornelius. For Bethlehem Estate see also I.M. Antonsen, "Plantagen Bethlehem på St. Croix i det attende århundrede," *Nationalmuseets Arbejdsmark* (1968).

288 Cornelius, who belonged to Peter de Wint, was interrogated in Christiansted Police Court on 1820-04-22. In the daily journal of the chief of police there are two entries concerning one Cornelius belonging to Peter de Wint. One that notes his arrest and one that notes that he received a punishment of seventy-five lashes, see 38.31.6. CB, PJ, entry 1820-04-19 and 1820-05-02.

289 38.9.11. CB, PRP, case 1800-10-13, see also 38.9.24. CB, PRP, case 1841, no. 27.

290 Cecilie, see 38.9.21. CB, PRP, case 1829-12-18; and Margrethe, see 38.9.24. CB, PRP, case 1841-02-15. For other rape cases see 38.6.25. CB, DP, verdict 1812-03-23; 38.6.29. CB, DP, verdict 1821-12-21; 38.9.24. CB, PRP, case 1839-06-29

291 *Kong Christian den Femtis Danske Lov*, 6-13-18 and 6-13-19. Koefoed, *Besovede kvindfolk*, 118.

292 38.11.4. VILA. Christiansted Byfoged, KP, case 1832-03-03.

293 3.81.219. Den Vestindiske Regering, Gruppeordnede sager: Retsvæsen. Mord på plantageforvalter P. Machin, 1832, 19-20.

294 3.81.219. Den Vestindiske Regering, Gruppeordnede sager: Retsvæsen. Mord på plantageforvalter P. Machin, 1832, 20-27.

295 38.9.21. CB, PRP, case 1831-02-21; and 2.27.6. GG, RP B, entry 1831 no. 56. For different interpretations of obeah and like spiritual practices in the Caribbean, see Brown, "Spiritual Terror and Sacred Authority in Jamaican Slave Society;" Browne, "The 'Bad Business';" N.H. Götz, *Obeah – Hexerei in der Karibik – zwischen Mackt und Ohnmacht* (Frankfurt am Main: Peter Lang, 1995); J.S. Handler, "Slave Medicine and Obeah in Barbados, ca. 1650 to 1834," *New West Indian Guide/Niewe West-Indische Gids* 74 (2000); J.S. Handler and K.M. Bilby, "On the Early Use and Origin of the Term 'Obeah' in Barbadoes and the Anglophone Caribbean," *Slavery & Abolition* 22, no. 2 (2001); D. Paton, "Witchcraft, Poison, Law, and Atlantic Slavery," *William and Mary Quarterly* 69, no. 2 (2012); D. Paton, *The Cultural Politics of Obeah: Religion, Colonialism and Modernity in the Caribbean World* (Cambridge: Cambridge University Press, 2015); J. Savage, "Between Colonial Fact and French Law: Slave Poisoners and the Provostial Court in Restoration-Era Martinique," *French Historical Studies* 29, no. 4 (2006); J. Savage, "'Black Magic' and White Terror: Slave Poisoning and Colonial Society in Early 19th Century Martinique," *Journal of Social History* 40, no. 3 (2007).

296 38.11.2. CB, KP, case 1819-12-08.

297 The question of how enslaved people understood their marital relationships and the norms they applied to regulate them has received attention in the history of Caribbean slavery. Mostly, however, enslaved people have been studied as members of extended kinship groups, as mothers, sisters, and aunts, fathers, brothers, and uncles. See M. Morrissey, *Slave Women in the New World: Gender Stratification in the Caribbean* (Lawrence: University Press of Kansas, 1989); Bush, *Slave Women in Caribbean Society 1650-1838*; Moitt, *Women and Slavery*; Morgan, *Laboring Women*; H. Altink, "'To Wed or Not to Wed?': The Struggle to Define Afro-Jamaican Relationships, 1834-1838," *Journal of Social History* 38, no. 1 (2004); B.W. Higman, "African and Creole Slave Family Patterns in Trinidad," *Journal of Family and History* 3, no. 2 (1978); B.W. Higman, "The Slave Family and Household in the British West Indies, 1800-1834," *Journal of Interdisciplinary History* 6, no. 2 (1975). Few contemporary historians would accept the ideas of Danish West Indian judges concerning slave unions; nonetheless, the notion that marriage among enslaved men and women, or, at least, divorce was somehow uncomplicated is still common. Historian of the British West Indies Barbara Bush, for instance, emphasizes the "ease of divorce in slave society," claiming that it had traditional West African precedents (Bush, *Slave Women in Caribbean Society 1650-1838*, 100-101), historical anthropologist Karen Olwig writes that unions

"were formed and dissolved at the wish of the partners," Olwig, *Cultural Adaptation*, 70, 77. These interpretations underscore the idea that enslaved men and women were guided by other norms and expectations than those of their European masters. In the interpretation I offer in this chapter, however, I emphasize the formal and ritual elements of enslaved marriages. By implication, I suggest that the domestic flexibility that characterized slaves' marriages may have been due more to slavery in the West Indies and its ramifications in West Africa than to particular African or Afro-Caribbean norms.

298   L. Holberg, *Introduction til Naturens- Og Folke-Rettens Kundskab. Uddragen Af de Fornemste Jurister, Besynderlig Grotii, Pufendorfs og Thomasii Skrifter*, Holbergs Samlede Skrifter (København: Gyldendalsk Boghandel, 1913), 627; Knudsen, *Lovkyndighed*, 51-82; Lazarus-Black, *Legitimate Acts*, 62, 249.

299   Hall, *Slave Society*, 45-47.

300   F4-8-20-21, Generalkirkeinspektionskollegiet, Indkomne sager, entry 1788-12-13; F4-3-2, Generalkirkeinspektionskollegiet, Kopibog for forestillinger og breve, entry 1786-12-18. See the term *"konkubine"* in *Ordbog over det danske Sprog* at http://ordnet.dk/ods (accessed 2016-05-26). Ann Laura Stoler has argued that concubinage served to confirm racial hierarchies. This may also have been the case in the Danish West Indies. Indeed, Christiansted's judges may have understood racial difference to be less relevant in relation to slave unions, since they were, above all, determined by slave status and seldom challenged the racial hierarchies established in the islands. Hence judges employed an expression, the 'natural marriage,' which reflected this fact. See Stoler, *Carnal Knowledge and Imperial Power: Race and the Intimate in Colonial Rule*, 51.

301   P. Ipsen, Koko's Daughters. Danish Men Marrying Ga Women in an Atlantic Slave Trading Port in the Eighteenth Century (Ph.D.-thesis, Københavns Universitet, 2008); P. Ipsen, "'The Christened Mulatresses': Euro-African Families in a Slave-Trading Town," *William and Mary Quarterly* 70, no. 2 (2013); P. Ipsen, *Daughters of the Trade, Atlantic Slavers and Interracial Marriage on the Gold Coast* (Philadelphia: University of Pennsylvania Press, 2015).

302   For examples of relationships described as natural marriages, see 38.9.11. CB, PRP, case 1800-10-13, 1802-04-24 and 1802-07-31; 38.6.21. CB, DP, verdict 1802-01-15; 38.5.28. CB, GRP, case 1804-07-27; 38.6.24. CB, DP, verdict 1806-11-25 and 1809-09-05; 38.6.28. CB, DP, verdict 1818-10-07, 1818-11-10 and 1820-01-11.

303   For examples of the use of terms referring to illicit sexuality among free people of color in the Danish West Indies, see 38.9.5. CB, PRP, case 1782-03-27; 38.6.20. CB, DP, verdict 1798-02-12 and verdict 1798-06-03; 38.9.10. CB, PRP, case 1800-03-18; 38.9.11. CB, PRP, case no. 1802-01, 1802-38, 1803-12 and case 1803-02-26; 38.9.14. CB, PRP, case 1806-09-10; 38.9.18. CB, PRP, case no. 1816-108 and 1820-31; 38.9.19. CB, PRP, case 1821-08-21; and 38.9.24. CB, PRP, case no. 1840-59.

304   38.9.3. CB, PRP, case 1774-10-12; and 38.9.14. CB, PRP, case 1806-04-22.

305   38.6.24. CB, DP, verdict 1807-12-15.

306   38.9.19. CB, PRP, case 1821-01-26.

307   38.9.02. CB, PRP, case 1769-12-16.

308   See the terms *hustru* and *ægtemand* in *Ordbog over det danske Sprog* at http://ordnet.dk/ods (accessed 2016-05-26). The prefix *ægte* derives from the old German terms for 'law' and 'marriage'. The prefix thus underlined the lawfulness of a marriage. See the entry *ægte* in *Dansk Etymologisk Ordbog. Ordenes Historie. Gyldendals Røde Ordbøger*, ed. Niels Åge Nielsen (København: Gyldendal, 2004).

309   For examples of trials in which terms denoting the legal nature of marital unions were used in relation to free inhabitants, see 38.9.5. CB, PRP, case 1782-03-16; 38.6.19. CB, DP, verdict 1796-01-23; 38.9.11. CB, PRP, case 1803-06-21; and 38.6.24. CB, DP, verdict 1807-12-15.

310   See the terms *mand* and *kone* in *Ordbog over det danske Sprog* at http://ordnet.dk/ods (accessed 2016-05-26).

311   Had an enslaved man referred to his partner as 'my woman', then the scribe would probably have chosen closer Danish equivalents such as the terms *kvinde* and *fruentimmer*. Scribes used such terms when they wanted to emphasize enslaved women's sex rather than their relationships to enslaved

men. A defamation case from 1802 illustrates this translation practice. During the case, the statement "mean woman" was translated into the Danish phrase "*slette fruentimmer;*" see 38.9.11. CB, PRP, case 1802-06-01. See also 38.6.17. CB, DP, verdict 1790-08-16; 38.6.27. CB, DP, verdict 1816-11-16; and 38.9.18. CB, PRP, case 1820-03-16.

312   See, for example, 38.5.19. CB, GRP, case 1783-07-02; and 38.9.19. CB, PRP, case 1822-09-26.

313   38.9.11. CB, PRP, case 1800-10-13; 38.9.11. CB, PRP, case 1802-04-24 and 1802-07-31.

314   38.5.19. CB, GRP, case 1781-02-24; 38.9.11. CB, PRP, case 1804-11-04; 38.9.12. CB, PRP, case 1804-07-16; and 38.11.2. CB, KP, case 1819-12-08.

315   For examples of verdicts where judges pointed to jealousy as a motive, see 38.6.8-9. CB, DP, verdict 1768-02-20; 38.6.14. CB, DP, verdict 1783-08-19-01; 38.6.21. CB, DP, verdict 1799-11-01; 38.6.23. CB, DP, verdict 1804-10-27; 38.6.28. CB, DP, verdict 1818-11-10; and 38.6.32. CB, DP, verdict 1845-08-11.

316   38.5.10. CB, GRP, case 1768-01-19.

317   A short architectural history of slave villages in the Danish West Indies is provided by W. Chapman, "Slave Villages in the Danish West Indies," *Vernacular Architecture Forum* (1991).

318   2.5.1. GG, Kopibøger til lokale myndigheder og personer, entry 1783-08-26.

319   Holsoe, "The Origin, Transport, Introduction and Distribution of Africans on St. Croix: An Overview," 42-43. See also 38.9.5. CB, PRP, case 1783-06-02.

320   38.9.5. CB, PRP, case 1783-06-02.

321   38.5.19. CB, GRP, case 1783-07-02.

322   38.9.5. CB, PRP, case 1783-06-02.

323   38.9.5. CB, PRP, case 1783-06-02. In the interrogation records of Christiansted Police Court Markitta appeared by the name Babetta, probably an alias. The context, however, clarifies that Babetta is the same woman as Markitta who appeared in Christiansted Lower Court.

324   38.9.5. CB, PRP, case 1783-06-02.

325   38.5.19. CB, GRP, case 1783-07-02.

326   38.9.5. CB, PRP, case 1783-06-02.

327   38.6.14. CB, DP, verdict 1783-08-19-01.

328   38.6.28. CB, DP, verdict 1820-01-11; and 38.31.6. CB, PJ, entry 1820-01-17.

329   38.11.2. CB, KP, case 1819-12-08.

330   38.11.2. CB, KP, case 1819-12-08.

331   38.6.28. CB, DP, verdict 1820-01-11.

332   38.6.28. CB, DP, verdict 1820-01-11.

333   38.11.2. CB, KP, case 1819-12-08.

334   38.11.2. CB, KP, case 1819-12-08.

335   38.11.2. CB, KP, case 1819-12-08.

336   38.11.2. CB, KP, case 1819-12-08.

337   38.11.2. CB, KP, case 1819-12-08.

338   38.11.2. CB, KP, case 1819-12-08.

339   38.9.19. CB, PRP, case 1822-09-26.

340   38.9.19. CB, PRP, case 1822-09-26.

341   2.28.7. GG, Sager til referatprotokoller B, entry 1822-10-10.

342   2.28.7. GG, Sager til referatprotokoller B, entry 1822-10-10.

343   For examples of slave couples sharing houses, see 38.9.11. CB, PRP, case 1802-04-24 and 38.9.23. CB, PRP, case 1840-01-31

344   Oxholm, *De Danske Vestindiske Öers Tilstand*, 55.

345   38.9.23. CB, PRP, case 1840-08-19.

346   For examples of slave houses that are locked, see 38.9.2. CB, PRP, 1773-12-20; 38.9.4. CB, PRP, case 1781-03-22; 38.9.18. CB, PRP, case 1819-11-10; and 38.9.24. CB, PRP, case 1841-02-15. See also Chapman, "Slave Villages in the Danish West Indies."

347 See, for example, 38.9.7. CB, PRP, case 1787-05-08; 38.9.12. CB, PRP, case 1804-07-16; and 38.9.15. CB, PRP, case 1811-04-16.

348 For tailoring maroons, see 38.9.11. CB, PRP, case 1802-09-13 and 38.9.2. CB, PRP, case 1774-07-02. For slaves stealing clothes, see 38.9.5. CB, PRP, case 1781-12-04 and 1782-10-03; 38.9.7. CB, PRP, case 1787-05-08; 38.9.11. CB, PRP, case 1800-12-11 and 1801-06-25; and 38.9.19. CB, PRP, case 1821-06-22. For clothes used as a means of exchange, see 38.9.5. CB, PRP, case 1781-09-11; 38.9.11. CB, PRP, case 1802-08-14; 38.6.32. CB, DP, verdict 1841-11-30.

349 38.6.23. CB, DP, verdict 1806-02-04.

350 38.9.20. CB, PRP, case 1828-05-01.

351 38.9.9. CB, PRP, case 1795-01-03; 38.9.11. CB, PRP, case 1802-11-15; and 38.9.16. CB, PRP, 1814-07-24.

352 38.9.22. CB, PRP, case 1835-01-07.

353 38.5.19. CB, GRP, case 1783-08-06.

354 38.9.9. CB, PRP, case 1794-06-27.

355 38.9.10. CB, PRP, case 1796-12-20.

356 38.9.20. CB, PRP, case 1828-09-23.

357 C. Geertz, *The Interpretation of Cultures* (New York: Basic Books, Inc., 1973), 3-30.

358 38.9.4. CB, PRP, case 1779-03-24.

359 2.5.1. GG, Kopibøger til lokale myndigheder og personer, entry 1779-03-29.

360 38.6.28. CB, DP, verdict 1818-11-10; 38.11.2. CB, KP, case 1818-10-28; and 5.5.3. Landsoverretten for de Vestindiske Øer, DP, verdict 1818-12-18.

361 38.22.40. CB, Fogedprotokoller, entry 1818-10-21.

362 38.22.40. CB, Fogedprotokoller, entry 1818-10-21.

363 38.11.2. CB, KP, entry 1818-10-28.

364 38.22.40. CB, Fogedprotokoller, entry 1818-10-21.

365 38.22.40. CB, Fogedprotokoller, entry 1818-10-21.

366 38.9.9. CB, PRP, case 1794-08-01.

367 38.9.9. CB, PRP, case 1795-05-21. For other examples of enslaved men castigating their wives, see 38.9.6. CB, PRP, case 1785-03-03; 38.9.9. CB, PRP, case 1794-06-27; 38.9.11. CB, PRP, case 1800-10-06; 38.9.14. CB, PRP, case 1807-05-22; 38.9.17. CB, PRP, case 1816-05-24; and 38.9.23. CB, PRP, case 1840-08-14.

368 38.11.2. CB, KP, entry 1818-10-28 and 38.22.40. CB, Fogedprotokoller, entry 1818-10-21.

369 38.6.21. CB, DP, verdict 1799-11-01. The sentence over Sally was commuted. This appears in a letter from 1808 from the public prosecutor to the governor during the second British occupation. The prosecutor did not, however, state what sentence Sally received instead of the original death sentence. See 3.56.2. Den Vestindiske Regering, Guvernementet på St. Croix, Indgåede breve til den engelske guvernør, entry 1809-02-022.

370 38.5.24. CB, GRP, case 1799-10-04.

371 38.9.11. CB, PRP, case 1800-10-13.

372 38.9.14. CB, PRP, case 1806-12-12.

373 38.9.15. CB, PRP, case 1808-05-17. For other examples of enslaved spouses expecting economic support, see 38.9.2. CB, PRP, case 1774-07-02; 38.9.5. CB, PRP, case 1783-05-24; 38.6.16. CB, DP, verdict 1788-06-13; 38.9.9. CB, PRP, case 1790-02-27; 38.9.11. CB, PRP, case 1800-10-13; 38.9.14. CB, PRP, case 1807-09-02; 38.9.18. CB, PRP, case 1820-08-03; 38.6.21. CB, DP, verdict 1825-07-23; 38.9.23. CB, PRP, case 1840-02-19.

374 38.9.8. CB, PRP, case 1788-05-02.

375 38.9.5. CB, PRP, case 1783-04-03; and 38.9.20. CB, PRP, case 1825-04-07.

376 38.5.24. CB, GRP, case 1799-10-04. Court Scribe Kinkel rendered this expression — convenience — in English. This was a notational practice used to indicate the verbatim nature of the transcription. The

practice of rendering words in English, often in Latin letters, in contrast to the Gothic hand used for the main body of text, was also used in defamation trials in which it was essential to determine exactly which swearwords had been used, see for example 38.9.11. CB, PRP, case 1802-01-06 and 1803-02-26; and 38.9.19. CB, PRP, case 1821-08-21.

377 See for example 38.9.11. CB, PRP, case 1800-10-06.

378 38.9.14. CB, PRP, case 1807-12-16.

379 38.31.2. CB, PJ, entry 1805-09-01.

380 38.31.2. CB, PJ, entry 1805-09-01.

381 Oldendorp, *Historie*, I, 727-728.

382 38.9.11. CB, PRP, case 1800-10-13.

383 *Kong Christian den Femtis Danske Lov*, 3-16-8.

384 38.5.28. CB, GRP, case 1804-07-27.

385 38.5.28. CB, GRP, case 1804-07-27.

386 38.22.27. CB, Fogedprotokoller, case 1804-06-16.

387 38.22.27. CB, Fogedprotokoller, case 1804-06-16; and 38.5.28. CB, GRP, case 1804-07-27.

388 38.5.28. CB, GRP, case 1804-07-27.

389 38.9.22. CB, PRP, case 1835-07-16.

390 M. Ferguson, *Subject to Others. British Women Writers and Colonial Slavery, 1670-1834* (New York and London: Routledge, 1992), 69-90.

391 J. George E. Brooks, "The *Signares* of Saint-Louis and Gorée: Women Entrepreneurs in Eighteenth-Century Senegal," in *Women in Africa: Studies in Social and Economic Change*, ed. Nancy J. Hafkin and Edna G. Bay (Palo Alto, CA: Stanford University Press, 1976), 34-38.

392 See M. Hinchman, "House and Household on Gorée, Senegal, 1758-1837," *Journal of the Society of Architectural Historians* 65, no. 2 (2006); J.F. Searing, *West African Slavery and Atlantic Commerce. The Senegal River Valley, 1700-1860* (Cambridge: Cambridge University Press, 1993), 93-128; George E. Brooks, "The Signares of Saint-Louis and Gorée," 19-44; Brooks, *Eurafricans in Western Africa*, 278-280.

393 3.61.3. Den Vestindiske Regering, Sager til referatprotokol A, 1815, no. 361; and http://www.unesco-asp.dk/da/transatlantic-slave-trade/skoleaktiviteter/227-an-african-venus-on-st-croix.html (accessed 2013-07- 29).

394 For the role of the house-yard complex in the Caribbean today, see S.W. Mintz, "Houses and Yards among Caribbean Peasantries," in Sidney W. Mintz, *Caribbean Transformations* (New York: Columbia University Press, 1989).

395 Robertson, "Africa into the Americas," 12.

396 Oldendorp, *Historie*, I, 725.

397 See for example 38.9.4. CB, PRP, case 1780-06-30; 38.9.11. CB, PRP, case 1800-08-20; and 38.9.19. CB, PRP, case 1821-06-15.

398 Johansen, "The Reality," 227.

399 38.6.19. CB, DP, verdict 1796-01-23.

400 For a detailed analysis of the African-Atlantic elements of gendered conflicts among slaves and their descendants in Brazil, see M.d.C. Soares, "Can Women Guide and Govern Men? Gendering Politics among African Catholics in Colonial Brazil," in *Women and Slavery: The Modern Atlantic*, ed. Gwyn Campbell, Suzanne Miers, and Joseph C. Miller (Athens, Ohio: Ohio University Press, 2008). For work on West Africa, see P. Manning, *Slavery and African Life: Occidental, Oriental, and African Slave Trades* (Cambridge: Cambridge University Press, 1990), 38-59; R. Law, *The Slave Coast of West Africa, 1550-1750* (Oxford: Clarendon Press, 1991), 38-59, 66; S.H. Broadhead, "Slave Wives, Free Sisters: Bakongo Women and Slavery c. 1700-1850," in *Women and Slavery in Africa*, ed. Claire C Robertson and Martin A. Klein (Madison: University of Wisconsin Press, 1983), 160-181; Greene, *Gender, Ethnicity, and Social Change*, 79-107; W. Rodney, *A History of the Upper Guinea Coast, 1545-1800* (New York: Monthly Review Press, 1970), 68, 106; Kopytoff, Igor, and S. Miers, "African 'Slavery' as

an Institution of Marginality," in *Slavery in Africa*, ed. Kopytoff, Igor, and Suzanne Miers (Madison: University of Wisconsin Press, 1977). Lovejoy also sees a "manipulation of the legal system" as a result of the trans-Atlantic slave trade P.E. Lovejoy, *Transformations in Slavery: A History of Slavery in Africa* (Cambridge: Cambridge University Press, 1983), 43-87.

401 For conditions in Fort Christiansværn, see Simonsen, "Legality outside the Courtroom."

402 38.6.14. CB, DP, verdict 1783-08-19.

403 38.6.5. CB, DP, verdict 1764-04-03 no. 99.

404 38.6.8-9. CB, DP, verdict 1769-04-01.

405 For examples of the use of the 1733 slave codes' article on the evidence needed to convict a slave, see 38.9.1. CB, PRP, case 1758-02-2; 38.6.7. CB, DP, verdict 1765-09-16; 38.6.8-9. CB, DP, verdict 1768-12-07, and verdict 1769-10-20; and 38.6.11. CB, DP, verdict 1772-10-03, and verdict 1773-09-09; 38.6.18. CB, DP, verdict 1793-08-12.

406 2.1.1. GG, PB, 1733-09-05; and 390. Generaltoldkammerets vestindiske og guineiske sager, Visdomsbog, 1733-1783, 359-363. For the 1755 slave code, see Kommercekollegiet, Dansk-norske sekretariat, nr. 17, forordninger, 1735-1770, 126-148.

407 *Kong Christian den Femtis Danske Lov*, 1-13-1 and 1-13-8.

408 Bagge, Frost, and Hjejle, *Højesteret, 1661-1961*, 93-96.

409 For verdicts based on presumptions, see 38.6.01-02. CB, DP, verdict 1758-12-07; 38.6.3. CB, DP, verdict 1760-01-04, 1760-01-11 & 1760-02-09; 38.6.4. CB, DP, verdict 1761-11-20, 1761-12-10 & 1762-01-11; 38.6.5. CB, DP, verdict 1764-04-03 no. 99 & 1764-04-03 no. 101; 38.6.7. CB, DP, verdict 1766-01-08 no. 1, no. 2 & no. 3; 38.6.8-9. CB, DP, verdict 1768-08-19, 1768-12-07, 1769-08-30 & 1769-10-20; 38.6.11. CB, DP, verdict 1772-10-03 no. 87 & 88; 38.6.13. CB, DP, verdict 1779-12-23, 1778-05-29, 1778-08-10 & 1779-06-23; 38.6.15. CB, DP, verdict 1784-11-29 & 1785-01-17; 38.6.16. CB, DP, verdict 1786-05-09; 38.6.17. CB, DP, verdict 1794-09-12; 38.6.18. CB, DP, 1795-03-21; 38.6.22. CB, DP, verdict 1802-06-23; 38.6.23. CB, DP, verdict 1805-11-12; 38.6.26. CB, DP, verdict 1813-12-06; 38.6.28. CB, DP, verdict 1818-10-07; 38.6.30. CB, DP, verdict 1824-01-27; 38.6.31. CB, DP, verdict 1832-03-22.

410 For verdicts in which slaves were convicted on the basis of presumptions formed from slave testimony, see 38.6.13. CB, DP, verdict 1778-05-29; 38.6.13. CB, DP, verdict 1779-06-23 and 1779-12-23; 38.6.15. CB, DP, verdict 1784-11-29; 38.6.16. CB, DP, verdict 1787-09-19 and 1788-06-13; 38.6.17. CB, DP, verdict 1794-09-12; 38.6.18. CB, DP, verdict 1795-03-21; 38.6.23. CB, DP, verdict 1805-11-12; 38.6.26. CB, DP, verdict 1813-12-06; 38.6.28. CB, DP, verdict 1818-10-07; 38.6.29. CB, DP, verdict 1822-10-01.

411 38.6.18. CB, DP, verdict 1795-03-21. Presumptions were also used in trials against Europeans; and in two cases presumptions led to the conviction of white West Indians for the killing or maltreatment of slaves, see 38.6.14. CB, DP, verdict 1781-08-11; and 38.6.18. CB, DP, verdict 1793-08-12.

412 390. Generaltoldkammerets vestindiske og guineiske sager, Visdomsbog, 1733-1783, 359-363.

413 38.6.13. CB, DP, verdict 1778-05-29.

414 38.6.13. CB, DP, verdict 1779-12-23.

415 See, for example, 38.6.15. CB, DP, verdict 1784-11-29.

416 For 187 of the 493 enslaved defendants in Christiansted Lower Court, from 1756 to 1848, judges noted that the defendant's own confession was one of the elements that explained their guilt, see 38.6.1-38.6.32. CB, DP, 1756 to 1848.

417 38.6.16. CB, DP, verdict 1786-09-20; and 38.6.18. CB, DP, verdict 1795-03-21; see also 38.6.21. CB, DP, verdict 1800-10-18.

418 38.6.14. CB, DP, verdict 1783-08-19. For more examples, see 38.6.14. CB, DP, verdict 1783-08-19; 38.6.21. CB, DP, verdict 1801-02-14; 38.6.23. CB, DP, verdict 1805-07-06; 38.6.28. CB, DP, verdict 1817-11-29; and 38.6.29. CB, DP, verdict 1823-09-27.

419 This estimate is based on the references provided in the 339 verdicts passed in Christiansted Lower Court, 1756-1848, see 38.6.1-32. CB, DP, 1756-1848.

420   38.6.22. CB, DP, verdict 1802-10-20.

421   *Kong Christian den Femtis Danske Lov*, 1-13-1 and 1-13-20. For unwavering and corresponding statements, see, for example, 38.6.13. CB, DP, verdict 1778-10-20 and 1779-06-23; 38.6.16. CB, DP, verdict 1786-07-22; 38.6.17. CB, DP, verdict 1789-10-30; 38.6.18. CB, DP, verdict 1793-08-12; 38.6.21. CB, DP, verdict 1799-08-26; 38.6.27. CB, DP, verdict 1816-11-16. For wavering statements, see 38.6.16. CB, DP, verdict 1786-09-20; 38.6.21. CB, DP, verdict 1799-08-26; 38.6.23. CB, DP, verdict 1805-11-12; 38.6.24. CB, DP verdict 1807-07-27; and 38.6.28. CB, DP, verdict 1817-11-29.

422   For examples of statements considered trustworthy because they were made under duress, see: Torture: 38.6.13. CB, DP, verdict 1778-10-20, 1779-06-23 and 1779-12-23. Confrontations: 38.6.13. CB, DP, verdict 1779-06-23; 38.6.15. CB, DP, verdict 1786-01-19; 38.6.22. CB, DP, verdict 1804-07-06; 38.6.23. CB, DP, verdict 1805-02-04; and 38.6.27. CB, DP, verdict 1816-11-16. Imminent death: 38.6.14. CB, DP, verdict 1783-08-19; 38.6.20. CB, DP, verdict 1798-02-12; and 38.6.28. CB, DP, verdict 1819-11-13.

423   38.6.13. CB, DP, verdict 1779-12-23.

424   38.9.5. CB, PRP, entry 1783-04-03.

425   38.6.5. CB, DP, verdict 1764-04-03.

426   38.6.23. CB, DP, verdict 1805-02-25.

427   38.6.15. CB, DP, verdict 1784-12-13.

428   For verdicts in which slave testimony was excluded because witnesses were not Christians, see 38.6.8-9. CB, DP, verdict 1768-02-27; 38.6.13. CB, DP, verdict 1778-08-10. And 38.6.13. CB, DP, verdict 1778-05-29, see also 38.6.15. CB, DP, verdict 1784-12-15.

429   38.6.18. CB, DP, verdict 1795-03-21; see also 38.6.14. CB, DP, verdict 1783-08-19; and 38.6.15. CB, DP, verdict 1784-12-15.

430   38.6.18. CB, DP, verdict 1795-03-21.

431   38.6.18. CB, DP, verdict 1795-03-21; and 2.16.1. GG, RP, entry 1795-03-30. For a case wherein Christianity was a disadvantage to the defendant, see 38.6.13. CB, DP, verdict 1779-06-23.

432   38.6.22. CB, DP, verdict 1802-10-20.

433   For the expression "history of the case," see 38.6.13. CB, DP, verdict 1779-04-08; 38.6.14. CB, DP, verdict 1783-08-19; 38.6.15. CB, DP, verdict 1784-11-29 and 1785-01-17; 38.6.24. CB, DP, verdict 1807-07-27; 38.6.27. CB, DP, verdict 1816-11-16; 38.6.28. CB, DP, verdict 1818-12-14; 38.6.28. CB, DP, verdict 1820-01-11; and 38.6.29. CB, DP, verdict 1823-09-27. For the expression "circumstances of the case," see 38.6.13. CB, DP, verdict 1776-10-23, 1778-05-29 and 1779-02-23; 38.6.15. CB, DP, verdict 1784-11-29; 38.6.16. CB, DP, verdict 1786-05-0; 38.6.18. CB, DP, verdict 1794-12-03; 38.6.20. CB, DP, verdict 1798-06-21; 38.6.21. CB, DP, verdict 1799-08-26, 1801-02-14 and 1801-07-03; 38.6.22. CB, DP, verdict 1803-11-12; 38.6.23. CB, DP, verdict 1804-11-02 and 1806-05-05; 38.6.25. CB, DP, verdict 1811-06-27; and 38.6.28. CB, DP, verdict 1817-10-01 and 1818-05-02. For the expression "the nature of the case," see for example 38.6.13. CB, DP, verdict 1779-04-08; and 38.6.28. CB, DP, verdict 1820-01-11.

434   Although the Danish words for history and story are identical (*historie*), judges employed the term to signify that their account was a reconstruction of past events. This is clear from judges' use of the adjective "historical" (*historisk*) that cannot be applied to a fictive account in Danish.

435   38.6.12. CB, DP, verdict 1775-01-16.

436   See, for example, 38.6.18. CB, DP, verdict 1795-03-21.

437   38.6.14. CB, DP, verdict 1781-03-24; 38.6.21. CB, DP, verdict 1800-10-18; 38.6.32. CB, DP, verdict 1840-07-11.

438   For other examples of this mode of describing enslaved people, see 38.6.13. CB, DP, verdict 1779-06-23 no. 121 & 1779-09-15; 38.6.15. CB, DP, verdict 1784-11-29; 38.6.17. CB, DP, verdict 1789-10-30; 38.6.19. CB, DP, verdict 1796-10-14; 38.6.24. CB, DP, verdict 1806-11-25 & 1809-02-06; and 38.6.29. CB, DP, verdict 1823-09-27.

439   38.5.10 CB, GRP, 1767-1768, case 1768-01-19; and 38.6.8-9. CB, DP, verdict 1768-02-20. For an inspiring analysis of how enslaved women could shape legal practices while being denied legal personality, see L.F. Edwards, "Enslaved Women and the Law: Paradoxes of Subordination in the Post-Revolutionary Carolinas," *Slavery & Abolition* 26, no. 2 (2005); L.F. Edwards, *The People and their Peace, Legal Culture and the Transformation of Inequality in the Post-Revolutionary South* (Chapel Hill: University of North Carolina Press, 2009).

440   38.6.13. CB, DP, verdict 1778-08-15.

441   38.6.15. CB, DP, verdict 1784-12-15.

442   38.6.7. CB, DP, verdict 1765-11-29.

443   38.6.13. CB, DP, verdict 1778-04-09.

444   38.6.13. CB, DP, verdict 1778-04-09.

445   The Danish West Indian Upper Court sentenced two other slaves to flogging under the gallows and transportation. Governor General Peter Clausen approved the verdicts against Dick and one of the other slaves, but commuted the sentence of the third slave after petitions from his owner; see 38.6.13. CB, DP, verdict 1778-04-09; 2.5.1. GG, Kopibøger til lokale myndigheder og personer, entry 1778-05-04 and 1778-06-22.

446   38.6.21. CB, DP, verdict 1802-01-15; and 38.9.11. CB, PRP, case no. 1801-63.

447   38.6.21. CB, DP, verdict 1802-01-15. It has not been possible to locate the gubernatorial resolution in the verdict against Jack.

448   38.6.11. CB, DP, verdict 1772-10-03.

449   38.6.23. CB, DP, verdict 1806-05-05.

450   38.6.23. CB, DP, verdict 1806-05-05.

451   38.6.25. CB, DP, verdict 1811-06-27. See also 38.6.23. CB, DP, verdict 1805-02-04; and 38.6.30. CB, DP, verdict 1824-01-17.

452   Falk-Jensen and Hjorth-Nielsen, *Candidati*, see under Lars Madsen Wiel.

453   38.6.11. CB, DP, verdict 1773-09-09.

454   Jensen, *For the Health*, 66-67.

455   38.9.4. CB, PRP, case 1779-05-07, note that Cudjoe's exclamation was transcribed in English in the court book; 38.6.13. CB, DP, verdict 1779-06-23.

456   38.6.15. CB, DP, verdict 1784-11-29.

457   3.81.73. Den Vestindiske Regering, Guvernementet på St. Croix, Gruppeordnede sager 2, Lokale myndigheder: Breve vedr. justits- og politivæsenet, entry 1786-07-28; and 38.6.15. CB, DP, verdict 1784-11-29.

458   38.9.5. CB, PRP, entry 1783-03-28.

459   38.6.15. CB, DP, verdict 1784-11-29.

460   38.6.15. CB, DP, verdict 1784-11-29.

461   Falk-Jensen and Hjorth-Nielsen, *Candidati*, see under Brown.

462   Eva's statement was recorded in March 1783 in Christiansted Police Court and was pasted into the register of verdict more than a year later in November 1784, see 38.9.5. CB, PRP, case 1783-03-38 and 38.6.15. CB, DP, verdict 1784-11-29.

463   38.6.15. CB, DP, verdict 1784-11-29.

464   38.6.15. CB, DP, verdict 1784-11-29.

465   38.9.6. CB, PRP, entry 1785-01-29.

466   J.O. Bro-Jørgensen, *Dansk Vestindien indtil 1755: Kolonisation og kompagnistyre*, ed. Johannes Brøndsted, vol. 1, *Vore Gamle Tropekolonier* (Denmark: Fremad, 1966), 255-256; Vibæk, *Dansk Vestindien 1755-1848*, 2, 94.

467   3.81.73. Den Vestindiske Regering, Guvernementet på St. Croix, Gruppeordnede sager 2, Lokale myndigheder: Breve vedr. justits- og politivæsenet, entry 1784-08-11, 1786-06-28, 1786-07-01 and 1786-07-28.

468   38.6.22. CB, DP, verdict 1803-08-24; 5.5.4. Landsoverretten for de Vestindiske Øer, DP, Litra S, verdict no. 1803-20; Rahbek, "Negerinden Peggy."

469   38.9.11. CB, PRP, case 1803-06-14.

470   38.6.22. CB, DP, verdict 1803-08-24.

471   38.9.11. CB, PRP, case 1803-06-14.

472   38.6.22. CB, DP, verdict 1803-08-24.

473   38.6.22. CB, DP, verdict 1803-08-24.

474   38.6.22. CB, DP, verdict 1803-08-24.

475   See Chapter 1.

476   5.5.4. Landsoverretten for de Vestindiske Øer, DP, Litra S, verdict no. 1803-20.

477   86.36. Reviderede Regnskaber, Vestindiske Regnskaber, Matrikler for St. Croix, 1803-1804, Hermon Hill, 58.

478   38.6.23. CB, DP, verdict 1804-11-02.

479   38.6.23. CB, DP, verdict 1804-11-02.

480   38.6.27. CB, DP, verdict 1816-11-16.

481   38.6.27. CB, DP, verdict 1816-11-16.

482   38.6.23. CB, DP, verdict 1804-11-02, and 5.5.3. Landsoverretten for de Vestindiske Øer, DP, verdict 1817-01-20.

483   38.9.11. CB, PRP, case 1802-05-19; and 38.6.22. CB, DP, verdict 1802-06-23.

484   424. Generaltoldkammerets vestindiske og guineiske sager, Dokumenter vedr. Kommissionen for Negerhandelens bedre indretning II, 1783-1806, letter from Bentzon to Governor General Schimmelmann, entry 1802-07-24.

485   See J.E. Petersen, Slaveoprøret på Skt. Jan i 1733. En strukturel og komparative analyse (MA-thesis, Aarhus Universitet, Historisk Institut, 1988); S.E. Greene, "From Whence They Came: A Note on the Influence of the West African Ethnic and Gender Relations on the Organizational Character of the 1733 St. John Slave Rebellion," in *The Danish West Indian Slave Trade*, ed. Arnold R. Highfiled and George F. Tyson (St. Croix: Virgin Islands Humanities Council, 1994); L. Sebro, "The 1733 Slave Revolt on the Island of St. John: Continuity and Change from Africa to the Americas," in *Scandinavian Colonialism and the Rise of Modernity, Small Time Agents in a Global Arena*, ed. Magdalena Naum and Jonas M. Nordin (New York: Springer, 2013).

486   C.G.A. Oldendorp, *Geschichte der Mission der evangelischen Brüder auf den caraibischen Inseln S. Thomas, S. Croix und S. Jan*, 2 vols. (Barby 1777).

487   38.31.2. CB, PJ, entry 1805-09-01.

488   Some years later one Count Rantzau related that his slaves believed that "ghosts" had been involved in theft from his front building and therefore they did not dare go there, see 38.9.15. CB, PRP, case 1809-06-09.

489   38.9.9. CB, PRP, case 1794-05-02.

490   38.6.17. CB, DP, verdict 1794-09-12.

491   38.6.21. CB, DP, verdict 1799-11-01.

492   38.5.24. CB, GRP, case 1799-10-04; and 38.6.21. CB, DP, verdict 1799-11-01.

493   38.9.12. CB, PRP, case 1804-07-16.

494   38.9.12. CB, PRP, case 1804-07-16.

495   2.16.3. GG, RP, entry 1804-07-31; and 38.9.12. CB, PRP, case 1804-08-10.

496   38.5.28. CB, GRP, case 1804-09-18.

497   38.6.23. CB, DP, verdict 1804-10-27; and 2.16.3. GG, RP, entry 1804-10-29.

498   Francky's accusations were voiced in Christiansted Police Court. They did not, however, appear in Christiansted Lower Court. This conclusion is based on the fact that there are no recorded interrogations of Francky and her alleged rapist, Mescir, in Christiansted Lower Court's interrogation records nor a verdict against either of them in the registers of verdicts of Christiansted Lower Court in

the year following the interrogation in the police court, see 38.5.22, GRP, November 1788 to November 1799; and 38.6.16-17, CB, DP, 1788-11-26 to 1789-11-29.

499   2.27.5. GG, RP B, entry 1830-01-18. There is no verdict against Davis in the registers of verdicts of Christiansted Lower Court from December 1829 to December 1830, see 38.6.30. CB, DP, 1829-12 to 1830-12.

500   2.27.16. GG, RP B, entry 1841-03-06, there are no other references to this case during 1841.

501   2.17.17. GG, Journaliserede og ikke-journaliserede skrivelser fra myndigheder m.m. i Dansk Vestindien, entry 1799-06-26 (the letter was written in English).

502   38.9.10. CB, PRP, case 1799-06-10.

503   2.17.17. GG, Journaliserede og ikke-journaliserede skrivelser fra myndigheder m.m. i Dansk Vestindien, entry 1799-06-26.

504   2.17.18. GG, Journaliserede og ikke-journaliserede skrivelser fra myndigheder m.m. i Dansk Vestindien, entry, 1799-10-07.

505   2.16.5. GG, RP, entry 1807, no. 127, 135 and 149.

506   38.31.2. CB, PJ, entry 1808-07-30. This conclusion is also based on the fact that there was no verdict against Lucas de Bretton, Sr., in Christiansted Lower Court's register of verdicts in the period June 1807 to December 1808, see 38.6.24. CB, DP 1807-06-12 to 1808-12-31. On Abrahamson see Vibæk, *Dansk Vestindien 1755-1848*, 2, 94-95.

507   For other examples, see 38.6.13. CB, DP, verdict 1779-04-08 and 1779-12-23; 38.6.14. CB, DP, verdict 1783-08-19; 38.6.15. CB, DP, verdict 1784-11-29, 1784-12-13 and 1786-01-19; 38.6.16. CB, DP verdict 1787-09-19 and 1788-06-13; 38.6.22. CB, DP, verdict 1803-08-19, 1804-04-23 and 1804-07-06; 38.6.23. CB, DP, verdict 1804-10-27, 1805-02-01 and 1805-11-12; 38.6.25. CB, DP, verdict 1812-07-07; and 38.6.26. CB, DP, verdict 1815-12-30.

508   38.6.3. CB, DP, verdict 1760-01-04; see also 38.6.13. CB, DP, verdict 1779-12-23.

509   For other examples, see 38.6.13. CB, DP, verdict 1779-04-08 and 1779-12-23; 38.6.14. CB, DP, verdict 1783-08-19; 38.6.15. CB, DP, verdict 1784-11-29, 1784-12-13 and 1786-01-19; 38.6.16. CB, DP verdict 1787-09-19 and 1788-06-13; 38.6.22. CB, DP, verdict 1803-08-19, 1804-04-23 and 1804-07-06; 38.6.23. CB, DP, verdict 1804-10-27, 1805-02-01 and 1805-11-12; 38.6.25. CB, DP, verdict 1812-07-07; and 38.6.26. CB, DP, verdict 1815-12-30.

510   38.6.28. CB, DP, verdict 1818-12-14; 38.6.26. CB, DP, verdict 1815-12-30. Modifiers like these were also used in the few cases in which whites were tried for their mistreatment of — indeed, their often deadly assaults on — enslaved people. In 1779, when two white West Indians were prosecuted for the abuse of their slave, the judge concluded that "although" the depositions of the witnesses showed that the slave in question had been severely mistreated by the defendants, it had not been proven that this treatment had caused the death of the slave in question. This conclusion was reached despite the many statements implicating the two defendants in the death of their slave (see 38.6.13. CB, DP, verdict 1779-04-08).

511   The Danish West Indian acquittal rates were similar to those in Jamaica in the mid-eighteenth century, where slaves had a 75 percent risk of conviction, see Paton, "Punishment," 933. In Virginia, slaves had a slightly higher risk of conviction, see P.J. Schwarz, *Twice Condemned: Slaves and the Criminal Laws of Virginia, 1705-1865* (New Jersey: The Lawbook Exchange, Ltd. Union, 1998), 40, 46-47.

512   This practice received formal sanction in 1820. However, it existed prior to its formal approval; see 3.56.2. Den Vestindiske Regering, Guvernementet på St. Croix, Indgåede breve til den engelske guvernør, entry 1809-02-22; and 2.10.1. GG, Kopibog, entry 1820-10-27. Metropolitan procedural law concerning capital punishment is described in Krogh, *Oplysningstiden*, 63-65.

513   38.6.4. CB, DP, verdict 1762-12-29

514   38.6.5. CB, DP, verdict 1764-02-08. For other examples, see 38.18.4. CB, Pådømte sager, verdict 1766-10-27; 38.6.8-9. CB, DP, verdict 1768-02-20; 38.6.12. CB, DP, verdict 1775-11-29; 38.6.14. CB, DP, verdict 1782-01-03; and 38.6.22. CB, DP, verdict 1802-10-20.

515 In the 183 gubernatorial decisions located in slave trials, only seven referred to the petitions of owners or patrons, see Telemark: 38.18.4. CB, Pådømte sager, 1764-1766, f. 191; Magdalena: 38.6.4. CB, DP, verdict 1761-04-16; Ginny: 38.18.4. CB, Pådømte sager, verdict 1766-10-23; Teigo: 2.5.1. GG, Kopibøger til lokale myndigheder og personer, entry 1778-05-04; Frederik: 2.5.1. GG, Kopibøger til lokale myndigheder og personer, entry 1775-12-11; Mingo: 2.5.1. GG, Kopibøger til lokale myndigheder og personer, entry 1775-12-13 and 1776-02-09; Frederik: 2.5.1. GG, Kopibøger til lokale myndigheder og personer, entry 1782-01-05. The importance of extra-legal community ties was probably larger than suggested by these figures; see W. Dooling, *Law and Community in a Slave Society: Stellenbosch District, South Africa, c. 1760-1820* (Cape Town, Centre for African Studies, University of Cape Town, 1992).

516 The governor general's decisions have been located for 183 of the 493 slaves tried by Christiansted Lower Court, 1755-1884. They are scattered in the following material:

Generalguvernementet:

2.2.3. GG, Korrespondance- og ordreprotokoller (kopibøger), entry 1818-11-12.

2.5.1. GG, Kopibøger til lokale myndigheder og personer, entry 1774-05-06, 1774-11-14, 1775-01-15, 1775-02-20, 1775-07-01, 1775-12-11, 1775-12-13, 1776-02-09, 1776-02-21, 1776-07-09, 1776-09-06, 1776-12-30, 1778-05-04, 1778-06-05, 1778-06-22, 1778-08-18, 1778-11-05, 1778-11-12, 1778-11-18, 1779-03-02, 1779-05-04, 1779-06-29, 1779-08-05, 1781-01-31, 1781-03-27, 1781-04-24, 1781-12-24, 1782-01-05, 1783-08-20, 1783-08-26, 1783-09-25.

2.6.6. GG, Koncepter til skrivelser overvejende til lokale myndigheder og personer, entry 1801-02-20

2.16.1. GG, RP, entry 1794-09-29, 1794-12-15, 1795-03-30; 2.16.2. GG, RP, entry 1802-09-11, 1802-10-23; 2.16.3. GG, RP, entry 1804-01-17, 1804-08-20, 1804-10-29, 1804-11-03, 1804-11-23, 1805-03-01, 1805-07-08, 1805-08-15; 2.16.4. GG, RP, entry 1805-10-22, 1805-11-13, 1805-12-05, 1806-02-06, 1806-04-09, 1806-11-26; 2.16.5. GG, RP, entry 1815-10-13, 1807-01-21, 1807-06-27; 2.16.6. GG, RP, entry 1816-01-02; 2.16.8. GG, RP, entry 1817-10-28, 1817-12-02; 2.16.9. GG, RP, entry 1819-01-11, 1819-11-16.

2.26.3. GG, Kopibog B, entry 1833-08-02.

2.27.3. GG, RP B, entry 1828-12-15; 2.27.7 GG, RP B, no. 106, no. 140, no. 161; 2.27.13. GG, RP B, entry 1837-04-24, 1837-06-20, 1837-12-27; 2.27.15. GG, RP B, entry 1839-04-11, 1840-08-19; 2.27.18. GG, RP B, entry 1845-05-27, 1845-08-18.

Den Vestindiske Regering (VR):

3.31.2. VR, Kopibog for skrivelser til lokaladministrationen m.fl., 1768-1776, entry 1771-04-09.

3.56.2. VR, Indgåede breve til den engelske guvernør, entry 1809-02-22.

3.59.3. VR, RP A, 1817, entry 1817-05-21; 3.59.8. VR, RP A, 1820-1821, entry 1822-04-16; 3.59.9. VR, RP A, 1821, entry 1821-08-09; 3.59.10. VR, RP A, 1822, entry 1822-09-05; 3.59.11. VR, RP A, 1823, entry 1823-10-30; 3.59.12. VR, RP A, 1824, entry 1824-01-23, 1824-02-02, 1824-09-18, 1824-10-19; 3.59.36. VR, RP A, 1838, entry 1838-09-10; 3.59.37. VR, RP A, 1839, entry 1839-12-10; 3.59.38. VR, RP A, entry 1840-06-01, 1840-06-20, 1840-07-15, 1840-07-20, 1840-08-19, 1840-08-29; 3.59.42. VR, RP A, 1843, entry 1843-11-15.

3.81.73. VR, Gruppeordnede sager 2, Lokale myndigheder: Breve vedr. justits- og politivæsenet, entry 1786-06-28.

Christiansted Byfoged:

38.6.4: CB, DP, verdict 1761-04-16.

38.18.2. CB, Pådømte sager, 1761, f. 178; 38.18.3 CB, Pådømte sager 1762-1763, f. 207, f. 294; 38.18.4. CB, Pådømte sager, 1764-1766, f. 183, f. 189, f. 194; 38.18.5. CB, Pådømte sager, 1767-1770, f. 198, f. 208, f. 212.

38.31.3. CB. PJ, entry 1811-04-14; 38.31.4. CB. PJ, entry 1812-01-15, 1813-02-06, 1813-06-22, 1814-09-21, 1814-10-31 and undated f. 374-375; 38.31.6. CB. PJ, entry 1820-01-17

Landsoverretten for de Vestindiske Øer:

5.7. Landsoverretten for de Vestindiske Øer, Alfabetisk navneregister til pådømte sager, 1806-1906

5.5.3. Landsoverretten for de Vestindiske Øer, DP, Litra Q-R, entry 1818-12-23, no. 12/1818.

517   2.5.1. Generalguvernementet 1716-1882. Kopibøger til lokale myndigheder og personer. 1773-1790, entry 1774-09-09

518   38.6.13. CB, DP, verdict 1779-02-23; and 2.5.1. GG, Kopibøger til lokale myndigheder og personer, entry 1779-03-02. There are no systematic studies of earlier Danish West Indian legal practice, but one can gain a general impression from W. Westergaard, *The Danish West Indies under Company Rule (1671-1754). With a supplementary chapter, 1755-1917* (New York: The Macmillan Company, 1917), 158-162. A look at Antigua suggests, however, that death sentences were widely used in the early and mid-eighteenth century. In Antigua approximately ten slaves were executed each year in the period from 1722 to 1763, see D.B. Gaspar, "From 'The Sense of Their Slavery': Slave Women and Resistance in Antigua, 1632-1763," in *More than Chattel: Black Women and Slavery in the Americas*, ed. David Barry Gaspar and Darlene Clark Hine (Bloomington: Indiana University Press, 1996), 226.

519   421. Generaltoldkammerets vestindiske og guineiske sager, Anmærkninger ved forslaget til negerloven. Tillige med supplement, grunde og analogi for samme, 22, 43-44 and 48.

520   38.6.21. CB, DP, verdict 1801-02-14.

521   2.16.7. GG, RP, entry 1817-01-16.

522   38.6.28. CB, DP, verdict 1818-12-14; see also 38.6.26. CB, DP, verdict 1815-12-30.

523   1789-02-20, "Fr. ang. nærmere Bestemmelse af Straffe for Tyve og Hælere," in *Chronologisk Register*.

524   38.6.26. CB, DP, verdict 1814-10-26.

525   38.6.26. CB, DP, verdict 1817-05-17.

526   38.6.28. CB, DP, verdict 1817-10-01. See also 38.6.26. CB, DP, verdict 1814-03-09. For another example of how the ordinance of 1789 was used in a verdict see 38.6.26. CB, DP, verdict 1813-09-18.

527   38.6.23. CB, DP, verdict 1804-10-27.

528   2.16.3. VILA. Generalguvernementet 1716-1882. RP (journaler) for indkomne skrivelser fra myndigheder m.m. i Dansk Vestindien, entry 1804-10-29.

529   38.6.23. CB, DP, verdict 1805-02-25.

530   38.6.23. CB, DP, verdict 1804-10-27. For similar arguments, see 38.6.22 CB, DP, verdict 1804-07-06; 38.6.24. CB, DP, verdict 1807-01-20; 38.6.25. CB, DP, verdict 1811-12-06, verdict 1813-03-01, and verdict 1811-06-27.

531   Morgan, *Laboring Women*, 16.

532   Beckles, *Centering Woman*, 2.

533   Morrissey, *Slave Women in the New World: Gender Stratification in the Caribbean*; L.M. Mair, *A Historical Study of Women in Jamaica, 1655-1844* (Kingston: University of the West Indies Press, 2006).

534   Morgan, *Laboring Women*, especially chapter 1; Garraway, *The Libertine Colony: Creolization in the Early French Caribbean*.

535   For more on the idea of slaves as degendered, see, for instance, Scully and Paton, "Introduction: Gender and Slave Emancipation in Comparative Perspective," 12; Beckles, *Centering Woman*, xxi, 2-21; Morrissey, *Slave Women in the New World: Gender Stratification in the Caribbean*, 31, 79. In more general terms, the anthropologist Claude Meillassoux describes this element of slavery when he conceptualizes slavery as a process of "de-sexualization" explaining that "in any social system to be a man or a woman means to be acknowledged as having certain functions and prerogatives linked to cultural notions of femininity or masculinity" (C. Meillassoux, *The Anthropology of Slavery: The Womb of Iron and Gold* (London: Athlone Press, 1991), 109. Orlando Patterson made possible a similar conclusion when he described slavery as instituting "social death" and "natal alienation." By using these terms he emphasized that, in principle, the only socially recognized relationship a slave can have is with his or her master; all other relationships are subjected to this one dominant relationship and can, at any time, be overruled by it. Therefore, the web of social relationships through which birth places the infant in gendered family and kinship structures does not exist for the slave, see O. Patterson, *Slavery and Social Death: A*

Comparative Study (Cambridge, MA: Harvard University Press, 1992), 13. For the Danish West Indies in particular, it is possible to find room for a similar conclusion in the work of the anthropologist Karen Fog Olwig who has described what she termed the "dehumanization" instituted by slavery in the Danish West Indies, see Olwig, *Cultural Adaptation*, 18-22. For a short critique of the idea of degendering, see J.L. Morgan, "Gender and Family Life," in *The Routledge History of Slavery*, ed. Gad Heuman and Trevor Burnard (London: Routledge, 2011), 143.

536   For the use of sexualization or similar terms see Bush, *Slave Women in Caribbean Society 1650-1838*, 13-20; Moitt, *Women and Slavery*, 15-17; D.G. White, *Ar'n't I A Woman?* (New York and London: W.W. Norton & Company, 1985), 27-48. Altink, "Deviant and Dangerous: Proslavery Representations of Jamaican Slave Women's Sexuality, ca. 1780-1834;" R.W. Slenes, "Black Homes, White Homilies: Perception of the Slave Family and of Slave Women in Nineteenth-Century Brazil," in *More than Chattel. Black Women and Slavery in the Americas*, ed. David Barry Gaspar and Darlene Clark Hine (Bloomington and Indianapolis: Indiana University Press, 1996).

537   Bush, *Slave Women in Caribbean Society 1650-1838*, 102-103; Moitt, *Women and Slavery*, 85-86. See also Morgan, *Laboring Women*, 185.

538   Burnard, *Mastery, Tyranny, and Desire: Thomas Thistlewood and His Slaves in the Anglo-Jamaican World*, 209-240; Beckles, *Centering Woman*, 125-139.

539   W. Johnson, "On Agency," *Journal of Social History* 37, no. 1 (2003), 118. See also Johnson, "Reading Evidence," 200.

540   Spivak, *A Critique of Postcolonial Reason: Toward a History of the Vanishing Present*, and Spivak, "Can the Subaltern Speak?." For introductions to post-colonial theory see P. Childs and R.J.P. Williams, eds., *An Introduction to Post-Colonial Theory* (Harlow, England: Pearson Education Ltd., 1997); *Postcolonial Theory: Contexts, Practices, Politics* (London: Verson, 1997); P. Williams and L. Chrisman, eds., *Colonial Discourse and Post-Colonial Theory: A Reader* (London: Harvester Wheatsheaf, 1993). See also G. Prakash, "Writing Post-Orientalist Histories of the Third World: Perspectives from Indian Historiography," *Comparative Studies in Society and History* 32, no. 2 (April 1990); G. Prakash, "Subaltern Studies and Postcolonial Criticism," *American Historical Review* 99, no. 5 (December 1994); and A.L. Stoler, *Along the Archival Grain. Epistemic Anxieties and Colonial Common Sense* (Princeton and Oxford: Princeton University Press, 2009). For critical discussions of postcolonial approaches to history, see F. Cooper, "Conflict and Connection: Rethinking Colonial African History," *American Historical Review* 99, no. 5 (1994); F.E. Mallon, "The Promise and Dilemma of Subaltern Studies: Perspectives from Latin American History," *American Historical Review* 99, no. 5; R. O'Hanlon and D. Washbrook, "After Orientalism: Culture, Criticism, and Politics in the Third World," *Comparative Studies in Society and History* 34, no. 1 (1992). In a Caribbean context Spivak has inspired, among others, and more or less directly, Beckles, *Centering Woman*; and Zacek, "Voices and Silences: The Problem of Slave Testimony in the English West Indian Law Court." The intersections between postcolonial history and critique and American history is also discussed by J.P. Greene, "Colonial History and National History: Reflections on a Continuing Problem," *William and Mary Quarterly* 64, no. 2 (2007); A.L. Stoler, "Tense and Tender Ties: The Politics of Comparison in North American History and (Post) Colonial Studies," *The Journal of American History* 88, no. 3 (2001).

541   In Spivak's own words: "The records I read showed the soldiers and administrators of the East India Company constructing the object of representation" and "[colonial representation] was the construction of a fiction whose task was to produce a whole collection of 'effects of the real'," Spivak, *A Critique of Postcolonial Reason: Toward a History of the Vanishing Present*, 202.

542   For the Americas, primarily the Caribbean, see Scully and Paton, "Introduction: Gender and Slave Emancipation in Comparative Perspective," 20, Trouillot, *Silencing*; Sheller, "Acting as Free Men: Subaltern Masculinities and Citizenship in Postslavery Jamaica; I. Rodríguez, ed. *The Latin American Subaltern Studies Reader* (Durham and London: Duke University Press, 2001); B. Joseph, "Proxies of

Power: Woman in the Colonial Archive," in *The Global Eighteenth Century*, ed. Felicity A. Nussbaum (Baltimore and London: Johns Hopkins University Press, 2003).

543   Trouillot, *Silencing*, 27.

544   Spivak, *A Critique of Postcolonial Reason: Toward a History of the Vanishing Present*, 235.

545   M. Craton, "Forms of Resistance to Slavery," in *The Slave Societies of the Caribbean*, ed. Franklin W. Knight, *General History of the Caribbean* (London: UNESCO Publishing, 1997); N.O. Bolland, "'The Hundredth Year of our Emancipation'. The dialectics of resistance in slavery and freedom," in *Working Slavery, Pricing Freedom: Perspectives from the Caribbean, Africa and the African Diaspora*, ed. Verene A. Shepherd (Kingston: Ian Randle Publishers, 2002); G. Heuman and T. Burnard, "Introduction," in *The Routledge History of Slavery*, ed. Gad Heuman and Trevor Burnard (London: Routledge, 2011); R. Drayton, "The Problem of the Hero(ine) in Caribbean History," *Small Axe* 1 (2011).

546   Hall, *Slave Society*, 58, 108-109.

547   E.V. Goveia, *The West Indian Slave Laws of the 18th Century* (Barbados: Caribbean University Press, 1970), 34, 40-41; A. Watson, *Slave Law in the Americas* (London: University of Georgia Press, 1989), 43, 72-74, 88, 98, 120-121.

548   Paton, "Punishment," 933. This conclusion is widely shared among historians of slave law, see, for example, R.J. Scott, "Slavery and the Law in Atlantic Perspective: Jurisdiction, Jurisprudence, and Justice," *Law and History Review* 29, no. 4 (2011), 924; Ghachem, *The Old Regime and the Haitian Revolution*, 5; Schafer, *Slavery, the Civil Law, and the Supreme Court of Louisiana*, 28; H. Jordaan, "Free Blacks and Coloreds, and the Administration of Justice in Eighteenth-Century Curaçao," *New West Indian Guide / Nieuwe West-Indische Gids* 84, no. 1 and 2 (2010), 84.

549   A.M. De la Fuente, "Slave Law and Claims-Making in Cuba: The Tannenbaum Debate Revisited," *Law and History Review* 22, no. 2 (2004), 349. See also C. Hünefeldt, *Paying the Price of Freedom. Family and Labor among Lima's Slaves, 1800-1854* (Berkeley: University of California Press, 1994); C. Aguirre, "Working the System: Black Slaves and the Courts in Lima, Peru, 1821-1854," in *Crossing Boundaries: Comparative History of Black People in Diaspora*, ed. Darlene Clark Hine and Jacqueline McLeod (Bloomington: Indiana University Press, 1999); L.L. Johnson, "'A Lack of Legitimate Obedience and Respect': Slaves and Their Masters in the Courts of Late Colonial Buenos Aires," *Hispanic American Historical Review* 87, no. 4 (2007); B. Premo, "An Equity Against the Law: Slave Rights and Creole Jurisprudence in Spanish America," *Slavery & Abolition* 32 (2011); G.G. Rodríguez, *Voices of the Enslaved in Nineteenth-Century Cuba. A Documentary History*, trans. Nancy L. Westrate (Chapel Hill: University of North Carolina Press, 2011).

550   M. Turner, "Modernizing Slavery: Investigating the Legal Dimension," *New West Indian Guide / Niewe West-Indische Gids* 73, no. 3 and 4 (1999), 5; R.N. Buckley, "The Admission of Slave Testimony at British Military Courts in the West Indies, 1800-1809," in *A Turbulent Time: The French Revolution and the Greater Caribbean*, ed. David Barry Gaspar and David Patrick Geggus (Bloomington: Indiana University Press, 1997).

551   Hall, *Slave Society*, 109.

552   Costa, *Crowns of Glory*, 72. For a similar point in regard to the colony of Berbice see M. Turner, "The 11 O'clock Flog: Women, Work and Labour Law in the British Caribbean," *Slavery & Abolition* 20, no. 1 (1999), 48.

553   Lazarus-Black, "Slaves, Masters and Magistrates," 267; M. Lazarus-Black, "John Grant's Jamaica: Notes Towards a Reassessment of Courts in the Slave Era," *The Journal of Caribbean History* 27, no. 2 (1993).

554   Paton, "Punishment," 934.

555   P.E. Olsen, "Negeroprør, termitter og landsarkivar Saxild: Om de dansk-vestindiske lokalarkivers skæbne," *Arkiv* 10, no. 3 (1985).

BIBLIOGRAPHY

Aguirre, Carlos, "Working the System: Black Slaves and the Courts in Lima, Peru, 1821-1854," in Darlene Clark Hine and Jacqueline McLeod, eds., *Crossing Boundaries: Comparative History of Black People in Diaspora* (Bloomington: Indiana University Press, 1999), 202-222.

Altink, Henrice, "Deviant and Dangerous. Proslavery Representations of Jamaican Slave Women's Sexuality, ca. 1780-1834," in Gwyn Campbell, Suzanne Miers and Joseph C. Miller, eds., *Women and Slavery: The Modern Atlantic* (Athens: Ohio University Press, 2008), 209-230.

———, "'An Outrage on all Decency': Abolitionist Reactions to Flogging Jamaican Slave Women, 1780-1834," *Slavery & Abolition* 23, no. 2 (2002), 107-122.

———, "'To Wed or Not to Wed?': The Struggle to Define Afro-Jamaican Relationships, 1834-1838," *Journal of Social History* 38, no. 1 (2004), 81-111.

Antonsen, Inger Mejer, "Plantagen Bethlehem på St. Croix i det attende århundrede," *Nationalmuseets Arbejdsmark* (1968), 113-122.

Ariés, Philippe, *Western Attitudes toward DEATH: From the Middle Ages to the Present* (Baltimore: Johns Hopkins University Press, 1974).

Bagge, Povl, Jep Lauesen Frost, and Bernt Hjejle, eds., *Højesteret, 1661-1961*, 2 vol. (København: GEC Gads Forlag, 1961).

Barr, Juliana, *Peace Came in the Form of a Woman. Indians and Spaniards in the Texas Borderlands* (Chapel Hill: University of North Carolina Press, 2007).

Bay, Edna G., *Wives of the Leopard. Gender, Politics, and Culture in the Kingdom of Dahomey* (Charlottesville: University of Virginia Press, 1998).

Beckles, Hilary, "Black Masculinity in Caribbean Slavery," in Rhoda Rheddock, ed., *Interrogating Caribbean Masculinities: Theoretical and Empirical Analyses* (Kingston: University of the West Indies Press, 2004), 225-243.

———, *Centering Woman: Gender Discourses in Caribbean Slave Society* (Kingston: Ian Randle Publishers, 1999).

Bendtsen, Lasse, "Domestic Slave Trading in St. Croix, 1764-1848," *Scandinavian Journal of History* 41, no. 4-5 (2016), 495-515.

———, Intern Slavehandel på St. Croix, 1750-1848 (MA-thesis, unpublished, Københavns Universitet, 2010).

Bennett, Lance W., and Martha S. Feldman, *Reconstructing Reality in the Courtroom* (London: Tavistock Publications, 1981).

Blackburn, Robin, *The Making of New World Slavery. From the Baroque to the Modern 1492-1800* (London: Verso, 1997).

———, *The Overthrow of Colonial Slavery 1776-1848* (London: Verso, 1988).

Block, Sharon, "Lines of Color, Sex, and Service: Comparative Sexual Coercion in Early America," in Martha Hodes, ed., *Sex, Love, Race: Crossing Boundaries in North American History* (New York: New York University Press, 1999), 141-163.

Bolland, Nigel O., "'The Hundredth Year of our Emancipation'. The dialectics of resistance in slavery and freedom," in Verene A. Shepherd, ed., *Working Slavery, Pricing Freedom. Perspectives from the Caribbean, Africa and the African Diaspora* (Kingston: Ian Randle Publishers, 2002), 320-337.

Brantlinger, Patrick, *Dark Vanishings. Discourse on the Extinction of Primitive Races, 1800-1930* (Ithaca, NY: Cornell University Press, 2003).

Brathwaite, Edward, *The Development of Creole Society in Jamaica 1770-1820* (Oxford: Clarendon Press, 1971).

Braude, Benjamin, "The Sons of Noah and the Construction of Ethnic and Geographical Identities in the Medieval and Early Modern Periods," *William and Mary Quarterly* 54, no. 1 (1997), 103-42.

Bredsdorff, Thomas, *Den brogede oplysning. Om følelsernes fornuft og fornuftens følelse i 1700-tallets nordiske litteratur* (København: Gyldendal, 2003).

Brereton, Bridget, "Text, Testimony and Gender: An Examination of some Texts by Women in the English-speaking Caribbean from the 1770s to the 1920s," in Verene Shepherd, Bridget Brereton and Barbara Bailey, eds., *Engendering History: Caribbean Women in Historical Perspective* (New York: St. Martin's Press, 1995), 63-93.

Bro-Jørgensen, J.O., *Dansk Vestindien indtil 1755: Kolonisation og kompagnistyre, Vore Gamle Tropekolonier* edited by Johannes Brøndsted vol. 1 (Denmark: Fremad, 1966).

Broadhead, Susan Herlin, "Slave Wives, Free Sisters: Bakongo Women and Slavery c. 1700-1850," in Claire C Robertson and Martin A. Klein, eds., *Women and Slavery in Africa* (Madison: University of Wisconsin Press, 1983), 160-181.

Brooks, George E., *Eurafricans in Western Africa: Commerce, Social Status, Gender and Religious Observance from the Sixteenth to the Eighteenth Century* (Athens, Ohio: Ohio University Press, 2003).

Brooks, Peter, and Paul Gewirtz, eds., *Law's Stories* (London: Yale University Press, 1996).

Brown, Christopher Leslie, *Moral Capital: Foundations of British Abolitionism* (Chapel Hill: University of North Carolina Press, 2006).

Brown, Kathleen M., *Good Wives, Nasty Wenches, and Anxious Patriarchs: Gender, Race, and Power in Colonial Virginia* (Chapel Hill: University of North Carolina Press, 1996).

Brown, Vincent, *The Reaper's Garden, Death and Power in the World of Atlantic Slavery* (Cambridge MA: Harvard University Press, 2008).

———, "Spiritual Terror and Sacred Authority in Jamaican Slave Society," *Slavery & Abolition* 24, no. 1 (April 2003), 24-53.

Browne, Randy M., "The 'Bad Business' of Obeah: Power, Authority, and the Politics of Slave Culture in the British Caribbean," *William and Mary Quarterly* 68, no. 3 (2011), 451-480.

Brøndsted, Johannes, ed., *Vore Gamle Tropekolonier*, Vol. 1-4 (Denmark: Fremad, 1966).

Buckley, Roger N., "The Admission of Slave Testimony at British Military Courts in the West Indies, 1800-1809," in David Barry Gaspar and David Patrick Geggus, eds., *A Turbulent Time: The French Revolution and the Greater Caribbean* (Bloomington: Indiana University Press, 1997), 226-250.

Burnard, Trevor, *Mastery, Tyranny, and Desire: Thomas Thistlewood and His Slaves in the Anglo-Jamaican World* (Chapel Hill: University of North Carolina Press, 2004).

Burnard, Trevor, and Gad Heuman, "Introduction," in Trevor Burnard and Gad Heuman, eds., *The Routledge History of Slavery* (London and New York: Routledge, 2011), 1-15.

Burnard, Trevor, and John Lean, "Hearing Slave Voices: The Fiscal's Reports of Berbice and Demerara-Essequebo," *Archives [Britain]* 27, no. 107 (2002), 120-133.

Busck, Steen, *Et landbosamfund i opbrud. Tradition og modernisering i Sundby sogn på Mors i tiden 1660-1800*, vol. 1 (Århus: Klim, 2011).

Bush, Barbara, *Slave Women in Caribbean Society 1650-1838* (Kingston: Ian Randle, 1990).

Carretta, Vincent, *Unchained Voices: An Anthology of Black Authors in the English Speaking World of the Eighteenth Century* (Lexington: University Press of Kentucky, 1996).

Cassidy, Frederic Gomes, and Robert Brock Le Page, *Dictionary of Jamaican English* (Cambridge: Cambridge University Press, 1967).

Chapman, William, "Slave Villages in the Danish West Indies," *Vernacular Architecture Forum* (1991), 108-120.

Chatterjee, Partha, *A Princely Imposter? The Strange and Universal History of the Kumar of Bhawal* (Princeton: Princeton University Press, 2002).

Childs, Peter, and R. J. Patrick Williams, eds., *An Introduction to Post-Colonial Theory* (Harlow, England: Pearson Education Ltd., 1997).

Christensen, Jørgen Bach, "Jord, slaver og plantere. Kolonisamfundet på St. Croix 1742-1804," in Peter Hoxcer Jensen, Leif Haar, Morten Hahn-Pedersen, Jessen Kaare Ulrich and Aksel Damsgaard-Madsen, eds., *Dansk kolonihistorie. Indføring og studier* (Århus: Historia, 1981), 137-151.

Clark, Anna, *Desire. A History of European Sexuality* (New York and London: Routledge, 2008).

Cooper, Frederick, "Conflict and Connection: Rethinking Colonial African History," *American Historical Review* 99, no. 5 (December 1994), 1516-1545.

Costa, Emilia Viotti da, *Crowns of Glory, Tears of Blood: The Demerara Slave Rebellion of 1823* (New York and Oxford: Oxford University Press, 1994).

Costanzo, Angelo, *Surprising Narrative: Olaudah Equiano and the Beginnings of Black Autobiography* (New York: Greenwood Press, 1987).

Craton, Michael, "Forms of Resistance to Slavery," in Franklin W. Knight, ed., *The Slave Societies of the Caribbean* General History of the Caribbean (London: UNESCO Publishing, 1997), 222-270.

———, *Testing the Chains. Resistance to Slavery in the British West Indies* (Ithaca and London: Cornell University Press, 1982).

Dansk biografisk leksikon, Gyldendal, http://denstoredanske.dk/Dansk_Biografisk_Leksikon (accessed 2016-04-08).

Dansk Etymologisk Ordbog. Ordenes Historie. Gyldendals Røde Ordbøger, edited by Niels Åge Nielsen (København: Gyldendal, 2004).

Dansk-vestindisk historie, Rigsarkivet, http://www.virgin-islands-history.dk/ (accessed 2017-05-01).

Dansk Vestindien – Kilder til historien, Rigsarkivet, https://www.virgin-islands-history.org/ (accessed 2016-11-14 & 2017-05-01).

Davis, Natalie Zemon, "Boundaries and the Sense of Self in Sixteenth-Century France," in Thomas C. Heller, Morton Sosna and David E. Wellbery, eds., *Reconstructing Individualism: Autonomy, Individuality, and the Sense of Self in Western Thought* (Palo Alto, CA: Stanford University Press, 1986), 53-63.

———, *Fiction in the Archives: Pardon Tales and Their Tellers in Sixteenth-Century France* (Palo Alto, CA: Stanford University Press, 1987).

———, "Judges, Masters, Diviners: Slaves' Experience of Criminal Justice in Colonial Suriname," *Law and History Review* 29, no. 4, special issue (2011), 925-984.

Davis, Thomas J., "Conspiracy and Credibility: Look Who's Talking, about What — Law Talk and Loose Talk," *William and Mary Quarterly* 59, no. 1 (2002), 167-174.

De Barros, Juanita, *Reproducing the British Caribbean, Sex, Gender, and Population Politics after Slavery* (Chapel Hill: University of North Carolina Press, 2014).

———, "'Setting Things Right': Medicine and Magic in British Guiana, 1803-38," *Slavery & Abolition* 25, no. 1 (April 2004), 26-50.

De la Fuente, Alejandro M., "Slave Law and Claims-Making in Cuba: The Tannenbaum Debate Revisited," *Law and History Review* 22, no. 2 (2004), 339-369.

Degn, Christian, *Die Schimmelmanns im atlantischen Dreickshandel. Gewinn und Gewissen* (Neumünster: Karl Wachholtz Verlag, 1984).

Dirks, Robert, *The Black Saturnalia: Conflict and its Ritual Expression on British West Indian Slave Plantations* (Gainesville: University of Florida Press, 1987).

Donoghue, Eddie, *Black Women/White Men: The Sexual Exploitation of Female Slaves in the Danish West Indies* (Trenton: Africa World Press, Inc., 2002).

Dooling, Wayne, *Law and Community in a Slave Society: Stellenbosch District, South Africa, c. 1760-1820* (Cape Town, Centre for African Studies, University of Cape Town, 1992).

Drayton, Richard, "The Problem of the Hero(ine) in Caribbean History," *Small Axe* 1 (2011), 26-45.

Dunn, Richard S., "Sugar Production and Slave Women in Jamaica," in Ira Berlin and Philip D. Morgan, eds., *Culture and Cultivation. Labor and the Shaping of Slave Life in the Americas* (Charlottesville: University Press of Virginia, 1993), 49-72.

Dübeck, Inger, "'alt hvis Politien egentlig vedkommer …' Forholdet mellem Danske Lov og den såkaldte politianordning," in Ditlev Tamm, ed., *Danske og Norske Lov i 300 år* (København: Jurist- og Økonomforbundets Forlag, 1983), 145-178.

———, "Voldtægtsforbrydelsen i retshistorisk belysning," *Historisk tidsskrift* 103, no. 1 (2003), 53-81.

Echeverri, Marcela, "'Enraged to the limit of despair': Infanticide and Slave Judicial Strategies in Barbacoas, 1788-98," *Slavery & Abolition* 30, no. 3 (2009), 403-426.

Edwards, Laura F., "Enslaved Women and the Law: Paradoxes of Subordination in the Post-Revolutionary Carolinas," *Slavery & Abolition* 26, no. 2 (2005), 305-323.

———, *The People and their Peace, Legal Culture and the Transformation of Inequality in the Post-Revolutionary South* (Chapel Hill: University of North Carolina Press, 2009).

Egerton, Douglas R., "Forgetting Denmark Vesey; Or, Oliver Stone Meets Richard Wade," *William and Mary Quarterly* 59, no. 1 (2002), 143-152.

Engelhardt, Juliane, *Borgerskab og fællesskab. De patriotiske selskaber i den danske helstat, 1769-1814* (København: Museum Tusculanums Forlag, 2010).

Falk-Jensen, A., and H. Hjorth-Nielsen, *Candidati og examinati juris 1736-1939* (København: G.E.C. Gad, 1954).

Feldbæk, Ole, and Ole Justesen, *Kolonierne i Asien og Afrika* (København: Politikens Forlag, 1980).

Ferguson, Moira, *Subject to Others. British Women Writers and Colonial Slavery, 1670-1834* (New York and London: Routledge, 1992).

Fogleman, Aaron Spencer, *Jesus Is Female: Moravians and Radical Religion in Early America* (Philadelphia: University of Pennsylvania Press, 2007).

Foucault, Michel, "The Subject and Power," *Critical Inquiry* 8 (Summer 1982), 777-795.

Fuentes, Marisa J., *Dispossessed Lives, Enslaved Women, Violence, and the Archive* (Philadelphia: University of Pennsylvania Press, 2016).

Garraway, Doris, *The Libertine Colony: Creolization in the Early French Caribbean* (Durham and London: Duke University Press, 2005).

Gaspar, David Barry, *Bondmen and Rebels: A Study of Master-Slave Relations in Antigua* (Durham: Duke University Press, 1985).

———, "From 'The Sense of Their Slavery': Slave Women and Resistance in Antigua, 1632-1763," in David Barry Gaspar and Darlene Clark Hine eds., *More than Chattel: Black Women and Slavery in the Americas* (Bloomington: Indiana University Press, 1996).

———, "'Rigid and Inclement': Origins of the Jamaica Slave Laws of the Seventeenth Century," in Bruce H. Mann and Christopher L. Tomlins, eds., *The Many Legalities of Early America* (Chapel Hill: University of North Carolina Press, 2001), 78-96.

———, "With a Rod of Iron: Barbados Slave Laws as a Model for Jamaica, South Carolina, and Antigua, 1661-1697," in Darlene Clark Hine and Jacqueline McLeod, eds., *Crossing Boundaries. Comparative History of Black People in Diaspora* (Bloomington: Indiana University Press, 1999), 343-366.

Gaspar, David Barry, and David Patrick Geggus, eds., *A Turbulent Time: The French Revolution and the Greater Caribbean* (Bloomington: Indiana University Press, 1997).

Gaspar, David Barry, and Darlene Clark Hine, eds., *More than Chattel: Black Women and Slavery in the America* (Bloomington: Indiana University Press, 1996).

Geertz, Clifford, *The Interpretation of Cultures* (New York: Basic Books, Inc., Publishers, 1973).

Geggus, David Patrick, "Slavery, War, and Revolution in the Greater Caribbean, 1789-1815," in David Barry Gaspar and David Patrick Geggus, eds., *A Turbulent Time: The French Revolution and the Greater Caribbean* (Bloomington: Indiana University Press, 1997), 1-50.

George E. Brooks, Jr., "The *Signares* of Saint-Louis and Gorée: Women Entrepreneurs in Eighteenth-Century Senegal," in Nancy J. Hafkin and Edna G. Bay, eds., *Women in Africa: Studies in Social and Economic Change* (Palo Alto, CA: Stanford University Press, 1976), 19-44.

Ghachem, Malick W., *The Old Regime and the Haitian Revolution* (Cambridge: Cambridge University Press, 2012).

———, "Prosecuting Torture: The Strategic Ethics of Slavery in Pre-Revolutionary Saint-Domingue (Haiti)," *Law and History Review* 29, no. 4, special issue (2011), 985-1029.

Gilroy, Paul, *The Black Atlantic: Modernity and Double Consciousness* (Cambridge, MA: Harvard University Press, 1993).

Ginzburg, Carlo, *The Cheese and the Worms: The Cosmos of a Sixteenth-Century Miller* (London: Routledge & Kegan Paul, 1980).

———, *Clues, Myths, and the Historical Method* (Baltimore: Johns Hopkins University Press, 1989).

———, *History, Rhetoric, and Proof* (Hanover and London: The University Press of New England, 1999).

Gold, Carol, *Danish Cookbooks. Domesticity and National Identity, 1616-1901* (Seattle: University of Washington Press and Museum Tusculanum Press, 2007).

———, *Educating Middle Class Daughters: Private Girls Schools in Copenhagen 1790-1820* (Copenhagen: Museum Tusculanum Press, 1996).

Gomez, Michael A., *Exchanging our Country Marks: The Transformation of African Identities in the Colonial and Antebellum South* (Chapel Hill: University of North Carolina Press, 1998).

Goveia, Elsa V., *Slave Society in the British Leeward Islands at the End of the Eighteenth Century* (Westport, CT: Greenwood Publishers, 1980 [1965]).

———, *The West Indian Slave Laws of the 18th Century* (Barbados: Caribbean University Press, 1970).

Green-Pedersen, Svend Erik, "Negro Slavery and Christianity: On Erik Pontoppidan's preface to L. F. Roemer Tilforladelig Efterretning om Kysten Guinea (A true account of the Coast of Guinea), 1760," *Transactions of the Historical Society of Ghana* 15, no. 1 (1974), 85-102.

———, "Slave Demography in the Danish West Indies and the Abolition of the Danish Slave Trade," in David Eltis and James Walvin, eds., *The Abolition of the Atlantic Slave Trade: Origins and Effects in Europe, Africa and the Americas* (Madison: University of Wisconsin Press, 1981), 231-257.

———, "Teologi og negerslaveri. Om Erik Pontoppidans fortale til L.F. Rømer: Tilforladelig Efterretning om Kysten Guinea, 1760," in Johny Leisner, Lorenz Rerup and Vagn Skovgaard-Petersen, eds., *Festskrift til Povl Bagge. På halvfjerdsårsdagen 30. november 1972* (København: Den Danske Historiske Forening, 1972), 71-87.

Greenblatt, Stephen J., *Marvelous Possessions: The Wonder of the New World* (New York: Clarendon Press, 1991).

Greene, Jack P., "Colonial History and National History: Reflections on a Continuing Problem," *William and Mary Quarterly* 64, no. 2 (2007), 235-250.

Greene, Sandra E., "From Whence They Came: A Note on the Influence of the West African Ethnic and Gender Relations on the Organizational Character of the 1733 St. John Slave Rebellion," in Arnold R. Highfiled and George F. Tyson, eds., *The Danish West Indian Slave Trade* (St. Croix: Virgin Islands Humanities Council, 1994), 47-67.

———, *Gender, Ethnicity, and Social Change on the Upper Slave Coast: A History of the Anlo-Ewe* (Portsmouth, NH: Heinemann, 1996).

Gross, Ariela J., *Double Character. Slavery and Mastery in the Antebellum Courtroom* (Princeton: Princeton University Press, 2000).

Gøbel, Erik, *The Danish Slave Trade and its Abolition* (Leiden and Boston: Brill, 2016).

———, *De styrede rigerne: Embedsmændene i den dansk-norske civile centraladministration 1660-1814* (Odense: Odense Universitets Forlag, 2000).

———, *Det danske slavehandelsforbud 1792, studier og kilder til forhistorien, forordningen og følgerne* (Odense: Syddansk Universitetsforlag, 2008).

———, *A Guide to Sources for the History of the Danish West Indies (U.S. Virgin Islands), 1671-1917* (Odense: University Press of Southern Denmark, 2002).

Götz, Nicola H., *Obeah – Hexerei in der Karibik – zwischen Mackt und Ohnmacht* (Frankfurt am Main: Peter Lang, 1995).

Hall, Catherine, *Civilising Subjects: Metropole and Colony in the English Imagination 1830-1867* (Chicago and London: University of Chicago Press, 2002).

Hall, Douglas, *In Miserable Slavery. Thomas Thistlewood in Jamaica 1750-1786* (London: Macmillan, 1992).

Hall, Gwendolyn Midlo, "African Ethnicities and the Meanings of 'Mina,'," in Paul E. Lovejoy, ed., *Identity in the Shadow of Slavery* (London: Continuum, 2000), 63-81.

———, *Africans in Colonial Louisiana: The Development of Afro-Creole Culture in the Eighteenth Century* (Baton Rouge: Louisiana State University Press, 1992).

———, *Slavery and African Ethnicities in the Americas: Restoring the Links* (Chapel Hill: University of North Carolina Press, 2005).

Hall, Kim F., *Things of Darkness. Economies of Race and Gender in Early Modern England* (Ithaca and London: Cornell University Press, 1995).

Hall, Neville A. T., *Slave Society in the Danish West Indies. St. Thomas, St. John and St. Croix* (Mona, Jamaica: University of the West Indies Press, 1992).

Halttunen, Karen, "Humanitarianism and the Pornography of Pain in Anglo-American Culture," *American Historical Review* 100, no. 2 (April 1995), 303-334.

Handler, Jerome S., "Slave Medicine and Obeah in Barbados, ca. 1650 to 1834," *New West Indian Guide/Niewe West-Indische Gids* 74 (2000), 57-90.

———, "Survivors of the Middle Passage: Life Histories of Enslaved Africans in British America," *Slavery & Abolition* 3, no. 1 (April 2002), 25-46.

Handler, Jerome S., and Kenneth M. Bilby, "On the Early Use and Origin of the Term 'Obeah' in Barbados and the Anglophone Caribbean," *Slavery & Abolition* 22, no. 2 (August 2001), 87-100.

Henningsen, Peter, "Rang og titler klingre skal omkring mit navn som bjælder: titulaturer, prædikater og patronymer i 1700-tallets Danmark," *1066. Tidsskrift for historie* 32, no. 2 (2002), 11-24.

Higginbotham, Evelyn Brooks, "African-American Women's History and the Metalanguage of Race," in Joan Wallach Scott, ed., *Feminism and History* (Oxford: Oxford University Press, 1997), 183-208.

Highfield, Arnold R., "Patterns of Accommodation and Resistance: The Moravian Witness To Slavery in the Danish West Indies," *The Journal of Caribbean History* 28, no. 2 (1994), 138-164.

Higman, B.W., "African and Creole Slave Family Patterns in Trinidad," *Journal of Family and History* 3, no. 2 (Summer 1978), 163-178.

———, "The Slave Family and Household in the British West Indies, 1800-1834," *Journal of Interdisciplinary History* 6, no. 2 (Autumn 1975), 261-287.

Hilliard, Kathleen, "Finding Slave Voices," in Robert L. Paquette and Mark M. Smith, eds., *The Oxford Handbook of Slavery in the Americas* (Oxford: Oxford University Press, 2010).

Hinchman, Mark, "House and Household on Gorée, Senegal, 1758-1837," *Journal of the Society of Architectural Historians* 65, no. 2 (2006), 166-187.

Hodes, Martha, ed., *Sex, Love, Race: Crossing Boundaries in North American History* (New York: New York University Press, 1999).

227

———, *White Women, Black Men: Illicit Sex in the Nineteenth-Century South* (New Haven and London: Yale University Press, 1997).

Hof- og Statskalenderen (published by various publishers and with various titles since 1734).

Holberg, Ludvig, *Introduction til Naturens- Og Folke-Rettens Kundskab. Uddragen Af de Fornemste Jurister, Besynderlig Grotii, Pufendorfs og Thomasii Skrifter*, Holbergs Samlede Skrifter (København: Gyldendalsk Boghandel, 1913 [1716]).

Holsoe, Svend E., "The Origin, Transport, Introduction and Distribution of Africans on St. Croix: An Overview," in Arnold R. Highfield and George F. Tyson, eds., *The Danish West Indian Slave Trade* (St. Croix: Virgin Islands Humanities Council, 1994), 33-46.

Hopkins, Daniel, "Jens Michelsen Beck's Map of a Danish West Indian Sugar-Plantation Island: Eighteenth-Century Colonial Cartography, Land Administration, Speculation and Fraud," *Terrae Incognitae* 25 (1993), 99-114.

Hornby, Ove, *Kolonierne i Vestindien* (København: Politikens Forlag, 1980).

Hsia, R. Po-chia, *Trent 1475: Stories of a Ritual Murder Trial* (New Haven and London: Yale University Press, 1992).

Hünefeldt, Christine, *Paying the Price of Freedom. Family and Labor among Lima's Slaves, 1800-1854* (Berkeley: University of California Press, 1994).

Haagensen, Reimert, *Beskrivelse over Eylandet St. Croix i America i Vest-Indien* (København: Lillies Enke, 1758).

———, *Description of the Island of St. Croix in America in the West Indies*, translated by Arnold R. Highfield (St. Croix: The Virgin Islands Humanities Council, 1995 [1758]).

Ipsen, Pernille, "'The Christened Mulatresses': Euro-African Families in a Slave-Trading Town," *William and Mary Quarterly* 70, no. 2 (2013), 371-398.

———, *Daughters of the Trade, Atlantic Slavers and Interracial Marriage on the Gold Coast* (Philadelphia: University of Pennsylvania Press, 2015).

———, Koko's Daughters. Danish Men Marrying Ga Women in an Atlantic Slave Trading Port in the Eighteenth Century (Ph.D.-thesis, unpublished, Københavns Universitet, 2008).

J.L. Carstens: En Almindelig Beskrivelse om alle de Danske, Americanske eller West-Jndiske Ey-Lande (København: Dansk Vestindisk Forlag, 1981 [1730s – 1740s]).

J.L. Carstens' St. Thomas in early Danish Times: A General Description of all the Danish, American or West Indian Islands, translated by Arnold R. Highfield (St. Croix: Virgin Islands Humanities Council, 1997 [1730s-1740s]).

James, C.L.R., *The Black Jacobins: Toussaint L'Ouverture and the San Domingo Revolution*, 2nd ed. (New York: Vintage Books, 1963 [1938]).

Jansson, Karin Hassan, *Kvinnofrid. Synen på våldtäkt och konstruktionen av kön i Sverige 1600-1800* (Uppsala: Uppsala University, 2002).

———, "Marriage, Family and Gender in Swedish Political Language, 1750-1820," in Pasi Ihalainen, Michael Bregnsbo, Karin Sennefelt and Patrik Winton, eds., *Scandinavia in the Age of Revolution. Nordic Political Cultures, 1740-1820* (Surrey: Ashgate, 2011), 193-204.

Jennings, Lawrence C., *French Anti-Slavery: The Movement for the Abolition of Slavery in France, 1802-1848* (Cambridge: Cambridge University Press, 2000).

Jensen, Niklas Thode, "'For the Benefit of the Planters and the Benefit of Mankind': The Struggle to Control Midwives and Obstetrics on St. Croix, Danish West Indies, 1800-1848," in Juanita de Barros, Steven Palmer and David Wright, eds., *Health and Medicine in the Circum-Caribbean, 1800-1968* Routledge Studies in the Social History of Medicine (New York: Routledge, 2009).

———, *For the Health of the Enslaved. Slaves, Medicine and Power in the Danish West Indies, 1803-1848* (København: Museum Tusculanum Press, 2012).

Johansen, Hans Christian, "The Reality behind the Demographic Argument to Abolish the Danish Slave Trade," in David Eltis and James Walvin, eds., *The Abolition of the Atlantic Slave Trade: Origins and Effects in Europe, Africa and the Americas* (Madison: University of Wisconsin Press, 1981), 221-230.

Johansen, Julie Fryd, "Landskolerne – skoler for slavebørn på landet," in Julie Fryd Johansen, Jesper Eckhardt Larsen and Vagn Skovgaard-Petersen, eds., *Skoler i palmernes skygge* (Odense: Syddansk Universitetsforlag, 2008), 103-122.

Johnson, Lyman L., "'A Lack of Legitimate Obedience and Respect': Slaves and Their Masters in the Courts of Late Colonial Buenos Aires," *Hispanic American Historical Review* 87, no. 4 (2007), 631-657.

Johnson, Michael P., "Denmark Vesey and His Co-Conspirators," *William and Mary Quarterly* 58, no. 4 (2001), 915-976.

———, "Reading Evidence," *William and Mary Quarterly* 59, no. 1 (2002), 193-202.

Johnson, Walter, "On Agency," *Journal of Social History* 37, no. 1 (Fall 2003), 113-124.

Jones, Cecily, *Engendering Whiteness. White Women and Colonialism in Barbados and North Carolina, 1627-1865* (Manchester: Manchester University Press, 2007).

Jordan, Winthrop D., "The Charleston Hurricane of 1822; Or, the Law's Rampage," *William and Mary Quarterly* 59, no. 1 (2002), 175-178.

———, *White over Black: American Attitudes Toward the Negro 1550-1812* (Chapel Hill: University of North Carolina Press, 1968).

Jordaan, Han, "Free Blacks and Coloreds, and the Administration of Justice in Eighteenth-Century Curaçao," *New West Indian Guide / Nieuwe West-Indische Gids* 84, no. 1 and 2 (2010), 63-86.

Joseph, Betty, "Proxies of Power: Woman in the Colonial Archive," in Felicity A. Nussbaum, ed., *The Global Eighteenth Century* (Balitmore and London: Johns Hopkins University Press, 2003).

Knap, Henning Højlund, "Danskerne og slaveriet: Negerslavedebatten i Danmark indtil 1792," in Peter Hoxcer Jensen, Leif Haar, Morten Hahn-Pedersen, Jessen Kaare Ulrich and Aksel Damsgaard-Madsen, eds., *Dansk kolonihistorie. Indføring og studier* (Århus: Historia, 1981), 153-174.

Knudsen, Pernille Ulla, *Lovkyndighed og vederhæftighed: sjællandske byfogeder 1682-1801* (København: Jurist- og økonomforbundets Forlag, 2001).

Koefoed, Nina Javette, *Besovede kvindfolk og ukærlige barnefædre. Køn, ret og sædelighed i 1700-tallets Danmark* (København: Museum Tusculanums Forlag, 2008).

Kong Christian den Femtis Danske Lov, edited by V.A. Secher (København: Schultz, 1891).

Kongelige Rescripter, Resolutioner og Collegialbreve for Danmark, Norge, udtogsviis udgivne, edited by Fogtman, Laurids, and T. Algreen-Ussing et al. (København, 1786-1871).

Kopytoff, Igor, and Suzanne Miers, "African 'Slavery' as an Institution of Marginality," in Kopytoff, Igor and Suzanne Miers, eds., *Slavery in Africa* (Madison: University of Wisconsin Press, 1977), 3-81.

Krogh, Tyge, *Det store natmandskomplot: En historie om 1700-tallets kriminelle underverden* (København: Samleren, 2000).

———, *Oplysningstiden og det magisk: Henrettelser og korporlige straffe i 1700-tallets første halvdel* (København: Samleren, 2000).

Langen, Ulrik, *Revolutionens skygger. Franske emigranter og andre folk i København 1789-1814* (Denmark: Lindhardt og Ringhof, 2005).

Law, Robin, "Ethnicities of Enslaved Africans in the Diaspora: On the Meaning of Mina (Again)," *History in Africa* 32 (2005), 247-267.

———, *The Slave Coast of West Africa, 1550-1750* (Oxford: Clarendon Press, 1991).

Lawaetz, Herman, *Brødremenighedens Mission i Dansk-Vestindien, 1769-1848* (København: Otto B. Wroblewski, 1902).

Lawrence, A.W., *Trade Castles & Forts of West Africa* (London: The Trinity Press, 1963).

Lazarus-Black, Mindie, "John Grant's Jamaica: Notes Towards a Reassessment of Courts in the Slave Era," *The Journal of Caribbean History* 27, no. 2 (1993), 144-159.

———, *Legitimate Acts and Illegal Encounters: Law and Society in Antigua and Barbuda* (Washington, D.C.: Smithsonian Institute Press, 1994).

———, "Slaves, Masters and Magistrates: Law and the Politics of Resistance in the British Caribbean, 1736-1834," in Mindie Lazarus-Black and Susan F. Hirsch, eds., *Law, Hegemony and Resistance* (New York: Routledge, 1994), 252-281.

Le Code Noir au le calvaire de Canaan, edited by Louis Sala-Molins (Paris: Presses Universitaires de France, 1987).

Lean, J.H., The Secret Lives of Slaves: Berbice 1819 to 1827 (Ph.D.-thesis, unpublished, University of Canterbury, 2002).

Lindvad, Felix, De afrikanske hjælpere i Brødremenigheden i Dansk Vestindien: En undersøgelse af menighedsfællesskabet og omvendelsen (MA-thesis, unpublished, Københavns Universitet, 2014).

Loftin, Joseph Evans, The Abolition of the Danish Slave Trade (Ph.D.-thesis, unpublished, Louisiana State University, 1977).

Lovejoy, Paul E., ed., *Identity in the Shadow of Slavery* (London: Continuum, 2000).

———, *Transformations in Slavery: A History of Slavery in Africa* (Cambridge: Cambridge University Press, 1983).

Lützen, Karin, *Byen Tæmmes. Kernefamilie, sociale reformer og velgørenhed i 1800-tallets København* (København: Hans Reitzels Forlag, 1998).

Mair, Lucille Mathurin, *A Historical Study of Women in Jamaica, 1655-1844*, edited and with an introduction by Hilary McD. Beckles and Verene A. Shepherd (Kingston: University of the West Indies Press, 2006).

Mallon, Florencia E., "The Promise and Dilemma of Subaltern Studies: Perspectives from Latin American History," *American Historical Review* 99, no. 5 (December 1994), 1491-1515.

Manning, Patrick, *Slavery and African Life: Occidental, Oriental, and African Slave Trades* (Cambridge: Cambridge University Press, 1990).

Martin, Phyllis M., *The External Trade of the Loango Coast, 1576-1870: The Effects of Changing Commercial Relations on the Vili Kingdom of Loango* (Oxford: Oxford University Press, 1972).

Mason, John Edwin, *Social Death and Resurrection: Slavery and Emancipation in South Africa* (Charlottesville and London: University of Virginia Press, 2003).

McBride, Dwigth A., *Impossible Witnesses: Truth, Abolitionism, and Slave Testimony* (New York: New York University Press, 2001).

Meillassoux, Claude, *The Anthropology of Slavery: The Womb of Iron and Gold* (London: The Athlone Press, 1991).

Mezey, Naomi, "Law as Culture," in Austin Sarat and Jonathan Simon, eds., *Cultural Analysis, Cultural Studies, and the Law* (Durham and London: Duke University Press, 2003).

Mintz, Sidney W., "Houses and Yards among Caribbean Peasantries," in Sidney W. Mintz, *Caribbean Transformations* (New York: Columbia University Press, 1989), 225-250.

Mintz, Sidney W., and Richard Price, *The Birth of African American Culture: An Anthropological Perspective* (Boston: Beacon Press, 1992 [1972]).

Moitt, Bernard, "Slave Women and Resistance in the French Caribbean," in David Barry Gaspar and Darlene Clark Hine, eds., *More than Chattel: Black Women and Slavery in the Americas* (Bloomington: Indiana University Press, 1996), 239-258.

———, *Women and Slavery in the French Antilles, 1635-1848* (Bloomington: Indiana University Press, 2001).

Moore-Gilbert, Bart, ed., *Postcolonial Theory: Contexts, Practices, Politics* (London: Verson, 1997).

Morgan, Jennifer L., "Gender and Family Life," in Gad Heuman and Trevor Burnard, eds., *The Routledge History of Slavery* (London: Routledge, 2011), 138-152.

———, *Laboring Women: Reproduction and Gender in New World Slavery* (Philadelphia: University of Pennsylvania Press, 2004).

Morgan, Philip D., "Conspiracy Scares," *William and Mary Quarterly* 59, no. 1 (2002), 159-166.

———, "The Cultural Implications of the Atlantic Slave Trade: African Regional Origins, American Destinations and New World Developments," *Slavery & Abolition* 18, no. 1 (1997), 122-145.

Morris, Thomas D., "Slaves and the Rules of Evidence in Criminal Trials," *Chicago-Kent Law Review* 68 (1993), 1209-1240.

———, *Southern Slavery and the Law, 1619-1860* (Chapel Hill: University of North Carolina Press, 1996).

Morrissey, Marietta, *Slave Women in the New World: Gender Stratification in the Caribbean* (Lawrence: University Press of Kansas, 1989).

Munch, Thomas, "Keeping the Peace. 'Good Police' and Civic Order in 18th-Century Copenhagen," *Scandinavian Journal of History* 32, no. 1 (2007), 38-62.

Mührmann-Lund, Jørgen, Borgerligt Regimente. Politiforvaltningen i købstæderne og på landet under den danske enevælde (Ph.D.-thesis, unpublished, Aalborg University, 2011).

Müller, Leos, Göran Rydén, and Holger Weiss, eds., *Global historia från periferin. Norden 1600-1850* (Lund: Studentlitteratur, 2010).

Nielsen, Per, ed., *Fra slaveri til frihed: Det dansk-vestindiske slavesamfund 1672-1848* (København: Nationalmuseet, 2001).

Nwokeji, G. Ugo, "African Conceptions of Gender and the Slave Traffic," *William and Mary Quarterly* 58, no. 1 (2001), 47-68.

O'Hanlon, Rosalind, and David Washbrook, "After Orientalism: Culture, Criticism, and Politics in the Third World," *Comparative Studies in Society and History* 34, no. 1 (January 1992), 141-167.

Okonjo, Kamene, "The Dual-Sex Political System in Operation: Igbo Women and Community Politics in Midwestern Nigeria," in Edna G. Bay and Nancy J. Hafkin, eds., *Women in Africa. Studies in Social and Economic Change* (Palo Alto, CA: Stanford University Press, 1976), 45-58.

Oldendorp, Christian Georg Andreas, *Geschichte der Mission der evangelischen Brüder auf den caraibischen Inseln S. Thomas, S. Croix und S. Jan*, 2 vols, edited by Johann Jakob Bossart (Barby, 1777).

———, *Historie der caribischen Inseln Sanct Thomas, Sanct Crux und Sanct Jan. Kommentierte Edition des Originalmanskriptes*, vol. II, edited by Gudrun Meir, Stephan Palmié, Peter Stein and Horst Ulbricht (Dresden: Verlag für Wissenschaft und Bildung, 2000).

———, *Historie der caribischen Inseln Sanct Thomas, Sanct Crux und Sanct Jan. Kommentierte Edition des Originalmanskriptes*, vol. I, edited by Gudrun Meir, Stephan Palmié, Peter Stein and Horst Ulbricht (Dresden: Verlag für Wissenschaft und Bildung, 2000).

———, *History of the Mission of the Evangelical Brethern on the Caribbean Islands of St. Thomas, St. Croix and St. John*, translated by Arnold R. Highfield and Vladimir Barac (Ann Arbor, MI: Karoma Publishers, Inc., 1987).

Oldfield, J. R., *Popular Politics and British Anti-Slavery: The Mobilisation of Public Opinion against the Slave Trade Trade, 1787-1807* (London: Frank Cass, 1998).

Olney, James, "'I Was Born': Slave Narratives, Their Status as Autobiography and as Literature," *Callaloo*, no. 20 (Winter 1984), 46-73.

Olsen, Marie Veisegaard, Frie afrocaribiske kvinder i Christiansted, St. Croix, Dansk Vestindien ca. 1780-1820 (MA-thesis, unpublished, Københavns Universitet, 2010).

———, "Sexual Relationships and Working Lives of Free Afro-Caribbean Women," *Scandinavian Journal of History* 41, no. 4-5 (2016), 565-585.

Olsen, Poul Erik, "Danske Lov på de vestindiske øer," in Ditlev Tamm, ed., *Danske og Norske Lov i 300 år* (København: Jurist- og Økonomforbundets Forlag, 1983), 289-321.

———, "De dansk-vestindiske øer og junigrundloven," *Historie* 18, ny række, no. 1 (1989), 1-28.

———, "Disse vilde karle: Negre i Danmark indtil 1848," in Bent Blüdnikow, ed., *Fremmede i Danmark* (Odense: Odense Universitets Forlag, 1987), 103-117.

———, "Fra ejendomsret til menneskeret," in Per Nielsen, ed., *Fra slaveri til frihed. Det dansk-vestindiske slavesamfund 1672-1848* (København: Nationalmuseet, 2001), 25-52.

———, "Godserne på St. Croix 1733-1800," *Bol og by* 2 (1996), 80-93.

———, "Negeroprør, termitter og landsarkivar Saxild: Om de dansk-vestindiske lokalarkivers skæbne," *Arkiv* 10, no. 3 (1985), 156-175.

Olwell, Robert, "'Loose, Idle and Disorderly': Slave Women in the Eighteenth-Century Charleston Marketplace," in David Barry Gaspar and Darlene Clark Hine, eds., *More than Chattel: Black Women and Slavery in the Americas* (Bloomington: Indiana University Press, 1996), 97-110.

Olwig, Karen Fog, "African Cultural Principles in the Caribbean Slave Societies," in Stephan Palmié, ed., *Slave Cultures and the Cultures of Slavery* (Knoxville: University of Tennessee Press, 1995), 23-39.

———, "African Culture in the Danish West Indies. The Slave Trade and its Aftermath," in Arnold R. and Tyson Highfield, George F., eds., *The Danish West Indian Slave Trade* (St. Croix: Virgin Islands Humanities Council, 1994), 69-87.

———, *Cultural Adaptation and Resistance on St. John: Three Centuries of Afro-Caribbean Life* (Gainesville: University of Florida Press, 1985).

———, *Global Culture, Island Identity: Continuity and Change in the Afro-Caribbean Community of Nevis* (Chur, Switzerland: Harwood Academic Publishers, 1993).

———, "Ret og lov, magt og afmagt, et eksempel fra Dansk Vestindien," *Historie. Jyske samlinger* Ny række, 17, no. 3 (1988), 387-400.

Ong, Walter J., *Orality and Literacy: Technologizing of the Word* (London and New York: Methuen, 1985).

Ordbog over det danske sprog. Historisk ordbog 1700-1950, Det Danske Sprog- og Litteraturselskab, http://ordnet.dk/ods (accessed 2016-05-06 & 2016-05-26).

Owensby, Brian P., *Empire of Law and Indian Justice in Colonial Mexico* (Palo Alto, CA: Stanford University Press, 2008).

Oxholm, Peter Lotharius, *De Danske Vestindiske Öers Tilstand i Henseende til Population, Cultur og Finance-Forfatning, i anledning af nogle Breve fra St. Croix indrykkede i det Politiske og Physiske Magazin for Marts og April Maaneder 1797 hvortil er föiet Beskrivelse om Sukkerets Fabrikation, med 4 Planer* (København: Johan Frederik Schultz, 1797).

Paquette, Robert L., "Jacobins of the Lowcountry: The Vesey Plot on Trial," *William and Mary Quarterly* 59, no. 1 (2002), 185-192.

Paton, Diana, *The Cultural Politics of Obeah: Religion, Colonialism and Modernity in the Caribbean World* (Cambridge: Cambridge University Press, 2015).

———, "Decency, Dependence and the Lash: Gender and the British Debate over Slave Emancipation, 1830-1834," *Slavery & Abolition* 17, no. 3 (December 1996), 163-184.

———, *No Bond but the Law: Punishment, Race, and Gender in Jamaican State Formation, 1780-1870* (Durham: Duke University Press, 2004).

———, "Punishment, Crime, and the Bodies of Slaves in Eighteenth-Century Jamaica," *Journal of Social History* 34, no. 4 (Summer 2001), 923-954.

———, "Witchcraft, Poison, Law, and Atlantic Slavery," *William and Mary Quarterly* 69, no. 2 (2012), 235-264.

Patterson, Orlando, *Slavery and Social Death: A Comparative Study* (Cambridge, MA: Harvard University Press, 1992).

———, *The Sociology of Slavery: An Analysis of the Origins, Development and Structure of Negro Slave Society in Jamaica* (London: Fairleigh Dickinson University Press, 1967).

Pearsall, Sarah M.S., *Atlantic Families. Lives and Letters in the Later Eighteenth Century* (Oxford: Oxford University Press, 2008).

Pearson, Edward A., "Trials and Errors. Denmark Vesey and His Historians," *William and Mary Quarterly* 59, no. 1 (2002), 137-142.

Pedersen, Merete Bøge, "Usædelige ugerninger – Utugt og straf indtil 1800-tallet," in Merete Bøge Pedersen and Anne Trine Larsen, eds., *Det bedste selskab. Festskrift til Jens Engberg i anledning af halvfjerdsårsdagen* (København: Selskabet til Forskning i Arbejderbevægelsens Historie, 2006), 89-103.

Petersen, Jan Erik, Slaveoprøret på Skt. Jan i 1733. En strukturel og komparative analyse (MA-thesis, unpublished, Aarhus Universitet, Historisk Institut, 1988).

233

Pope, Pauline Holman, Cruzan Slavery: An Ethnohistorical Study of Differential Responses to Slavery in the Danish West Indies (Ph.D.-thesis, unpublished, University of California, 1969).

Possing, Birgitte, *Viljens Styrke: Natalie Zahle – En biografi om dannelse, køn og magtfuldkommenhed* (København: Gyldendal, 1992).

Prakash, Gyan, "Subaltern Studies and Postcolonial Criticism," *American Historical Review* 99, no. 5 (December 1994), 1475-1490.

———, "Writing Post-Orientalist Histories of the Third World: Perspectives from Indian Historiography," *Comparative Studies in Society and History* 32, no. 2 (April 1990), 383-408.

Premo, Bianca, "An Equity Against the Law: Slave Rights and Creole Jurisprudence in Spanish America," *Slavery & Abolition* 32 (2011), 495-517.

Putman, Lara, "Rites of Power and Rumors of Race: The Circulation of Supernatural Knowledge in the Greater Caribbean, 1890-1940," in Diana Paton and Maarit Forde, eds., *Obeah and Other Powers: The Politics of Caribbean Religion and Healing* (Durham: Duke University Press, 2012), 244-267.

Rahbek, K. L., "Negerinden Peggy: En sandfærdig begivenhed, uddraget af Sagens Documenter," *Minerva* (juli-september 1804), 298-321.

Resnick, Daniel P., "The Société des Amis des Noirs and the Abolition of Slavery," *French Historical Studies* VII, no. 4 (Fall 1972), 558-569.

Rezende, Elizabeth, Cultural Identity of the Free Colored in Christiansted, St. Croix, Danish West Indies 1800-1848 (Ph.D.-thesis, unpublished, The Union Institute, 1997).

Robertson, Claire, "Africa into the Americas? Slavery and Women, the Family, and the Gender Division of Labor," in David Barry Gaspar and Darlene Clark Hine, eds., *More than Chattel: Black Women and Slavery in the Americas* (Bloomington: Indiana University Press, 1996), 3-40.

Robertson, Claire C., and Martin A. Klein, "Women's Importance in African Slave Systems," in Claire C. Robertson and Martin A. Klein, eds., *Women and Slavery in Africa* (Madison: University of Wisconsin Press, 1983), 3-25.

Robertson, David, "Inconsistent Contextualism: The Hermeneutics of Michael Johnson," *William and Mary Quarterly* 59, no. 1 (2002), 153-158.

Rodney, Walter, *A History of the Upper Guinea Coast, 1545-1800* (New York: Monthly Review Press, 1970).

Rodríguez, Gloria García, *Voices of the Enslaved in Nineteenth-Century Cuba. A Documentary History*, translated by Nancy L. Westrate (Chapel Hill: University of North Carolina Press, 2011 [1996]).

Rodríguez, Ileana, ed., *The Latin American Subaltern Studies Reader* (Durham and London: Duke University Press, 2001).

Rosenvinge, J.L.U. Kolderup, *Grundrids af den danske politiret: Til brug ved Forelæsninger* (København: Den Gyldendalske Boghandels Forlag, 1825).

Rossem, Cefas van, and Hein van der Voort, eds., *Die Creol Taal. 250 years of Negerhollands texts* (Amsterdam: Amsterdam University Press, 1996).

Rugemer, Edward B., "The Development of Mastery and Race in the Comprehensive Slave Codes of the Greater Caribbean during the Seventeenth Century," *William and Mary Quarterly* 70, no. 3 (2013), 429-458.

Røge, Pernille, "Why the Danes Got There First – A Trans-Imperial Study of the Abolition of the Danish Slave Trade in 1792," *Slavery & Abolition* 35, no. 4 (2014), 576-592.

Said, Edward W., *Orientalism: Western Conceptions of the Orient* (London: Penguin Books, 1995 [1978]).

Savage, John, "Between Colonial Fact and French Law: Slave Poisoners and the Provostial Court in Restoration-Era Martinique," *French Historical Studies* 29, no. 4 (Fall 2006), 565-594.

———, "'Black Magic' and White Terror: Slave Poisoning and Colonial Society in Early 19th Century Martinique," *Journal of Social History* 40, no. 3 (Spring 2007), 635-662.

Schafer, Judith Kelleher, *Slavery, the Civil Law, and the Supreme Court of Louisiana* (Baton Rouge: Louisiana State University Press, 1994).

Schmidt, Klaus Arøe, Det kongelige civile vestindiske embedskorps 1800 til 1848 med særligt henblik på sammensætning og karriereforhold (MA-thesis, unpublished, Københavns Universitet, 1980).

Schou, J.H., and J.L.A. Kolderup-Rosenvinge, eds., *Chronologisk Register over de Kongelige Forordninger og Aabne Breve, som fra Aar 1670 af ere udkomne* (København, 1777-1850).

Schwarz, Philip J., *Slave Laws in Virginia* (Athens and London: University of Georgia Press, 1996).

———, *Twice Condemned: Slaves and the Criminal Laws of Virginia, 1705-1865* (Clark, NJ: The Lawbook Exchange, Ltd. Union, 1998).

Scott, James C., *Domination and the Arts of Resistance: Hidden Transcripts* (New Haven and London: Yale University Press, 1990).

Scott, Joan Wallach, "Gender: A Useful Category of Historical Analysis," in Joan Wallach Scott, ed., *Feminism and History* (Oxford: Oxford University Press, 1997), 152-180.

Scott, Rebecca J., "Slavery and the Law in Atlantic Perspective: Jurisdiction, Jurisprudence, and Justice," *Law and History Review* 29, no. 4 (2011), 915-924.

Scully, Pamela, *Liberating the Family? Gender and British Slave Emancipation in the Rural Western Cape, South Africa, 1823-1853* (Portsmouth, NH: Heinemann, 1997).

———, "Rape, Race, and Colonial Culture: The Sexual Politics of Identity in the Nineteenth-Century Cape," *American Historical Review* 100, no. 2 (1995), 335-359.

Scully, Pamela, and Diana Paton, eds., *Gender and Slave Emancipation in the Atlantic World* (Durham: Duke University Press, 2005).

———, "Introduction: Gender and Slave Emancipation in Comparative Perspective," in Pamela Scully and Diana Paton, eds., *Gender and Slave Emancipation in the Atlantic World* (Durham and London: Duke University Press, 2005), 1-34.

Searing, James F., *West African Slavery and Atlantic Commerce. The Senegal River Valley, 1700-1860* (Cambridge: Cambridge University Press, 1993).

Sebro, Louise, "The 1733 Slave Revolt on the Island of St. John: Continuity and Change from Africa to the Americas," in Magdalena Naum and Jonas M. Nordin, eds., *Scandinavian Colonialism and the Rise of Modernity, Small Time Agents in a Global Arena* (New York: Springer, 2013).

———, "Kreoliseringen af eurocaribierne i Dansk Vestindien – sociale relationer og selvopfattelse," *Fortid og nutid* 2 (2005), 83-102.

———, *Mellem afrikaner og kreol. Etnisk identitet og social navigation i Dansk Vestindien 1730-1770* (Lund: Historiska Institutionen ved Lunds Universitet, 2010).

Sensbach, Jon F., *Rebecca's Revival: Creating Black Christianity in the Atlantic World* (Cambridge, MA: Harvard University Press, 2005).

———, *A Separate Canaan: The Making of an Afro-Moravian World in North Carolina, 1763-1840* (Chapel Hill: University of North Carolina Press, 1998).

Sheller, Mimi, "Acting as Free Men: Subaltern Masculinities and Citizenship in Postslavery Jamaica," in Pamela Scully and Diana Paton, eds., *Gender and Slave Emancipation in the Atlantic World* (Durham and London: Duke University Press, 2005), 79-98.

Shepherd, Verene, Bridget Brereton, and Barbara Bailey, eds., *Engendering History: Caribbean Women in Historical Perspective* (New York: St. Martin's Press, 1995).

Sidbury, James, "Plausible Stories and Varnished Truths," *William and Mary Quarterly* 59, no. 1 (2002), 179-184.

Sielemann, Rasmus Basse, Natures of Conduct: Governmentality and the Danish West Indies (Ph.D.-thesis, unpublished, Københavns Universitet, 2015).

Simonsen, Gunvor, "Legality outside the Courtroom: Practices of Law and Law Enforcement in the Danish West Indies at the End of the Eighteenth Century," *Quarderni Fiorentini. Per La Storia del Pensiero Giuridico Moderno* 33-34 (2005), 921-961.

———, "Magic, Obeah and Law in the Danish West Indies, 1750s-1840s," in Holger Weiss, ed., *Ports of Globalisation, Places of Creolisation: Nordic Possessions in the Atlantic World during the Era of the Slave Trade* (Leiden: Brill, 2015), 245-279.

———, "Moving in Circles: African and Black History in the Atlantic World," *Nuevo Mundo Mundos Nuevos* (2008), 15.

———, "Northern Europe and the Atlantic World," in Trevor Burnard, ed., *Oxford Online Encyclopaedia of the Atlantic World* (Oxford: Oxford University Press, 2011).

———, "Nye og gamle perspektiver på dansk kolonihistorie," *1066 – Tidsskrift for Historie* 2 (2003), 3-13.

Skrubbeltrang, Fridlev, *Dansk Vestindien 1848-1880: Politiske Brydninger og Social Uro*, Vore Gamle Tropekolonier edited by Johannes Brøndsted vol. 3 (Denmark: Fremad, 1967).

Slenes, Robert W., "Black Homes, White Homilies: Perception of the Slave Family and of Slave Women in Nineteenth-Century Brazil," in David Barry Gaspar and Darlene Clark Hine, eds., *More than Chattel. Black Women and Slavery in the Americas* (Bloomington and Indianapolis: Indiana University Press, 1996), 126-146.

Smith, Jørgen, "Inkvisitionskommission i København. Tortur i Danmark," *Politihistorisk Selskab. Årsskrift* (1997), 61-71.

Smolenski, John, "Hearing Voices: Microhistory, Dialogicality and the Recovery of Popular Culture on an Eighteenth-Century Virginia Plantation," *Slavery & Abolition* 24, no. 1 (April 2003), 1-23.

Soares, Maria de Carvalho, "Can Women Guide and Govern Men? Gendering Politics among African Catholics in Colonial Brazil," in Gwyn Campbell, Suzanne Miers and Joseph C. Miller, eds., *Women and Slavery: The Modern Atlantic* (Athens: Ohio University Press, 2008), 79-99.

Spivak, Gayatri Chakravorty, "Can the Subaltern Speak?," in Cary Nelson and Lawrence Grossberg, eds., *Marxism and the Interpretation of Culture* (Basingstoke: Macmillan Education Ltd, 1988), 271-313.

———, *A Critique of Postcolonial Reason: Toward a History of the Vanishing Present* (Cambridge, MA: Harvard University Press, 1999).

Steedman, Carolyn, "Enforced Narratives. Stories of Another Self," in Tess Cosslett, Celia Lury and Summerfield Penny, eds., *Feminism and Autobiography* (Routledge: London, 2000), 25-39.

Stein, Peter, and Hein van der Voort, eds., *Christian Georg Andreas Oldendorp: Criolisches Wörterbuch sowie das anonyme, J.C. Kingo zugeschriebene Vestindisk Glossarium*, Lexicographica vol. 69 (Tübingen: Max Niemeyer Verlag, 1996).

Stevnsborg, Henrik, "'Samfundets' og 'statens' strafferetspleje. Lovgivning og praksis i københavnske prostitutionssager i slutningen af det 17. og begyndelsen af det 18. århundrede," *Historisk tidsskrift* 82, no. 14. rk. bd. III (1982), 1-26.

Stoler, Ann Laura, *Along the Archival Grain. Epistemic Anxieties and Colonial Common Sense* (Princeton and Oxford: Princeton University Press, 2009).

———, *Carnal Knowledge and Imperial Power: Race and the Intimate in Colonial Rule* (Berkeley: University of California Press, 2002).

———, "Tense and Tender Ties: The Politics of Comparison in North American History and (Post) Colonial Studies," *The Journal of American History* 88, no. 3 (December 2001), 829-865.

Sweet, James H., *Domingos Álvares, African Healing, and the Intellectual History of the Atlantic World* (Chapel Hill: University of North Carolina Press, 2011).

———, *Recreating Africa: Culture, Kinship, and Religion in the African-Portuguese World, 1441-1770* (Chapel Hill: University of North Carolina Press, 2003).

Tamm, Ditlev, *Retshistorie – Danmark – Europa – globale perspektiver* (København: Jurist- og Økonomforbundets Forlag, 2005).

The Atlantic Slave Trade and Slave Life in the Americas: A Visual Record, compiled by Jerome Handler and Michael Tuite, Virginia Foundation for the Humanities and University of Virginia, http://www.slaveryimages.org/ (accessed 2015-01-01).

Thomsen, Asbjørn Romvig, *Lykkens smedje? Social mobilitet og social stabilitet over fem generationer i tre sogne i Salling 1750-1850* (Viborg: Landbohistorisk Selskab, 2011).

Thornton, John, *Africa and Africans in the Making of the Atlantic World, 1400-1800*, 2nd ed. (Cambridge: Cambridge University Press, 1998).

———, "Central African Names and African-American Naming Patterns," *William and Mary Quarterly* 50, no. 4 (October 1993), 727-742.

Tomlins, Christopher, "The Many Legalities of Colonization: A Manifesto of Destiny for Early American Legal History," in Bruce H. Mann and Christopher L. Tomlins, eds., *The Many Legalities of Early America* (Chapel Hill: University of North Carolina Press, 2001), 1-20.

Trier, C.A., "Det dansk-vestindiske Negerindførselsforbud af 1792," *Historisk Tidsskrift* 5 (1904), 405-508.

Trotman, David Vincent, *Crime in Trinidad: Conflict and Control in a Plantation Society, 1838-1900* (Knoxville: University of Tennessee Press, 1986).

Trouillot, Michel-Rolph, *Silencing the Past: Power and the Production of History* (Boston: Beacon Press, 1995).

Turner, Mary, "The 11 O'clock Flog: Women, Work and Labour Law in the British Caribbean," *Slavery & Abolition* 20, no. 1 (April 1999), 38-58.

———, "Modernizing Slavery: Investigating the Legal Dimension," *New West Indian Guide / Niewe West-Indische Gids* 73, no. 3 and 4 (1999), 5-26.

———, *Slaves and Missionaries: The Disintegration of Jamaican Slave Society 1787-1834* (Kingston: University of the West Indies Press, 1998 [1982]).

Tyson, George F., "On the Periphery of the Peripheries: The Cotton Plantations of St. Croix, Danish West Indies, 1735-1815," *The Journal of Caribbean History* 26, no. 1 (1992), 1-36.

Tyson, George. F, and Arnold R. Highfield, eds., *The Danish West Indian Slave Trade* (St. Croix: Virgin Islands Humanities Council, 1994).

Unesco Associated Schools Project, The Transatlantic Slave Trade, http://www.unesco-asp.dk/da/transatlantic-slave-trade.html (accessed 2013-07-29).

Vansina, Jan, *Oral Tradition as History* (Madison: University of Wisconsin Press, 1985).

Vibæk, Jens, *Dansk Vestindien 1755-1848: Vestindiens Storhedstid, Vore Gamle Tropekolonier* edited by Johannes Brøndsted vol. 2 (Denmark: Fremad, 1966).

Watson, Alan, *Slave Law in the Americas* (London: University of Georgia Press, 1989).

West, Hans, *Beretning om det danske Eiland St. Croix i Vestindien fra Junii Maaned 1789 til Junii Maaneds Udgang 1790* (København, 1790).

———, *Bidrag til Beskrivelse over Ste Croix med en kort udsigt over St. Thomas, St. Jean, Tortola, Spanish Town and Crabeneiland* (København: Friderik Wilhelm Thiele, 1793).

———, *Hans West's Accounts of St. Croix in the West Indies,* translated by Nina York and Arnold R. Highfield (US Virgin Islands: The Virgin Islands Humanities Council, 2004 [1790 and 1793]).

Westergaard, Waldemar, *The Danish West Indies under Company Rule (1671-1754). With a supplementary chapter, 1755-1917* (New York: The Macmillan Company, 1917).

White, Deborah Gray, *Ar'n't I A Woman?* (New York and London: W.W. Norton & Company, 1985).

Williams, Patrick, and Laura Chrisman, eds., *Colonial Discourse and Post-Colonial Theory: A Reader* (London: Harvester Wheatsheaf, 1993).

Waaben, Knud, "A.S. Ørsted og negerslaverne i København," *Juristen* 46 (1964), 321-343.

Zacek, Natalie, "Voices and Silences: The Problem of Slave Testimony in the English West Indian Law Court," *Slavery & Abolition* 24, no. 3 (December 2003), 24-39.

Österberg, Eva, and Sølvi Sogner, eds., *People Meet the Law: Control and Conflict Handling in the Courts, Nordic Countries in the Post-Reformation and Pre-Industrial Period* (Oslo: Universitetsforlaget, 2000).

INDEX